S0-BLX-209

THE ORIGINS OF THE PARTITION OF INDIA
1936–47

This volume is sponsored by the
Inter-Faculty Committee for South Asian Studies
University of Oxford

To the memory of
my father

Oxford University South Asian Studies Series

THE ORIGINS OF THE PARTITION OF INDIA 1936–1947

ANITA INDER SINGH

DELHI
OXFORD UNIVERSITY PRESS
BOMBAY CALCUTTA MADRAS

Oxford University Press, Walton Street, Oxford OX2 6DP

New York Toronto
Delhi Bombay Calcutta Madras Karachi
Petaling Jaya Singapore Hong Kong Tokyo
Nairobi Dar es Salaam
Melbourne Auckland
and associates in
Berlin Ibadan

Second impression 1989

SBN 0 19 561955 2

Typeset by Taj Services Ltd., Noida, U.P.
Printed by Rekha Printers Pvt. Ltd., New Delhi 110020
Published by S.K. Mookerjee, Oxford University Press
YMCA Library Building, Jai Singh Road, New Delhi 110001

Contents

Preface

The origins of the partition of India have been traced to the medieval period of Indian history, so it might well be asked why 1936 is chosen as the starting point for this book One reason is that there is insufficient evidence on social relations during the medieval era to establish whether or not two nations were innate in that society, and there is little point in repeating the controversies surrounding the material that does exist. Secondly, some aspects of communal politics in India before 1935 have been discussed recently, among others, by R. J. Moore, Mushir-ul-Hasan, Gail Minault, and David Page.[1] Moore's latest book, *Escape from Empire* dealt with British policy between 1945–7, while M. N. Das's *Partition and Independence of India*[2] concentrated on the Mountbatten viceroyalty. There are, therefore, many gaps in our knowledge of the interplay of British, Congress and Muslim League strategies after 1936 which culminated in partition, which this book attempts to fill; and, both in scope and in terms of the questions raised, it differs from many earlier works on the communal problem and the partition of India. 1936 is also a useful starting point as it furnishes the immediate background to the coalition controversy between the Congress and the League in the UP in 1937, regarded by many as a milestone on the road to partition. One of the questions raised by this book is why agreement eluded the Congress and Muslim League to the point of civil war. Was it because of irreconcilable political differences between them? What alternatives did the Congress, which did not want partition, have which might have enabled it to defeat the League's claim for a sovereign Pakistan?

If it cannot be proved whether there were 'always' two nations in India, but only majority and minority communities, then at what point in time did the religious minority become a nation? Did the

[1] R.J. Moore, *The Crisis of Indian Unity 1917–1940* (Oxford, 1974); M. Hasan, *Nationalism and Communalism in Indian Politics* (New Delhi, 1979); G. Minault, *The Khilafat Movement* (Delhi, 1982); D. Page, *Prelude to Partition* (Delhi, 1982).
[2] R. J. Moore, *Escape from Empire* (Oxford, 1983); M.N. Das, *Partition and Independence of India* (New Delhi, 1982).

introduction of separate electorates and responsible government bring about this transformation? Or did the demand for a sovereign Muslim state in March 1940 express the aspirations of an historic nation struggling to be born? Above all did Jinnah owe his standing in all India politics to the interests and tactics of the British or to grass-roots support?

Many questions relate to British policy and tactics. The Labour government's directive to the Cabinet Mission in March 1946 stressed that power would only be transferred to Indians if they agreed to a settlement which would safeguard British economic and military interests in India. But in Feburary 1947, the Labour government announced that it would wind up the Raj by June 1948, even if no agreement had emerged. Less than four months later, Lord Mountbatten announced that the British would transfer power on 15 August 1947, suggesting that much happened during this interval which persuaded the British to bring forward the date for terminating the empire by almost one year. Also, the British have often claimed that they had to partition because the Indian parties failed to agree. But until the early 1940s the differences between them had been a pretext for the British to reject the Congress demand for independence. The British had earlier regarded the Congress–League rift as the bulwark of their rule. Why then did they divide and quit in 1947, when these differences were exacerbated?

Mountbatten has said that he would not have agreed to partition if he had known that Jinnah would be dead 'in X months'.[3] But for all Jinnah's obduracy, people do not get what they want simply because they ask for it—someone is usually willing to give it to them or is unable to stop them. Having demanded a sovereign Pakistan in March 1940, would Jinnah have accepted anything less? If so, on what terms? The high-handedness of the Congress and the 'divide and rule' policy of the British have both been blamed for the partition of India. While it is not our intention to whitewash either the British or the Congress, the question does arise whether they and the League dealt with each other at cross-purposes, and whether Jinnah's insistence on a sovereign Pakistan must account for its realization as much as the failure of the Congress and British to persuade him to join the Constituent Assembly for a united India. These

[3] L.Collins and D. Lapierre, *Mountbatten and the Partition of India Vol. 1, 22 March–15 August, 1947* (New Delhi, 1982) p. 39.

are some of the questions which this book will attempt to answer.

As the main question posed by this book is what led to the partition of India in August 1947, I have concentrated on those developments which, in my opinion, provide the most answers, and some explanation is probably needed about the emphasis given to certain issues. For example, the League's election campaign in the Punjab and its attempt to gain power in that province between 1944–7 are given more weight than, say, its election campaign in Bengal, because the possibility of an intercommunal coalition in the Punjab posed the greatest threat, in the eyes of the League, to the emergence of Pakistan. In Bengal, the League ministry had been able to cultivate grass-roots support during the war; the greatest electoral battles were not fought in this province in 1945–6. Again, details of the discussions between Mountbatten and the British cabinet in May 1947 are not detailed, partly because they merit separate treatment, partly because the emphasis is on why the British accepted the principle of partition and not on the technicalities of the transfer of power. For the same reasons, the slender possibility of a united Bengal receiving independence in 1947 is not discussed in depth; nor is the problem of the princely states.[4]

Finally, I would like to clarify my usage of some of the terms used in this book, especially where they comprised the categories used by the authors of the sources consulted. With evidence from British, Congress, League[5] and Mahasabha sources, I have often had to sort out what each of them meant by labels such as 'communal', 'problem of minorities', 'Hindu-Muslim problem', etc. I have used 'communalism' and 'communal problem' to describe thinking in terms of religious identity. I do not use 'Hindu-Muslim problem' when quoting from sources, because, until 1946–7, there is little

[4] See ibid; some of these issues have been discussed in V.P. Menon's *The Story of the Integration of the Indian States* (1956); and *The Transfer of Power in India* (Madras paperback, 1968); W.H. Morris-Jones, 'The Transfer of Power, 1947: A View from the Sidelines', *Modern Asian Studies,* 16, 1, 1982, pp. 1–32; R.J. Moore, *Escape from Empire*; official documents have been published in *TOP*, vols. 10–12.

[5] At the time of writing, Indian scholars do not have access to Muslim League papers. But fairly good accounts of League attitudes and politics can be gleaned from newspapers, four of which espoused the cause of the League. These were *Dawn*, started in 1942 by Jinnah himself; the *Eastern Times* of Lahore, the *Star of India* and the *Morning News* of Calcutta, which was edited by a leading member of the Calcutta and Bengal Leagues. Reports of British officials and Congress leaders have also been helpful.

evidence of the communities being at *all* levels. One of the reasons why it can be used is because the Muslim League claimed to have established a Muslim homeland on the subcontinent in 1947. But is India the homeland of Hindus only? Also, the term 'Hindu-Muslim problem' tends to assume that Hindus and Muslims are homogenous entities: their religious affiliation marks them off from other groups socially, economically, culturally, politically. In a sense this is true—a person may identify himself as a Hindu, Muslim, Sikh, Christian or whatever. Merely by doing so, he does not create a social or political problem. The problem arises when a unified 'Hindu or 'Muslim' religious, political, social or economic consciousness is assumed (usually without evidence); which leaves no room for political and other intellectual differences within a particular community. According to this scheme of things, there cannot be Congress Hindus, Mahasabha Hindus, Communist Hindus, anti-Congress Hindus; nor can we have Muslim League or non-Muslim League Muslims. Indeed, as the Muslim League claimed, 'Muslims' were only those who supported it.

One should also distinguish between a community as a religious minority or majority—the census figures tell us that—and a political majority, which owes its position to its political platform and the amount of support it receives from voters for its political programme. For example, we can see that Muslims were a religious majority in the NWFP in 1937, but the Muslim League was a political minority. This distinction is vital when we discuss Indian or Pakistani nationalism.

Generally speaking, the British helped to confuse issues by labelling the Congress as Hindu, and *loyalist* Muslim opposition to it as 'Muslim' opposition to a Hindu Congress. Loyalist Hindu opposition to the Congress was ignored by the British, presumably because it may have been politically inexpedient for them. Talking about political division, both the League and the Hindu Mahasabha thought the economic programmes of the Congress were too radical in the 1930s. Both wanted a continuing long-term British presence in India, while the Congress had started talking about complete independence, involving the severance of all ties with the British Crown after 1930.

The term, 'problem of minorities' raises the question why the divide occurred largely between Hindus and Muslims in 1947; and to a lesser extent between Sikhs and Muslims—and not say, between

Hindus and Christians or Christians and Muslims. 'Problem of minorities' has also been used most often in a political context. We find that Muslims were the only minority to whom the British gave guarantees about their political position in British-sponsored constitutions on the ground that they would be able to safeguard their religious, cultural, social and economic interests. Similar guarantees were never given to other minorities. The question is why, and the answers would probably tell us at least as much about British perceptions of Indian society and politics and of their interests and tactics in India as about the 'problem of minorities'.[6]

The 'problem of minorities' is misleading because it refers only to Muslims at the all India level, leaving out Sikhs, Christians and other minorities, and even the Hindu minorities in the Muslim majority provinces. This last observation could explain why the Congress had 'Minorities Departments' in the Muslim minority provinces but not in the Muslim majority provinces—which may have been a psychological stumbling block to their ability to make a bid for Muslim support in the provinces which were to form the backbone of Pakistan. In fact, this categorization is probably the reason why scholars have only discussed 'Hindu-Muslim' differences and have not attempted to explain why, in the face of similar differences between say, Hindus and Christians or Christians and Sikhs, no politico-communal conflict emerged between these communities; why the Muslims were the only minority to whom the British gave constitutional guarantees.

[6] Some of these points are discussed more fully in Anita Inder Singh, 'Nehru and the Communal Problem, 1936–1939', (unpublished M. Phil dissertation submitted to Jawaharalal Nehru University, 1976), chapter 1; and my 'Decolonization in India; The Statement of 20 February 1947', *International History Review* May, 1984.

Abbreviations

AICC	All India Congress Committee
AIML	All India Muslim League
BDC	Bhulabhai Desai Correspondence
BSRC	B. Shiva Rao Correspondence
CC	Cunningham Correspondence
CP	Central Provinces and Berar
Correspondence	S.S. Pirzada, *Leaders' Correspondence with Mr. Jinnah* (Bombay, 1944).
CWC	Congress Working Committee
DC	Deputy Commissioner
FR	Fortnightly Report
GHQ	General Headquarters
HC	Haig Correspondence
HMG	His Majesty's Government
HP	Home Political (Internal) Department
ICS	Indian Civil Service
IAR	*Indian Annual Register*
INA	Indian National Army
LC	Linlithgow Correspondence
KPP	Krishak Praja Party
MGC	Mahatma Gandhi Correspondence
MLA	Member of Legislative Assembly
MLPB	Muslim League Parliamentary Board
MLWC	Muslim League Working Committee
NAP	National Agriculturist Party
NC	Nehru Correspondence
NDC	National Defence Council
NWFP	North-West Frontier Province
PC	Durga Das, (ed.) *Sardar Patel Correspondence, 1945–50* (10 vols., Ahmadabad, 197–4).
PCC	Pradesh Congress Committee
PTC	Purshottamadas Thakurdas Correspondence

Pirpur Report: Report of the Inquiry Committee appointed by the Council of the All India Muslim League to inquire into

Muslim Grievances in Congress Provinces (November 1938).

Pirzada, *Documents*: S.S. Pirzada (ed.) *Foundations of Pakistan: All India Muslim League Documents*, Vol. 2 (Karachi, 1970).

RPC	Rajendra Prasad Correspondence
SW	S. Gopal (ed.), *Selected Works of Jawaharlal Nehru* (12 vols., New Delhi, 1972–79)
(T)	Telegram
TBSC	T.B. Sapru Correspondence
TOP	P.N.S. Mansergh (ed.), *The Transfer of Power* (9 vols., HMSO, 1970–80)
UP	United Provinces
UPML	United Provinces Muslim League
VCO	Viceroy's Commissioned Officer
ZC	Zetland Collection

Acknowledgements

This book is based largely on my Oxford D.Phil thesis. Grants from the Oxford Graduate Studies Committee, the Bartle Frere and Radhakrishnan Memorial Funds, helped me to complete the thesis. I wish to thank my supervisor, Professor Ronald Robinson, who helped me to say what I wanted to say. I have found extremely useful the advice of my examiners, Professor Nicholas Mansergh and Sir Penderel Moon. Professor Thomas Metcalf, Professor W.H. Morris Jones, Professor Bipan Chandra, Mr Richard Symonds, Mr W.H. Saumarez-Smith, Mr Henry Taylor, Mr Arthur Williams and Dr Tapan Raychaudhuri have all read the manuscript and have made many valuable suggestions. Professor Sarvepalli Gopal has given me the most generous encouragement thoughout the period of the writing of this book. For moral support, without which this book could not have been written, I am grateful to my mother, Vanita and Asoke Mukerji—and very special thanks to Amrita and Ranjan Kapur.

CHAPTER 1

Elections and the Congress in Office

April 1936 to September 1939

> 'Minorities means a combination of things. It may be that a minority has a different religion from the other citizens of a country. Their language may be different, their race may be different, their culture may be different, and the combination of all these various elements—religion, culture, race, language, arts, music and so forth makes the minority a separate entity in the State, and that separate entity as an entity wants safeguards. Surely, therefore, we must face this question as a political problem'.
>
> MUHAMMAD ALI JINNAH, 1935.[1]

> 'It is, after all, a side issue, and it can have no real meaning in the larger scheme of things'.
>
> JAWAHARLAL NEHRU, 1936.[2]

These two statements, made by the men who led the main all-India parties in the elections of 1936 and who played a leading role in the negotiations for the transfer of power in 1946–7, indicate their very different approaches to the communal problem, which influenced decisively the British decision to transfer power to two successor states in 1947. In 1947, what for Nehru and his colleagues in the Congress had always been the real issue—the achievement of independence by India—was settled. But it was accompanied by the partition of India on a religious basis which was the antithesis of the secular Indian nationalism on which the Congress had always prided itself, and which suggested that, the 'side issue' of 1936 had become inextricably woven with the main issue in 1947. It was not

[1] Jamil-ud-din Ahmad (ed.), *Speeches and Writings of Mr. Jinnah*, vol. 1, 6th edn. (Lahore, 1960), pp. 5–6.

[2] Presidential address to the Lucknow Congress, 12 April 1936; hereafter referred to as Lucknow, S. Gopal (ed.), *Selected Works of Jawaharlal Nehru* (New Delhi, 1975), hereafter referred to as *SW*, vol. 7, p. 190.

before 1940 that Jinnah demanded a separate Muslim state. One of the arguments of this thesis is that the League's position—after the elections—induced its demand for Pakistan. It is these developments between 1937 and 1939 that we shall try to analyse in this chapter.

Elections to the provincial legislature under the Government of India Act of 1935 occupied the attention of all political parties in 1936. An electorate of some 36 million, as compared to an electorate of 7 million in 1920, and representing 30 per cent of the adult population,[3] would elect 1585 representatives to the provincial legislatures. The Act of 1935 was the first constitutional measure introduced by the British in India which envisaged that the parties winning a majority of seats in the legislatures would form ministries which would function on the basis of joint and collective responsibility.[4]

Both the Congress and the League were dissatisfied with the Act and held that it did not go far enough to satisfy the political aspirations of Indians. Nehru had described the act as 'a charter of bondage',[5] and a Congress resolution of 1936 stated that the future constitution of India could only be framed by a Constituent Assembly based on adult franchise.[6] The League had criticized the Federal part of the Act as 'most reactionary', but decided to work the provincial part 'for what it is worth'.[7] It was expected that the Congress would sweep the polls in the Hindu majority provinces, and the League, or other parties led by Muslim leaders, would win in the Muslim majority provinces. Their opposition to the federal part of the Act would be counterbalanced by the presence of the 115 Princely States which would join the federation in accordance with the federal part of the Act.[8]

In spite of their opposition to the Act, both Congress and the League decided to contest the provincial elections, if only to make use of the election campaign to spread their respective messages to the electorate.

[3] *Indian Franchise Committee Report*, vol. 1 (Calcutta, 1932), p. 33.

[4] *Government of India Act* (New Delhi, 1936).

[5] M. Gwyer and A. Appadorai (eds), *Speeches and Documents on the Indian Constitution 1921–47*, vol. 1 (Oxford, 1957), p. 386.

[6] Ibid., p. 385. [7] Ibid., pp. 384–5.

[8] For the politics behind the making of the Act of 1935, see R. J. Moore, *The Crisis of Indian Unity, 1917–40* (Oxford, 1970).

In 1936, there appeared to be some reason for Nehru's optimism on the communal problem. The Hindu Mahasabha, the leading Hindu communal organization, had no influence among the Hindu masses, and had been dismissed by Congress leaders as politically irrelevant.[9] On the Muslim side, Jinnah, then the most outstanding Muslim leader at the all India level, had expressed willingness to 'forget the Communal Award and to apply our mind to larger questions affecting India'.[10]

Jinnah's own position in Indian politics was far from secure. In 1931, he had exiled himself to England after being ignored by Congress, the British, and most sections of Muslim political opinion.[11] An invitation from Liaqat Ali Khan, a prominent Muslim Leaguer from the UP, to return to India and to 'put new life into the Muslim League and save it',[12] had resulted in his attempt, in 1936, to organize the League for elections to the provincial legislatures.

The League had been more or less defunct since 1920. In 1927, its total membership was 1330. Between 1931 and 1933 its annual expenditure did not exceed Rs 3,000. Decisions of the Council of the Muslim League were taken by a very small minority, with only 10 out of its 310 members forming a quorum. Since the central office of the League was situated in Delhi, Leaguers from provinces far away from Delhi hardly ever attended party meetings.[13]

The League's popular appeal was negligible. Part of the reason for this lay in the social conservatism of its members. Wealth, social position and education determined entry into the League. Between 1924 and 1926, only 7 out of 144 resolutions passed had touched upon

[9] Anita Singh, 'Nehru and the Communal Problem, 1936–1939', unpublished M. Phil Thesis submitted to Jawaharlal Nehru University, 1976, p. 103.

[10] *Bombay Chronicle*, 3 April 1936.

[11] Jinnah himself admitted that in 1931, 'Muslims were unhappy with me because of my views regarding joint electorates. My Hindu friends were angry with me because of the fourteen points that I advocated . . . The British Parliamentarians were also resentful because I had characterized the Round Table Conference itself as a fraud'. Quoted in K. B. Sayeed, *Pakistan: the Formative Phase* (London, 1968), p. 291.

[12] Hector Bolitho, *Jinnah Creator of Pakistan* (London, 1954), p. 105.

[13] This paragraph is based largely on C. Khaliquzzaman, *Pathway to Pakistan*, (Lahore, 1961), pp. 137–8; K.B. Sayeed, *Pakistan the Formative Phase*, pp. 176–7, and Z. H. Zaidi (ed.), *Introduction to M. A. Jinnah-Ispahani Correspondence 1936–48* (Karachi, 1976), pp. 10–14, and Z. H. Zaidi, 'Aspects of the Development of Muslim League Policy' in C. H. Philips and M. D. Wainwright (eds.), *The Partition of India* (London, 1970), p. 246.

social and economic problems. The last time these issues had been debated was in 1928.[14] The League had never contested elections on an all-India basis,[15] and the extent of support for it in the Muslim majority provinces was doubtful. It could only provide a rallying point for Muslims at the all-India level on questions such as representation in the services and in legislatures; and when these had been settled, as, for example, in the Communal Award of 1932, the League appeared to have little to offer Muslims in the provinces.[16]

The Act of 1919 had introduced responsible government in the provinces. This set the scene for the emergence of parties and politicians whose base and horizons were essentially provincial, and whose political alliances cut across communal divisions.[17] They had, therefore, little interest in Jinnah's all-India Muslim politics.

In the Punjab, for example, Fazli Husain, whose Unionist party had governed the province since 1920, believed that Muslims, whose majority in the province was only marginal, could not achieve anything without the cooperation of the Hindu and Sikh minorities. The need for Hindu and Sikh support partly determined the intercommunal character of the Unionist party, which represented agrarian interests in the Punjab.[18]

Jinnah received, then, a crushing rebuff when he asked Fazli Husain to join the Muslim League Parliamentary Board in 1936. Jinnah was told of

> 'the advisability of keeping his finger out of the Punjab pie . . . we cannot possibly allow "provincial autonomy" to be tampered with in any sphere, and by anybody, be he a nominee of the powers who have given this autonomy or a President of the Muslim League or any other association or body.'[19]

In Bengal, an opportunity for Muslim unity arose when Hindus in Calcutta started an agitation against the Communal Award in August 1936. The Award had given Muslims 48.6 per cent of the

[14] Zaidi, Introduction to *Jinnah-Ispahani Correspondence*, pp. 13–14.

[15] Zaidi, 'Muslim League Policy', p. 253.

[16] Zaidi, Introduction to *Jinnah-Ispahani Correspondence*, pp. 13–15.

[17] On the effects of the Act of 1919 see D. Page, *Prelude to Partition: The Indian Muslims and the Imperial System of Control 1920–1932* (New Delhi, 1982).

[18] Ibid and Azim Husain, *Fazli Husain* (Bombay, 1946).

[19] Sikander Hyat Khan to Fazli Husain, 1 May 1935, Fazli Husain papers, quoted in Zaidi, Introduction to *Jinnah–Ispahani Correspondence*, p. 16.

seats in the legislature, and the British had envisaged that landlords would support them and raise their majority to 51.4 per cent. Hindus alleged that they had not been represented in proportion to their population in the province, while Muslims had been allowed weightage in all Muslim minority provinces. But a cleavage soon arose between the parties which had united against the Hindus. The United Muslim Party had been started by the Nawab of Dacca to contest the provincial elections and it represented big landlords, lawyers and businessmen. It could not make common cause with the Krishak Proja Party of Fazlul Huq, which had been founded as the Nikil Banga Proja Samity in 1929,[20] and which espoused the interests of poor peasants and small landowners. As the majority of poor peasants in Bengal were Muslims, Huq could claim that his party represented the Muslim majority of Bengal. But the intercommunal character of his political alliances can be seen by his maintenance of links with Hindu and Congress leaders even while he was Vice-President of the Bengal Provincial Muslim League.[21]

Jinnah initially managed to bring together the United Muslim Party and the KPP. But Huq walked out of the agreement because Leaguers refused to accept his demand that they also join the KPP and incorporate in the League's election manifesto a promise to abolish the Permanent Settlement in Bengal. The big *zamindars* of Dacca's United Muslim Party would not agree to this, so Jinnah brushed aside Huq's proposals as not being 'practical politics'. But the final break between Huq and Jinnah seems to have been caused by Huq's opposition to the nomination of 4 non-Bengali businessmen to the Muslim League Parliamentary Board.[22]

In Bihar, the United Muslim and Ahrar parties could not sink personal differences and unite with the League. In the Central Provinces and Madras, disagreements about the nomination of candidates proved the stumbling block in the way of Muslim unity. In Sind, leaders of the Azad Muslim Party did not want their initiative in provincial matters to be fettered by an all India parliamentary board. So, personal and provincial rivalries prevented the formation of a single Muslim party in most provinces.[23]

[20] Shila Sen, *Muslim Politics in Bengal, 1937–1947* (New Delhi, 1976), pp. 74–5.
[21] Zaidi, Introduction to *Jinnah–Ispahani Correspondence*, pp. 8–9.
[22] Ibid., p. 22 and Sen, *Muslim Politics*, pp. 76–8.
[23] Zaidi, *Muslim Politics*, pp. 248–9.

It was in the United Provinces, with the Muslim Unity Board, that Jinnah was able, eventually, to make an alliance. The Board had been formed at the time of the Unity Conference of 1933, when representatives of two leading Muslim organizations, the Muslim Conference and the Nationalist Muslims, led by Khaliquzzaman, agreed to form a joint front to promote the political interests of Muslims.[24] The Board seems to have had little sympathy with the Muslim League, against whom some of its own candidates successfully contested for Muslim seats in the Central Legislature in the elections of 1934.[25]

The success achieved by the Unity Board in the elections—it won a third of the Muslim seats in the Legislature[26]—probably explains Jinnah's eagerness to reach a settlement with it. Why the Unity Board responded so enthusiastically to Jinnah's call for Muslim unity is not so easily discernible. Perhaps, as Sir Harry Haig, the Governor, wrote, it was because the name of the Muslim League carried considerable influence in the UP.[27] Khaliquzzaman, who skilfully balanced himself between three parties, does not give a very satisfactory account of the events which prompted him and other leaders of the Unity Board to respond to Jinnah's appeal. He simply says that the Board was at first willing to consider a Congress request to put up Muslim candidates to contest the Muslim League and the National Agriculturist Party[28] in the coming elections. Later, however, one of the leaders of the Unity Board, Ahmad Said, seemed to be in agreement with Jinnah on what is vaguely described as 'the future policy of Muslims', and felt that Jinnah was 'prepared to go very far' to satisfy the Board.[29]

Jinnah and the leaders of the Unity Board appeared to agree that the Muslim League 'consisted mostly of big landlords, title-holders and selfish people, who looked to their class and personal interests more than to communal and national interests and who had always

[24] For an account of the circumstances leading to the formation of the Unity Board, see Khaliquzzaman, *Pathway to Pakistan* (Lahore, 1961), pp. 117–20.

[25] Ibid., p. 130. [26] Ibid., p. 142.

[27] Haig to Linlithgow, 21 May 1936, *HC*, vol. 5.

[28] The formation of the NAP was encouraged by Sir Malcolm Hailey, Governor of the UP, to counterpoise the Congress. See P.D. Reeves, 'Landlords and Party Politics in the United Provinces 1934–1937', in D.A. Low (ed.) ***Soundings in Modern South Asian History*** (London, 1968), pp. 261–82.

[29] Khaliquzzaman, *Pathway to Pakistan*, pp. 140–1.

been ready to sacrifice them to suit British policy.' Jinnah wished to purify and revive the League. In this connection, he intended to ask the League to give him a mandate to form a parliamentary board for the purposes of the forthcoming elections. He promised the Unity Board a majority on the parliamentary board, and stressed the need for a united Muslim front. One difference remained between the Unity Board and the Muslim League. The Unity Board was committed to the goal of independence; the Muslim League was not. Jinnah reassured the Unity Board. 'When I give you a majority in the Parliamentary Board you can do everything'.[30]

It was against this background that the twenty-fourth session of the Muslim League opened at Bombay on 11 April 1936. The two hundred delegates who assembled there sought primarily the 'all-round uplift of the Muslims.[31] From the outset, dissimilarities between the League and the Congress on political issues were evident. Whatever the differences between Nehru and his colleagues on the Congress Working Committee, they were all agreed on one point—the winning of independence by India. But Syed Wazir Hasan, far from taking an anti-imperialist stand in his presidential address to the Muslim League, spoke of 'the fortunate connection between India and the British Crown'. He defined 'ultimate object of the constitutional advancement of the Muslims of India' as 'the attainment of responsible government for our mother-land'. *Swaraj, purna swaraj*, 'self-government', 'complete independence', 'responsible government', 'substance of independence', and Dominion Status, were to be, among other things, 'under the aegis . . . of the Crown of the Emperor of India'.[32] A resolution passed at this session of the Muslim League did not demand independence: it referred to 'India's most cherished goal of complete responsible government'.[33]

The election manifestoes of the Congress[34] and the League[35] further reflected the differences in their objectives and ideals. The manifesto of the League was vaguely worded, and was characterized by an absence of commitment on any issue. It made a show of concern for the religious rights of Muslims, which it professed to

[30] Ibid., p. 141.

[31] S.S. Pirzada, (ed.) *Foundations of Pakistan: All-India Muslim League Documents*, vol. 2 (Karachi, 1970), p. 235.

[32] Ibid., pp. 241, 248–9. [33] Ibid., p. 261.

[34] The Congress Election Manifesto, 22 August, 1936, *SW*, vol. 7, pp. 459–64.

[35] Khaliquzzaman, *Pathway to Pakistan*, p. 417.

protect. It asked for the repeal of all repressive laws, reduction in the cost of administration and military expenditure, and called for the social, educational and economic uplift of the rural population.

The Congress manifesto, drafted by Nehru, rejected the new constitution 'in its entirety', while the Muslim League manifesto made no mention of it. The manifesto of the League also made no reference to the future political development of India. Independence was not demanded, and, it was clear that the Muslim League did not desire the severance of the British connection. It is, in fact, significant that one of the reasons for the failure of negotiations between Jinnah and the Ahrars, who had a radical social programme, was Jinnah's refusal to promise them that a demand for independence would be made in the election manifesto of the Muslim League.[36]

The Congress manifesto reflected the growing mass support for the organization, and stressed the crucial role to be played by the masses in the struggle for freedom.[37] The Muslim League manifesto merely asked for the creation of 'a healthy public opinion and general political consciousness throughout the country'. In this connection, it should be noted that the Muslim League, in its session at Bombay, had rejected a proposal to reduce the membership fee from one rupee to four annas.[38]

It seems rather strange that British officials in 1936, and many writers since then,[39] thought that the social and economic objectives of the Congress and the League were similar. British officials thought that the manifesto of the League was as socialistic as that of the Congress! Haig in fact considered the NAP as a counterpoise to both the Congress and the Muslim League in the UP.[40] The election manifesto of the League resembled not the Congress manifesto, but the manifestoes of the National Agricultural Parties of Agra and Oudh, whose formation had been encouraged by the British in 1934

[36] M. Noman, *Muslim India: The Rise and Growth of the All-Indian Moslem League* (Allahabad, 1942), p. 329. On the Ahrars, see also P. Hardy, *The Muslims of British India* (Cambridge, 1972), p. 216.

[37] *SW*, vol. 7, p. 460. [38] *IAR*, 1936, vol. 1, p. 295.

[39] See, for example, FR for Punjab for first half of June, 1936, HP File No. 18/6/36; S. Gopal, *Jawaharlal Nehru: A Biography*, vol. 1, 1889–1947 (London, 1975), p. 223; S.R. Mehrotra, 'The Congress and the Partition of India,' in Philips & Wainwright (eds), *Partition of India*, p. 193.

[40] Haig to Linlithgow, 29 October 1936, *HC*, vol. 112.

to counter what they regarded as the political, and social radicalism of the Congress.[41]

As the provincial elections approached, Nehru reiterated in his presidential address to the Faizpur Congress in December 1936 the struggle against imperialism, the issues of social and economic freedom, the demand for a Constituent Assembly, his hostility to the Indian States system, and the need for greater mass participation in the Congress.[42] The address emphasised his belief that the contest in India was 'between two forces—the Congress as representing the will to freedom of the nation, and the British Government in India and its supporters who oppose this urge and try to suppress it.'[43]

Jinnah did not agree. There was a third party in India, he sharply informed Nehru, and that was the Muslims' Party;[44] revealing a vital difference in his attitude to political questions from Nehru's. For Nehru, the issue was that of independence. 'He who is for it must be with the Congress and if he talks in terms of communalism he is not keen on independence'.[45] Jinnah's sole aim was to establish the Muslim League as the only representative of Muslim affairs and to maintain it as such in the forefront of Indian politics.

Nehru's reply to Jinnah revealed his disdain for the political and long-term role a communal organization such as the League could play on the Indian political scene. He expressed unhappiness over Jinnah's reference to a 'third party', for, as he saw it, between British imperialism and Indian nationalism Jinnah would have Muslims remain as a political group apart, apparently playing off one against

[41] The election manifesto of the NAP of Agra: 'To devise means for peace, prosperity and good government of the country; to adopt all constitutional means in order to promote self-government in India; to create a healthy public opinion; to protect and advance by all constitutional means the interests of the people generally and of the agricultural population particularly in these provinces; to help and advance the political, social, educational and economic uplift of the province; to encourage industries and cottage and agricultural industries particularly; . . . to regulate exchange policy in the interests of the country; to reduce expenditure and effect substantial economy in every branch of the government administration'. The manifesto of the NAP of Oudh also called for 'the relief of agricultural indebtedness' and 'the reduction of the burden of taxation'. See P.D. Reeves, 'Landlords and Party Politics', pp. 292–3.

[42] Presidential address to the Faizpur Congress, 27 December 1936, *SW*, vol. 7, pp. 598–614.

[43] 'Line up with the Congress', 18 September 1936, Ibid., p. 468.

[44] *Bombay Chronicle*, 4 January 1937.

[45] 'Line up with the Congress', *SW*, vol. 7, pp. 468–9.

the other, and seeking communal advantage even at the cost of the larger public good.[46] This was 'communalism raised to the nth power'. Nehru explained, with a patient sarcasm, the unacceptability of the 'logical conclusion' of Jinnah's statement—'that in no department of public activity must non-Muslims have anything to do with Muslim affairs'.[47] He ridiculed the 'new test of orthodoxy' being enunciated by Jinnah—that Muslims were 'only those who follow Mr Jinnah and the Muslim League'.[48]

Nehru decried the communal philosophy of the League, as he pointed out that 'real issues', pertaining to economic and political problems, could not be considered communally.[49] He attached no significance to 'third parties', 'middle and undecided groups', for, in the long run, they had no role to play. The Congress represented Indian nationalism 'and is thus charged with a historic destiny'.[50]

Nehru was contemptuous of the indifference of the League to the question of independence, and of its distance from the masses. 'It represents a group of Muslims no doubt, highly estimable persons but functioning in the higher regions of the upper middle classes and having no contacts with the Muslim masses and few even with the lower middle class'.[51] He welcomed cooperation with the League, but only on the basis of anti-imperialism and the good of the masses. He ruled out pacts between handfuls of upper class people which ignored the interests of the masses.[52]

Jinnah chafed under Nehru's derisive view of the Muslim League even as he attacked what he regarded as Nehru's claim to be the 'sole custodian of the masses'. With a sarcasm that matched that of Nehru, he challenged the Congress claim that it was a national organization and defended the communal character of the League. 'The League does not believe in assuming a non-communal label with a few adventurers or credulous persons belonging to other communities thrown in and who have no backing of their people, and thus pass off as the only party entitled to speak and act on behalf of the whole of India'.[53]

Jinnah's stand on political and economic questions was also revealed. He asserted that the Muslim League would maintain a sepa-

[46] 'The Congress and Muslims,' 10 January 1937, *Eighteen Months in India*, hereafter referred to as *EMII* (Allahabad, 1938), p. 152.

[47] Ibid., pp. 150–1. [48] Ibid., p. 151.

[49] Ibid., p., 152. [50] Ibid., p. 153. [51] Ibid., p. 154.

[52] Ibid., pp. 155–6. [53] *Leader*, 23 January 1937.

rate identity; and he made a show of the League's importance, gratuitously laying down the terms under which the League would cooperate with any party in the struggle for freedom. The Muslim League 'is prepared to join hands with any progressive party in the fight for the country's freedom, but to achieve this the question of minorities must be settled satisfactorily'. Jinnah expressed his disagreement with 'certain methods and means to which the Congress stands pledged.' He informed Nehru that 'Even a large bulk of patriotic and nationalistic Hindus are not members of the Congress. Because they do not believe in the Congress methods'.[54]

The British had the most interest in the electoral fortunes of the Congress, which they regarded as a test of its strength against them. Even as they predicted a Congress victory in most provinces,[55] British officials discussed the possibility of an opposition to it, especially in view of the emphasis on independence and economic reform in its election manifesto. In the UP, the British were supporting the National Agriculturist Party against the Congress; Linlithgow hoped that Nehru's expounding of his radical economic theories would consolidate the Right throughout India for the purpose of the elections.[56] It is interesting, in view of the fact that both the Congress and the British sought the hand of the Muslim League only three years later, that there are only the most cursory references—or none at all—to the election campaign of the League in official reports, and, at this time, the British do not seem to have envisaged its emergence as an opposition of any significance. Perhaps it was because the League was considered similar to the Congress in its socialistic tendencies—and Jinnah the arch enemy of the Raj![57]—and, of course, the League had not been able to consolidate its position, as the leading Muslim organization, especially in the Muslim-majority provinces.

The elections revealed the strength of the Congress as an all India force. The Congress contested 1161 seats in the general constituencies and won 716, securing a clear majority in six out of the eleven

[54] Ibid.

[55] See, for example, Brabourne to Linlithgow, 13 November 1936; Keane to Linlithgow, 28 October 1936; Sifton to Linlithgow, 3 November 1936; Hyde Gowan to Linlithgow, 10 November 1936; *LC*, vol. 112.

[56] Linlithgow to Zetland, 27 August 1936, Ibid., vol. 3.

[57] Raja of Mahmudabad, 'Some Memories', in Philips and Wainwright (eds), *Partition of India*, p. 384.

provinces of British India. It emerged as the largest single party in three other provinces. The extent of the success of the Congress confounded most political pundits,[58] and one British official could only remark, somewhat grudgingly, that it remained to be seen whether the Congress would actually fulfil its promises.[59] Officials unanimously attributed the victory of the Congress to the absence of any organized opposition against it, [60] the attraction of the names of Gandhi and Nehru,[61] and 'wild promises' of the reduction of rent.[62] The enormous extent of the new franchise was regarded as a great advantage to the Congress, especially in Bihar and in the UP, where Congress election propaganda had been directed more against landlords than against the British.[63] Here the Congress defeated, often in straight fights, big landlords who were thought to have exercised exceptionally great influence over their tenants,[64] and whom the British had hoped would be able to check any rising tide of Congress fortunes. In the NWFP also, the Congress defeated the Khans—the great feudal landowners—usually by very big margins.[65]

The Congress fared best in the UP, where it captured 133 out of 288 seats in the Legislative Assembly. It was in a position to form governments in Bihar, where it won 95 out of 152 seats; in Bombay, where it secured 88 out of 175; in the CP, where it emerged victo-

[58] See, for example, FR for Assam for first half of January 1937; FR for Orissa for second half of January 1937; HP file no. 18/2/37; and FR for UP for first half of February 1937, HP file no. 18/2/37; Anderson to Linlithgow, 8 February 1937, *LC*, vol. 112.

[59] Haig to Linlithgow, 13 February 1937, *LC*, vol. 112.

[60] FR for Bihar for first half of February 1937, HP file no. 18/2/37; Keane to Linlithgow, 15 December 1936; Anderson to Linlithgow, 3 December 1936; Hyde Gowan to Linlithgow, 10 November 1936; Sifton to Linlithgow, 9 February 1937; all these letters to Linlithgow in *LC*, vol. 112.

[61] See, for example, FR for UP for first half of February 1937; FR for Bihar for second half of February 1937; HP file no. 18/2/37.

[62] Haig to Linlithgow, 9 February 1937, *LC*, vol. 112; FR for Assam for second half of January 1937, HP file no. 18/1/37; and FR for Bihar for first half of February 1937, HP file no. 18/2/37.

[63] Griffith to Linlithgow, 9 November 1936; Haig to Linlithgow, 26 January and 4 February 1937; *LC*, vol. 112; FR for Assam for first half of January 1937, HP file no. 18/1/37; FR for Bihar for first half of February 1937; HP file no. 18/2/37.

[64] Haig to Linlithgow, 13 February 1937; *LC*, vol. 112; and FR HP file no. 18/2/87 for Bihar for first half of February 1937.

[65] Griffith to Linlithgow, 22 February 1937, *LC*, vol. 112.

rious winning 71 out of 112 seats; in Madras and Orissa, where it obtained 150 out of 215 and 36 out of 60 seats respectively in the Legislative Assemblies. The Congress routed the Hindu Mahasabha in the UP and in the Punjab, and disabled it politically.

Handicapped during its election campaign by a shortage of Muslim workers,[66] the Congress achievement with Muslim seats was somewhat less remarkable. It contested only 56 out of the 482 Muslim seats in British India, and won 28. It did not secure a single Muslim seat in the UP, Bengal and in the Punjab. It did not contest any Muslim seats in Sind, Bombay, Bihar and the UP, and failed to win any Muslim seat in Bengal, the CP and the Punjab. Its greatest successes with Muslim seats were achieved in Madras where it obtained 4, and in the NWFP, where it won 15.

The success of the Congress in the NWFP was only one indication that its overall failure in Muslim constituencies did not necessarily reflect communal trends. The Muslim League fared very badly in the Muslim majority provinces and was not in a position to form a government in any of them. Of the 117 seats allotted to Muslims in Bengal it won 38. In the Punjab it contested 7 and obtained only 2 out of 84 Muslim seats; and in Sind it won only 3 out of 33 Muslim seats. Its inability to put up a sufficient number of Muslim candidates in these provinces showed that it lacked a popular base in the Muslim majority provinces. The fact that an intercommunal party based on the agrarian interests of all communities won a majority in the Punjab showed that communal questions did not play a decisive part in the elections. The same could be said of Bengal, where the success of the Congress and the KPP pointed to the popularity of radical economic programmes.[67] Taking into account the rout of the Hindu Mahasabha in the general constituencies at the hands of the Congress, and the lack of success of the League in the Muslim majority provinces, it can be concluded, then, that communal questions did not play a major role in the elections of 1937.

The election results proved that neither the Congress nor the League could claim to represent Muslims. But the success of the Congress in the general constituencies showed its popularity on the all India level; for the Muslim League, the future did not appear very promising as it had failed to capture a majority of the Muslim

[66] G.B. Pant to Rajendra Prasad, 21 January 1937, *RPC* File II/37, Col. 1, reel 5.
[67] FR for Bengal for first half of February 1937, HP file no. 18/1/37.

votes; and more significantly, it was not in a position to form a government on its own in any province. This realization lay behind the almost conciliatory posture taken up by Jinnah after the elections. He therefore expressed the League's willingness to cooperate 'with any group or party if the basic principles are determined by common consent.'[68]

Jinnah, however, was never the man to humble himself, or, as he put it later, 'to bow our head before Anand Bhawan'.[69] It was characteristic of him to declare that 'Minus verbiage and slogans there is no substantial difference between the policy of the Muslim League and the Congress', refer to 'fundamental differences' between them, and to dissuade Muslims from signing the pledge of another party 'for the sake of ministers',[70] all in the same breath. Jinnah's position in March 1937 was an unenviable one. Not only had the Muslim League failed to capture a majority of Muslim votes; there were few signs of the Muslim unity which Jinnah had tried to build up since 1934, as provincial Muslim leaders of the League were showing no interest in a united Muslim front, and some Leaguers were even suggesting that it would be better if the Congress and the Muslim League could reach some sort of understanding.[71] Jinnah, therefore, had to reconcile his personal antagonism towards the Congress with the conciliatory mood of the League towards it, as well as of the need of the League to cooperate with it, without appearing to be confessing the League's weakness and swallowing his pride. This is illustrated by a statement in which he said that there was no difference between the Congress and the 'Moslems' except that the latter stood for the establishment of the rights of the minority community, while at the same time he attacked Congress propaganda which, he said, had no other object than capturing votes.

Jinnah's statements anticipated a Congress decision on the question of office acceptance.[72] Much to the dismay of Nehru and the radicals in the Congress, the AICC, on 18 March 1937, voted, by 127 votes to 70, in favour of acceptance of office by the Congress, subject to the condition that Governors of provinces would not use the special powers vested in them by Section 93 of the Government of India Act. The AICC decision provided Jinnah with an oppor-

[68] *Leader*, 1 March 1937. [69] *Leader*, 12 May 1937.

[70] *Leader*, 15 March 1937. [71] *Leader*, 16 March 1937.

[72] See, for example, *Bombay Chronicle*, 19 March 1937. Also Gopal, *Nehru*, pp. 217–19; Tomlinson, *Congress and the Raj* (London, 1976), pp. 62–3.

tunity to renew his offer of cooperation with congress ministries. Jinnah now highlighted points of agreement between the League and the Congress.

> 'I congratulate the right wing of the Congress leaders for having carried the Congress with them. They have adopted the formula which practically is the same as was adopted by the All-India Moslem League on April 12, 1936, namely, that in the present conditions we should utilize the constitution for what it is worth . . . . Now struggling as we are for national self-government, perhaps it will be easier for the All-India Muslim League parties to cooperate with other progressive parties as the Congress is also lined up.'

Characteristically, however, Jinnah scoffed at Congress attempts to gain assurances that the Governors would not use their special powers of interference. Any such assurance, said Jinnah, would be futile as the Governor was the ultimate authority in the province according to the Instrument of Accession of the Act. 'It may, however, appeal to the imagination of some people that the Congress has laid down something novel'.

Jinnah skilfully veiled his apprehension about the future of the League as he persisted in upholding its separate identity. He exhorted Muslims to rally round the Muslim League banner. [73] It was not possible for Muslims and Hindus to merge their identities; and while it was most feasible for them to march together towards the goal of freedom, he did not want Muslims to do this to please every particular person or organization. He did not want them to be camp followers but to be in the vanguard.[74]

Nehru was not inclined to respond sympathetically to Jinnah's call, and his terms, for cooperation, especially at a time when he felt confident that the Congress itself could win over the Muslim masses on the basis of economic issues. Nor was he dismayed that the Congress had won only a fraction of the Muslim seats in the elections. During the election campaign the Congress had found a willing response from the Muslim masses 'and a desire to line up with our freedom movement'. Until now the Congress had not made much effort to work among the Muslim masses, and it was essential that the Congress take 'full advantage of this new interest and awakening', and make 'a special effort' to enrol more Muslim members, 'so that our struggle for freedom may become even more broadbased than it is, and the Muslim masses should take the prominent part in

[73] *Leader*, 22 March 1937. [74] *Leader*, 24 March 1937.

it which is their due.'[75] The Congress was not interested in pacts with a few persons representing communal organisations, 'with no common political background, meeting together and discussing and quarrelling.'[76] Clearly, Nehru, whether or not he saw the motives behind Jinnah's cautious overtures to the Congress, turned them down.

'It is remarkable that Jinnah and Shaukat Ali have worked themselves in a mad fury just because we have decided to work among the masses'.[77] The inception of the Congress Muslim mass contact programme, and Nehru's declaration that the Congress hoped to rouse the Muslim masses in its favour could hardly have been welcomed by a communal organization such as the League. Whatever Nehru may have said to the contrary,[78] this could only mean that the success of the programme would lead to the rout of the Muslim League as a political organization. To Jinnah, it must have seemed an insult, added to the injury, that not only was the Congress indifferent to the idea of cooperating with the Muslim League, but also that it was inaugurating a campaign, the very success of which would spell the political extinction of the League. The very reasons which made Nehru confident of its success roused Jinnah's fears. The appeal of Congress programmes to voters had been proved in the elections. If, as Nehru himself admitted, the Congress had not been very successful in winning Muslim seats, the League had not fared very well either. It had obtained only 4.8 per cent of the Muslim vote, and won only 43 out of 272 Muslim seats in the Muslim majority areas.[79] So far, it had also failed to enlist the support of Sikandar Hyat Khan and Fazlul Huq, whose parties were leading ministries in the Punjab and Bengal respectively. Not only had the League fared badly in the elections; it could not even count on successful parties led by Muslim leaders.

The implications of the Congress Muslim Mass Contact programme being quite clear, Jinnah's sharp reaction to its inauguration was not surprising. He regretted that Nehru should have found a solution which would produce more bitterness and frustrate the object that every nationalist had at heart.[80] To Jinnah, the Congress

[75] *Leader*, 3 April 1937.
[76] 'The Congress and Muslims,' 4 April 1937, *EMII*, p. 161.
[77] K.M. Ashraf to S.A. Brelvi, 23 April 1937, AICC file G-68, 1937, p. 137.
[78] Nehru to Ismail Khan, 5 February 1938, *NC*, vol. 39.
[79] Calculated from election returns of 1937. [80] *Leader*, 22 April 1937.

attempt 'under the guise of establishing mass contact with the Musalmans, is calculated to divide and weaken and break the Musalmans, and is an effort to detach them from their accredited leaders'.[81]

Jinnah's consternation was not eased by the attempts being made by some members of the Muslim League parliamentary board in the UP for cooperation between the Congress and the League in the province. Discussions between G.B. Pant and Khaliquzzaman, leader of the provincial MLPB, started almost as soon as the elections were over, and were encouraged by 'the amicable manner' in which the elections had been fought by both the Congress and the League.[82] For during the elections there had not been much conflict between the two parties, and in some places they had cooperated against the National Agriculturist Party. The Congress had supported the Muslim League candidate, where there was no Congress Muslim candidate, 'if he was not an obvious reactionary'.[83]

Uncertainty prevailed in Muslim League ranks in the UP after the elections. Some Muslim Leaguers were sympathetic to the 'interim' government headed by Chhatari,[84] while Khaliquzzaman spurned an offer to join it. Pant reportedly offered the League two seats in a possible Congress ministry[85] and earned Nehru's displeasure.[86] At a time when he stressed the need for unity and discipline among Congress legislative parties,[87] the Congress objectives of independence and mass betterment,[88] Nehru was not inclined to support moves for pacts with communal organizations which had no common political and economic policy, were dominated by reactionaries, and looked to the British for favours.[89] Nehru thus rebuffed the overtures of the League for a Congress-League ministry, even as he chided Congressmen who talked 'in terms of pacts and compromises with Muslims or other religious groups'.[90]

[81] Pirzada, *Documents*, p. 270.

[82] Khaliquzzaman, *Pathway to Pakistan*, p. 153; see also note by Donaldson dated 14 August 1940, Reforms Office file 89/40-R; referred to hereafter as Donaldson.

[83] Nehru to Rajendra Prasad, 21 July 1937, *NC*, vol. 85, and Donaldson.

[84] Chhatari was invited by the British to form an 'interim' government in the UP following the Congress refusal to form a ministry in the province because it had not received an assurance from the Governor that he would not interfere in the working of the ministry.

[85] Haig to Linlithgow, 7 April 1937, *HC*, vol. 17A.

[86] Nehru to Pant, 30 March 1937, AICC file E-1, 1936–1937, p. 7.

[87] *EMII*, p. 126. [88] Ibid., p. 157. [89] Ibid., p. 160. [90] Ibid., p. 157.

The negotiations between Pant and Khaliquzzaman did not get off to a very promising start. On 2 April Pant informed Nehru that he had received no definite response to a suggestion made by him that nationalist Muslims join the Congress actively both inside and outside the legislature.[91]

Meanwhile, the manoeuvres of Khaliquzzaman for a Congress-League settlement on the one hand; the announcement of the Congress Muslim mass contact programme on the other, created some consternation in the UP Muslim League. Many provincial Leaguers were alarmed at the political implications of the Congress programme, and it was believed that a majority of them were not likely to support Khaliquzzaman's overtures to the Congress. Even as Khaliquzzaman wavered between taking the risk of being defeated in the Muslim League[92] and fulfilling his ambition of securing a ministerial post in a Congress government, a majority of the members of the UP Muslim League appeared willing to take a lead from Jinnah.[93] Jinnah now made open his opposition to Khaliquzzaman's flirtation with the Congress. '. . . I want to make it clear,' he admonished Khaliquzzaman, 'that it will be useless for any individual or individuals to effectively carry the Muslims behind them if any settlement is arrived at with a particular group or even . . . with the whole province. I say that it is a pity that these roundabout efforts are being made. The only object of it can be to create some differences between Mussalmans.'[94]

Jinnah's warning went home. On 7 May, at a meeting of the UP Muslim League at which he was also present, it was decided that the Muslim League would not merge with the Congress or lose its independence either inside or outside the legislature. Khaliquzzaman was asked to make it plain to the Congress that Muslim Leaguers would not accept Congress decisions on matters affecting the Communal Award.[95] A resolution was passed which emphasized the differences in the aims of the Congress and the League. It said that the Muslim League party in the legislature could not and should not join the Congress in its policy of wrecking the Constitution.[96] The

[91] Pant to Nehru, *NC*, 2 April 1937, vol. 79.
[92] Haig to Linlithgow, 23 April 1937, *HC*, vol. 17A.
[93] Haig to Linlithgow, 7 May 1937, Ibid.
[94] *Leader*, 10 May 1937. [95] *Bombay Chronicle*, 8 May 1937.
[96] *Leader*, 10 May 1937.

resolution was considered a personal triumph for Jinnah: Khaliquzzaman accepted the situation.[97]

The animosity displayed by the Muslim League towards the Congress on the occasion of the Bundelkhand by-election symbolised 'the alarm that has been caused among the Muslims generally by the Congress attempts to capture the Muslim masses', the strong feeling among them 'that if the community is to retain its individuality, no efforts must be spared in resisting the attempts of the Congress to absorb them'.[98] The existence of such feeling showed how a political conflict with the League could be construed as an attack on Muslims as a community. In June 1937, the seat of the constituency of Jhansi-Hamirpur-Orai in Bundelkhand fell vacant owing to the death of its holder, K.B. Habibullah, who had belonged to the Muslim League. Both the Congress and the League put up their own candidates—Nisar Ahmed Sherwani and Rafiuddin respectively—to contest the by-election for the seat. For the League, it was a question of survival. For, in spite of Jinnah's call for Muslim unity, there were signs of restlessness within the ranks of the Muslim League over its policies. Syed Wazir Hasan, who had presided over the Muslim League session in April 1936, now appealed to Muslims to join the fight for independence led by the Congress.[99] On the eve of the by-election, A.H. Qureshi and Hakim Riazuddin, two Vice-Presidents of the Jhansi Muslim League, resigned from their posts and advised Muslims not to join the League.[100]

Jinnah now demonstrated his strategy for survival. On 30 June 1937, a statement, allegedly written by him, appeared in the Urdu newspaper *Khilafat*, which made a frankly communal appeal to the Muslim voter.

> 'My only object in organising the Muslim League, and the Muslim League Parliamentary Board, and putting forward the programme for the "Nazm" (Organization) of Musalmans . . . is that Mussalmans should unite among themselves as they have been ordered to do by God and his Prophet . . . Thank God our efforts are proving fruitful. Our success and progress is becoming an eye-sore to the enemies of Islam. They want to frighten and bully us. Their putting up a candidate for the by-election from Bundelkhand in opposition to the Muslim League is also one of such efforts.'

[97] Haig to Linlithgow, 8 May 1937, *HC*, vol. 17A.
[98] Haig to Linlithgow, 24 May 1937, Ibid.
[99] *Bombay Chronicle*, 12 June 1937.
[100] *Bombay Chronicle*, 26 June 1937.

The appeal exhorted Muslims to vote for Rafiuddin 'so that it will mean a crushing reply to the non-Muslim organisation and in future it will not dare to interfere in the affairs of Musalmans . . . . I assure you in my capacity as the President of the Muslim League and the Muslim League Parliamentary Board, that God willing the Shariat Islami, special rights of Musalmans, their culture and their language will be saved from the interference of outsiders'.[101]

Jinnah denied authorship of the statement[102] but it is significant that he did not condemn the exploitation of religious sentiment for political ends. Meanwhile, Shaukat Ali raised the cry of 'Islam in danger'. Exhorting Muslims to vote for Rafiuddin, Shaukat Ali said, 'Do it in the name of Islam, in the name of religion and its honour'.[103]

Nehru was astounded at the tactics of the League—'this is communalism in excelsis'[104]—even as he was determined that the Congress must face the challenge with all its strength.[105]

But even as Nehru urged that the Congress should approach the Muslim electorate in Bundelkhand 'on economic lines', and not compete with the Muslim League on its own ground,[106] Sherwani asked him to arrange for visits of prominent ulema to help him in his election campaign,[107] and a disapproving Nehru noted that Sherwani thought 'too much of the Maulvi type of individuals'.[108] For some Congress workers in Bundelkhand, appearances were everything. One of them requested that only Muslim volunteers be sent to campaign for Sherwani, 'and, if possible, with all the outward signs of a "Muslim" (I mean beards etc.)'.[109]

The Muslim League emerged victorious at Bundelkhand. Rafiuddin secured 4,700 votes; Sherwani obtained 2,000. The success of the Muslim League was a personal triumph for Jinnah. But its real significance lay in the nature of the League's challenge to the Congress. Bribery and the cry of 'religion in danger' contributed to its

[101] *Bombay Chronicle*, 2 July 1937.

[102] *Bombay Chronicle*, 2 July 1937.

[103] *NC*, part II, file 114, p. 8, from extract entitled 'Maulana Shokat Ali Sahib,' pp. 6–8.

[104] *Bombay Chronicle*, 1 July 1937.

[105] Nehru to Kidwai, 1 July 1937, AICC file G-61, 1937, p. 213.

[106] Nehru to Sherwani, 3 July 1937, Ibid., p. 105.

[107] Sherwani to Nehru, 2 July 1937, Ibid., pp. 161–2.

[108] Nehru to M.L. Saxena, 23 June 1937, Ibid., p. 247.

[109] Asst. Secy., UPCC, to R.A. Kidwai, 6 July 1937, Ibid., p. 157.

victory. Congress propaganda started only two days before the election and was entirely political and economic. So Congress leaders were not disheartened by the party's defeat at Bundelkhand and were satisfied that when the Muslim peasant was asked why he was voting for the Congress, 'he confessed frankly that he did so because he expected the Congress to reduce his rent.'[110]

Even as the battle for Bundelkhand was on, Khaliquzzaman and Ismail Khan approached Pant with the question of seats in a possible Congress ministry in the UP. On learning of this at the beginning of July, Maulana Azad met Khaliquzzaman who told him that he would give him a blank cheque provided he and Ismail were included in a ministry. Azad looked suspiciously on this move, and he and other members of the Congress Working Committee disliked the bargaining for seats in the ministry. They were wary of taking in two persons 'who, from the Congress point of view, were weak,' who had been fighting the Congress and who only seemed interested in the spoils of office, at the cost of Muslims who had always been staunch supporters of the Congress. Yet the Congress Working Committee were willing to consider the proposal as it held out the possibility of the winding up of the Muslim League in the UP and its absorption in the Congress; which would undoubtedly clear the political field of communal troubles. It would also 'knock over the British Government which relied so much on these troubles'.

At a time when the need for organizational unity and discipline appeared to be of paramount importance to Congress leaders, stringent conditions were offered to the UP Muslim League parliamentary group, and it was decided that Khaliquzzaman and Ismail would be taken into a Congress ministry only if they accepted all of them.[111] The Congress expected Muslim Leaguers to abide by decisions taken by the Congress party both inside and outside the legislature, and called for the dissolution of the Muslim League Parliamentary Board in the UP. Thereafter, the Muslim League would support Congress candidates during by-elections. Members of the League would also be bound by any Congress decision to resign from the legislature or from the ministry.[112]

Khaliquzzaman writes that he rejected the terms, which, to him,

[110] Nehru to Prasad, 21 July 1937, *NC*, vol. 85.
[111] Ibid. [112] Khaliquzzaman, *Pathway to Pakistan*, p. 161.

meant signing 'the death warrant' of the provincial Muslim League Parliamentary Board as well as of the Muslim League organization.[113] According to Nehru, however, he agreed to all the conditions except two: the winding up of the Parliamentary Board and the agreement not to set up separate candidates at by-elections; and said that he personally would agree to even these two conditions but that he did not have the authority to do so. Azad then informed him that he could not give him a final answer.

Meanwhile, Nehru felt 'very uncomfortable and was instinctively repelled by all this talk on an opportunistic basis'. He also feared that any settlement with the League would be temporary. The Congress Working Committee insisted that the League should accept all the conditions. Khaliquzzaman then promised to ask the Muslim League Executive to consider the question of by-elections. But now, Nehru did not encourage him at all.[114]

Khaliquzzaman writes that a few days later, on 24 July, Azad presented him with a modified version of the conditions laid down by the Congress for a coalition. Khaliquzzaman then demanded that 'the Muslim League Party members in the UP Assembly will be free to vote in accordance with their conscience, on communal matters', which would include religion, religious ceremonies, languages, culture, services, etc.[115] The Congress refused to accept such a provision, as it would have given the League a communal veto on many matters, and the possibility of a Congress–League coalition in the UP ended.

According to Maulana Azad, the negotiations foundered when Nehru, with his 'theoretical bias', turned down Khaliquzzaman's proposal to include both himself and Ismail Khan in the UP ministry.[116] But Nehru does not seem to have been directly involved in the negotiations, or even been fully informed of all that had taken place since March, until the beginning of July.[117] In any case, as Nehru himself pointed out, he alone was not responsible for the final decision. G.B. Pant, Rafi Ahmad Kidwai[118] and Azad,[119]

[113] Ibid., p. 161.
[114] Nehru to Prasad, 21 July 1937, *NC*, vol. 85.
[115] Khaliquzzaman, *Pathway to Pakistan*, pp. 162–3.
[116] M.A.K. Azad, *India Wins Freedom*, (New York, 1960) pp. 187–8.
[117] Nehru to Prasad, 21 July 1937, *NC*, vol. 85.
[118] *The Hindu*, 8 February 1959.
[119] Azad had opposed a Congress–League pact even in March. (Nehru to Abdul

among others, were also instrumental in arriving at the decision not to form a coalition with the League. From Wardha, Gandhi signalled his approval of the terms of the Congress offer to the League.[120] There was also no necessity for the Congress to form a coalition with any party as it had a clear majority in the UP. It was, in fact, the League which got valuable assistance from the Congress in the election: the direct benefits of the electoral understanding went to the League.[121]

'A ministry,' wrote Nehru to Jinnah in April 1938, 'must have a definite political and economic programme and policy.'[122] Such a basis for a coalition did not exist between the Congress and the Muslim League. The League, like its Hindu counterpart, the Hindu Mahasabha, was strictly a communal organization, more interested in claiming special privileges from the British, with whom it avoided any conflict. The Congress, on the other hand, was irrevocably opposed to British imperialism. The Congress was also interested in agrarian reform and feared that the League, which was largely a representative of the big zamindars of the UP, would stymie its attempts in that direction.[123] The Muslim League did, in fact, oppose the Tenancy Bill which was introduced by Pant's ministry in 1938.[124] How an economic problem could be given a communal colouring was illustrated by Khaliquzzaman's statement before the Cabinet Mission in 1946 that to strike at the zamindari in the UP was to strike at the root of Muslim existence.[125]

The conduct of Muslim Leaguers, including Khaliquzzaman and Ismail,[126] was at variance with their professed desire for a coalition.

Walli, 30 March 1937, AICC file G-5 (KW) (i), 1937, p. 139.) It is clear (Nehru to Prasad, 21 July 1937) that he was a party to the final decision not to form a coalition with the Muslim League.

[120] Nehru, 22 July 1937, *NC*, vol. 25. [121] Donaldson.

[122] Nehru to Jinnah, 6 April 1938, Pirzada, *Correspondence*, p. 1124.

[123] *The Hindu*, 8 February 1959.

[124] Papers relating to the Muslim League and the UP Tenancy Act, *NC*, part II, file 55.

[125] Meeting between Cabinet Delegation, Wavell, Ismail, Chundrigar, Raufshah and Khaliquzzaman on 8 April 1946, P.N.S. Mansergh (ed.) *The Transfer of Power 1942–1947*, hereafter referred to as *TOP*, vol. 7 (H.M.S.O., 1977) p. 166.

[126] Khaliquzzaman seems to have been a party to what was probably a communal appeal, which greatly dismayed Nehru. (Nehru to Khaliquzzaman, 27 June 1937, *NC*, vol. 39). Ismail has made an appeal to Muslim voters which was very similar to Jinnah's. 'I hope the Muslims now fully realize the political exigency of nominating

Jinnah opposed, all along, Khaliquzzaman's efforts to bring the negotiations to a successful conclusion. Khaliquzzaman himself vacillated between the prospect of a ministerial future and his anxiety not to lose influence in the Muslim League; and he eventually chose to abide by the dictates of Jinnah. Throughout the negotiations, he was also insistent that he would not collaborate in the ministry with Congress Muslims.[127] The differences in the aims of the Congress and the Muslim League, the fact that at no time did the League give the Congress an assurance that it would cooperate fully with it, justified the Congress decision not to form a coalition with the League.[128] Jinnah's opposition to the negotiations between provincial Leaguers and the Congress showed that the failure could not have been the reason behind his call for a sovereign Muslim state in March 1940.

The main significance of the failure of the negotiations for a Congress–League coalition in the UP was that it provided the Muslim League with excellent propaganda material to 'expose' the 'Hindu' bias of the Congress. Disagreements with the League on political and economic issues were made to imply that the Congress was biased against Muslims as a community. Jinnah alleged that the Congress had, 'by their words, deeds and programme shown, more and more, that the Musalmans cannot expect any justice or fair play at their hands. Wherever they were in a majority and wherever it

---

their own candidate to the legislatures . . . The League Parliamentary Board has been formed with a view to choose candidate (sic) for the legislature, who will safeguard the political and religious rights of the Muslims besides their culture and language. I hope you also realize the gravity of the situation with which we are faced in Bundelkhand. A non-Muslim organization has set up a nominee against the chosen representative of a Muslim organization . . . the victory of the former will falsify the Muslim right to choose their own representative and our community, in result, may face the gravest consequences . . . Therefore I appeal to you to call a halt to the intervention of the non-Muslim organization in our problems by electing the representative of the Muslim League'. *The Hindustan Times*, 30 June 1937.

[127] Donaldson.

[128] Interestingly, Haig correctly prophesized the outcome of the negotiations for a coalition between the Congress and the League in February 1937. 'There are rumours that the Congress will make considerable efforts to win over the whole of the Muslim League group, realising that if they do this and thus split the Muslims seriously, they will render the whole opposition ineffective . . . Nevertheless, it seems doubtful whether for the Ministry they will pass over the handful of genuine Congress Muslims in favour of those who are clearly not in real sympathy with the Congress aims.' Haig to Linlithgow, 17 February 1937, *HC*, vol. 16.

suited them, they refused to co-operate with the Muslim League parties and demanded unconditional surrender and the signing of their pledges'.[129]

Jinnah's presidential address to the Muslim League in October 1937 was, in fact, a declaration of war against the Congress. His political strategy was starting to crystallize. It consisted of attacking the Congress, and of equating Congress governments with 'Hindu' Raj. Jinnah alleged that the Congress was 'pursuing a policy which is exclusively Hindu', that it was imposing Hindi, *Bande Mataram* and the national flag on 'all and sundry'. By identifying the Congress with the majority community, Jinnah sought to create Muslim apprehensions against the Congress. 'On the very threshold of what little power and responsibility is given, the majority community have clearly shown their hand: that Hindustan is for the Hindus'.[130] The failure of the negotiations was depicted, not as the consequence of the absence of a common political programme between the Congress and the League, but as an example of the Congress' conception of nationalism, which, as the Pirpur Report alleged later, was based on 'the establishment of a national state of the majority community in which other nationalities and communities have only secondary rights'.[131] It was made to appear that the 'sectarianism' of the Congress, and not the League's own lack of popular support, was responsible for the fact that it had been 'deprived' of political power in the provinces, even as Jinnah acknowledged that the Congress leadership did not have a very high opinion of the Muslim League. 'No settlement with the majority is possible, as no Hindu leader speaking with any authority shows any concern or genuine desire for it'.[132]

Even as he railed against the Congress, Jinnah tacitly confessed the political inefficacy of the League, as he urged Muslims to 'develop power and strength' till they were 'fully organized, and have acquired that power and strength which must come from the solidarity and the unity of people'.[133] The Muslim League now seemed to have realized the importance of building up mass support. Provincial branches of the League were reorganized, and the membership fee was lowered from one rupee to two annas.[134] A comprehensive socio-economic programme was also framed. The program-

[129] Pirzada, *Documents*, p. 267. [130] Ibid., pp. 267–8.
[131] *Pirpur Report*, p. 2. [132] Pirzada, *Documents*, p. 269.
[133] Ibid., p. 269. [134] Zaidi, 'Muslim League Policy'. p. 259.

me included the fixation of working hours and minimum wages for factory workers, the reduction of rural and urban debts, the promotion of indigenous industries, and the advancement of primary, secondary and university education.[135]

But 'power' and 'strength' could not be built up until Jinnah had gained a foothold in the Muslim majority provinces. His ability to achieve this depended on the position of provincial Muslim politicians, rather than on the strength of any communal sentiment. In Bengal, no single party had obtained a majority in the elections. As leader of the largest single group, Fazlul Huq had some difficulty in forming a ministry. The provincial Congress was willing to form a coalition with him,[136] but the Congress High Command called a halt to the negotiations because of Huq's refusal to promise that his government would release political prisoners. Huq then turned to an assortment of groups—the Hindu Nationalist Group, the Europeans and the Scheduled Castes—for support. The family of his old adversary, the Nawab of Dacca, was given three posts in the ministry.[137]

The accommodation with Dacca and his group lost Huq the support of a radical group in the KPP, led by Nausher Ali and Shamsuddin, who crossed the floor of the House. Deserted by a section of his own followers, Huq now made overtures to the League, which was the largest single Muslim group in the Assembly. Declaring that 'no problem . . . relating to the administration of India can be solved without the League,'[138] he successfully wooed Jinnah in order to ensure the support of the provincial League for his ministry. At the Lucknow session of the League, he rounded on the Congress in terms that would have done credit to Jinnah himself. Acceptance of Congress offers, said Huq, would have meant signing 'with my own hands the death warrant of Islam.' Coalition with the Congress could only be 'on such terms as amount to the virtual effacement of the Muslims as a separate political entity.'[139]

But the strains were never far from the surface in this political marriage of convenience. Ispahani, one of Jinnah's most loyal lieutenants in Bengal, complained that the moment the ministry was

[135] Pirzada, *Documents*, p. 280.

[136] John Gallagher, 'The Congress in Bengal: The Period of Decline 1930–1939,' *Modern Asian Studies*, 7, 7, 1973, p. 643.

[137] Zaidi, Introduction to *Jinnah–Ispahani Correspondence*, p. 26.

[138] *IAR*, 1938, vol. 1, p. 377. [139] Ibid., p. 386.

formed, 'the League was shelved. No meeting of the League Board or Party, no League Whips, leaders or other office bearers.'[140] Yet Jinnah himself believed that he could only strengthen his hand through compromise and patience. He had no intention of throwing away the gains his alliance with Huq had brought him.

> 'You must not mix up the aims we have with the achievements. The aims are not achieved immediately they are laid down. But I think, on the whole, Bengal has done well and we must be thankful for small mercies. As you go on, of course with patience and tact, things are bound to develop and improve more and more in accordance with our ideals and aims'.[141]

Why Sikander Hyat Khan joined up with Jinnah at the Lucknow session of the League is not quite certain. Sikander himself was known to have little sympathy with the 'virulent communalism' of the League. But sympathy for the League of a section of Muslim Unionists, caused by their alarm that the Congress would have no regard for the 'position of Muslims' in a federal government, persuaded Sikander, in the interests of maintaining unity within the party, to join the Muslim League.[142] It is also possible that Sikander saw the growing strength of the Congress as a threat to his own political interests. Ahmad Yar Khan Daulatana, Chief Secretary of the Unionist Party, said that Congress attempts to organize a Muslim Mass Contact Campaign in the Punjab would open a fresh chapter of communal controversy,[143] as it would attack one of the bases of Unionist strength.

The path to an understanding with Unionists was not a smooth one for Jinnah. Sikander wanted the Unionists to control the League's parliamentary board in the Punjab and also the finances of the League.[144] Whether he achieved this objective is not known, but it was not until April 1938 that Muslim Unionists actually signed the membership forms of the League.[145] The understanding appears to have been that Jinnah would not interfere in provincial politics, while he would speak for Muslims at the all India level.[146]

[140] Ispahani to Jinnah, 23 July 1937, *Jinnah–Ispahani Correspondence*, p. 83.
[141] Jinnah to Ispahani, 4 April 1937, Ibid., p. 81.
[142] P. Moon, *Divide and Quit*, p. 17. [143] *Bombay Chronicle*, 8 May 1937.
[144] Iqbal to Jinnah, 10 November 1939, G. Allana, *Pakistan Movement: Historic Documents*, 2nd edition (Lahore, 1968), pp. 148–9.
[145] Emerson to Linlithgow, 12 April 1938, *LC*, vol. 86.
[146] Emerson to Linlithgow, 21 October 1937, *LC*, vol. 113.

The NWFP remained a Congress province; Allah Baksh would not subscribe to the communalism of the League in Sind; but the arrangements with Huq and Sikander enabled Jinnah to assert that 'The All-India Muslim League has now come to live and play its just part in the world of Indian politics; and the sooner this is realized and reckoned with, the better it will be for all interests concerned.' Jinnah, however, remained aware that the League was not in a position to bargain on its own terms with the Congress.

> 'An honourable settlement can only be achieved between equals; and unless the two parties learn to respect and fear each other, there is no solid ground for any settlement. Offers of peace by the weaker party always mean a confession of weakness, and an invitation to aggression . . . Politics means power and not relying only on cries of justice or fairplay or goodwill.'[147]

Jinnah did not appear to be interested in any compromise with the Congress, as he emphasised the political differences between it and the League. He criticized yet again the economic programmes of the Congress. 'All the talk of hunger and poverty is intended to lead the people towards socialistic and communistic ideas, for which India is far from prepared'. The Congress demand for a Constituent Assembly was scathingly described as 'the height of all ignorance'.[148] Jinnah could not bring himself to visualize a situation where the British might leave India, leaving behind political authority in the hands of the Congress. He revealed what was to develop into regular strategy later: to wait for the Congress to express an opinion first; even to throw a challenge about the course of action he might take, without stating his own intentions at all. The British were talking about the inauguration of Federation. What, enquired Jinnah, was the Congress going to do? without himself revealing the League's position.

What infuriated Jinnah was the indifference of the Congress to the League. He was, in fact, looking for a way to bring the Congress High Command 'to its senses'; and he challenged Nehru to come and sit with the Muslims in order to formulate a constructive, practical and ameliorative programme which would give immediate relief to the poor.[149] Fazlul Huq, who had by now joined the League, alleged that the Congress press had given distorted accounts of his

[147] Pirzada, *Documents*, p. 280. [148] Ibid., p. 270.
[149] *Bombay Chronicle*, 27 December 1937.

activities on a tour of Eastern Bengal simply because he was a Muslim, and threatened to use 'a stern rod' on those who preached communalism and disturbed the peace of the country.[150]

If the leadership of the Muslim League had been looking for the best way to influence Congress leaders so that they would attach some importance to the League as a political organization, the statements of Jinnah and Huq accomplished the purpose. Both Gandhi and Nehru were roused not only to take up Jinnah's challenge, but also to initiate correspondence with him on communal matters; and, in a way, accorded the League the status it sought—as spokesman of the Muslims. 'I had no desire whatever to carry on a controversy,' wrote Nehru to Ismail Khan, 'but in view of Mr. Jinnah's "Challenge" to me, I had to say something in reply'.[151]

For his part, Gandhi doubted that he could do anything to bring the Congress and the League together, after Jinnah's declaration of war against the Congress at the Lucknow session of the Muslim League.[152]. Jinnah's reply to Gandhi made no bones about what he wanted. 'We have reached a stage when no doubt should be left'. The Congress should recognize the League as the authoritative and representative organization of Muslims, and Gandhi should negotiate on behalf of the Congress and the Hindus. 'It is only on this basis that we can proceed further and further and devise a machinery of approach'.[153] Gandhi turned down the suggestion, saying that he could represent neither the Congress nor the Hindus.[154]

Knowing of Gandhi's reaction by 8 March, it is unlikely that Jinnah was serious in making the same demand of Nehru on 17 March,[155] or indeed, that any of his points for discussion with Nehru had any purpose behind them at all. 'Obviously the Muslim League is an important communal organization and we deal with it as such,' replied Nehru. But there were Muslims in the Congress, in trade and peasant unions, and in zamindar associations, which had both Hindu and Muslim members. There were also special Muslim organizations such as the Jamiat-ul-ulema and the Ahrars. Moreov-

[150] *IAR*, 1937, vol. 2, pp. 466–7.
[151] Nehru to Ismail, 2 January 3938, *NC*, vol. 39.
[152] Gandhi to Jinnah, 3 February 1938, *IAR*, 1938, vol. 1, p. 360.
[153] Jinnah to Gandhi, 3 March 1938, Ibid., p. 361.
[154] Gandhi to Jinnah, 8 March 1938, Ibid., p. 362. Also *Harijan*, 30 April 1938.
[155] Jinnah to Nehru, 17 March 1938, Pirzada, *Correspondence*, p. 99.

er, Nehru felt that the importance of organizations depended on their inherent strength and not on outside recognition.

Jinnah's suggestion that the two leaders discuss the Fourteen Points lacked substance.[156] The Fourteen Points, as Nehru rightly remarked, 'were somewhat out of date'. Many of their provisions had already been effected; others required constitutional changes which were beyond the competence of the Congress.[157]

Guarantees for Muslims in the services and protection of their rights, were minor constitutional changes, and any case the Congress wanted to do away 'completely with the present constitution and replace it by another for a free India.'[158]

Nehru assured Jinnah that the Congress was not trying to impose Hindi or to injure Urdu. Referring to his article, 'The Question of Language,' he told Jinnah that the Congress wanted to introduce Hindustani, which could be written in either the Urdu or the Devanagri script.[159] On the Communal Award, Nehru reiterated that the Congress sought alterations only on the basis of mutual consent of the parties concerned. 'I do not understand how any one can take objection to this attitude and policy.' But he emphasised that the Award was anti-national. 'If we think in terms of independence, we cannot possibly fit in this Award with it.'[160]

Nehru did not take very seriously Jinnah's demand for coalition ministries. A ministry must have a definite political and economic policy. Any other kind of ministry would be a disjointed and ineffective body, with no clear mind or direction. 'What seems to me far more important', continued Nehru, 'is more basic understanding of each other'—implying that such an understanding did not exist at that moment—'bringing with it the desire to co-operate together.' Any cooperation must be based on independence and the interests of the masses.

What prompted Congress leaders to seek an understanding with the Muslim League was their desire to strengthen the nationalist front against Federation,[161] and their fear that an unreconciled Jin-

[156] Jinnah to Nehru, 17 March 1938, Ibid., pp. 113–15.
[157] Nehru to Jinnah, 3 April 1938, Ibid., p. 115.
[158] Ibid., p. 113–14.
[159] Ibid., p. 120.
[160] Ibid., p. 115.
[161] P. Sitarammaya, *The History of the Indian National Congress*, vol. 2, 1935–1947, (Bombay, 1947), p. 74.

nah might not sympathize with them and might even try to thwart their effort.[162] The intensification of communal bitterness in public life also troubled them, and it is interesting that communal friction was increasing even as the correspondence between Jinnah and Gandhi and Nehru continued. Communal tension prevailed in many cities including Nagpur, Lahore, Benares, Jubbulpore and Allahabad during the last fortnight of March, and April 1938.[163] Official sources held the League responsible for the tense communal situation,[164] and pointed out that it reflected the strained relations between the Congress and the League.[165]

The anxiety of Congress leaders to reach an understanding with the Muslim League did not diminish, and, even as Jinnah's correspondence with Nehru came to an end, he was due to meet Gandhi at the end of April 1938. Jinnah was thinking of capitalizing on the eagerness of Congress leaders for a settlement, and had admitted that the strong communal tone of his speeches to the League on 17 April had been calculated at securing some tactical advantage in his approaching conversations with Gandhi.[166]

Jinnah, however, overestimated the chances of getting Congress leaders to agree to his main demand—recognition of the Muslim League as the sole representative of the Muslims. His talks with Gandhi failed on this score. Subhas Chandra Bose, who had become president of the Congress in February 1938, then continued the discussions, and turned down Jinnah's demand on the ground that the Congress could not give up its national character.[167] Congress leaders, including Bose, Azad, Prasad, Patel and Gandhi informed Jinnah that they favoured an amicable settlement of the communal question, but there could be no infringement of Congress programmes and policies.[168] As it turned out, the discussions between Jinnah and Bose never progressed beyond the stage of 'the examination of credentials'.[169] On 5 June, Jinnah informed Bose that the Execu-

[162] Survey of secret information relating to Congress attitude towards Federation, Enclosure 8; Linlithgow to Zetland, 6 April 1938, *ZC*, vol. 15.

[163] *Bombay Chronicle*, 17, 18 March 1938.

[164] FRs for UP for first and second half of March; also for Bihar, CP, March, 1938; HP file no. 18/3/38.

[165] Linlithgow to Zetland, 27 March 1938, *ZC*, vol. 15.

[166] Linlithgow to Zetland, 27 April 1938, *ZC*, vol. 15.

[167] Bose to Jinnah, 14 May 1938, Pirzada, *Correspondence*, p. 62.

[168] *Bombay Chronicle*, 13 May 1938,

[169] Linlithgow to Zetland, 24 May 1938, *ZC*, vol. 15.

tive Council of the Muslim League had passed a resolution which reiterated that the Congress must recognize the League as the only representative body of Muslims in India. Also, the Congress could not invite representatives of other Muslim organizations to participate in any talks that might take place.[170]

Bose rejected the proposals once more, saying that it would be 'not only impossible, but improper' for the Congress to agree that the League was the sole representative of Muslims.[171] The correspondence between Jinnah and Bose continued in this vein until October.[172] On 16 December, the Congress Working Committee finally rejected the demand and also stated that it was not in a position to do anything further in the direction of starting negotiations with the League with a view to arriving at a settlement of the Hindu-Muslim question.[173] On the same day the Working Committee passed a resolution which defined the Hindu Mahasabha and the Muslim League as communal organizations, and forbade any Congress member from belonging to either of them and the Congress simultaneously.[174]

If, by the close of 1938, it was clear to Jinnah that the Congress would never accept his claim to represent all Muslims, he had to create an atmosphere which would dissuade Muslims from sympathizing with it. His main political weapon since 1937 had been attacks on the Congress, and he had to give some substance to them. This the League attempted in the Pirpur Report, which was published in November 1938.

Perhaps the greatest significance of the assumption of office by the Congress was the opportunity which it provided the Muslim League to stir up Muslim opinion against the alleged communal bias of Congress governments. The League did not challenge the Congress on political issues publicly to any great extent, perhaps because the election had proved the appeal of the Congress stand on these issues. Instead, the League sought to embarrass Congress governments, by alleging that Congress governments were either incapable or unwilling to safeguard the religious and cultural rights of

[170] Jinnah to Bose, 5 June 1938, Pirzada, *Correspondence*, pp. 64–5.
[171] Bose to Jinnah, 25 July 1938, Ibid., p. 66.
[172] Jinnah to Bose, 10 October 1938, Ibid., pp. 69–74.
[173] *National Herald*, 17 December 1938.
[174] *Bombay Chronicle*, 16 December 1938.

Muslims, and had no intention of fulfilling the assurances made to minorities in the Karachi Resolution of 1931.

There was little justification for the charge that Congress governments discriminated against Muslims. The allegations stemmed from the failure of the Congress and the League to resolve differences on political issues. But in a situation where ideological differences often took on a religious colouring, the accusations levelled against Congress governments put Congress leaders very much on the defensive. As the majority of Indians were Hindus by religion, the Congress, a broad nationalist front which represented the majority of Indians, regardless of class or creed, knew that it often appeared representative of Hindus only. The defensive reactions of Congress leaders to these allegations shows how easily propaganda builds up into myths, which are then accepted as facts on the basis of which policies are formulated—keeping in mind, of course, the political context.

The inquiry conducted by the Pirpur Committee into Muslim grievances in Congress provinces contended that with the acceptance of office by the Congress, Muslims were being discriminated against not only by Congress officials and workers, but also that 'People of a particular community were encouraged to believe that the government was not theirs'.[175]

Congress governments were in fact accused of deliberately engaging in actions, or of formulating policies, that offended the religious sentiments of Muslims. Among the issues raised by the Pirpur Report were the singing of *Bande Mataram* and the hoisting of the Congress flag in public places, attacks on the religious right of Muslims to slaughter cows, and the suppression of the Urdu language by Congress governments. A resolution passed by the League was quoted which contended that *Bande Mataram* was 'positively anti-Islamic and idolatrous in its inspiration and ideas . . .'.[176] The tricolour was described as 'purely a party flag and nothing more . . . the foisting of the so-called national flag on the unwilling minorities' was 'an expression of the narrow communalism of the majority community'. The flag should represent the 'true feelings and sentiments of the Muslim community' merely in showing of the Muslim colour was not of much significance. The implication was, of course, that Hindus, Hindu communalism and Congress govern-

[175] *Pirpur Report*, p. 15. [176] Ibid., p. 17.

ments were all synonymous. Hindus in educational institutions had been encouraged 'to ignore the feelings of the Muslims,' and they lost no opportunity to offend Muslim sentiments.[177]

'The question of cow slaughter has been one of the causes of conflict between the Hindus and Muslims of India.'[178] Muslims were said to have been intimidated to give up cow sacrifice and the eating of beef. Action had been organized to prevent the sale of cows to Muslims, and Hindus had resorted to violent measures to do this. It was also alleged that some Congress governments had refused to grant licences to Muslim butchers for selling beef.[179] Such action was being taken 'in the name of law and order and on the false ground that the Muslims did not prove the custom to sacrifice cow or that they proposed to kill cows openly or that it was a nuisance in the eyes of some people . . .'.[180] This was looked on as deliberate discrimination against the religious rights of Muslims. 'Muslims have been enjoined by their religion to prevent idol worship and other idolatrous practices. Will the Government abolish or restrict idol-worship and prohibit public exhibition of idols in processions in the name of law and order, if some Muslims object to it or form an unlawful assembly to secure their object?'[181] It was also alleged that Gandhi's emphasis on cow protection, and his advocacy of charkha, showed an apprehension that Congress Raj was Hindu Raj and offended the religious sentiments of Muslims.

Congress governments were also accused of discrimination against Urdu and of trying to impose Hindi on Muslims. Muslims, it was implied, spoke only Urdu, and the imparting of education in vernaculars would lead to their cultural degeneration and would also place Muslim students at a disadvantage in competition with boys of other communities, 'who are fortunate enough to receive their education in their own mother tongue'.[182] Some Congress governments were not opening Urdu schools where there was a demand for them, or were not giving grants to them, or were abolishing Urdu classes in schools.[183] The Vidya Mandir Scheme introduced in the Wardha scheme of education was criticized on the ground that the word Mandir, connoting idol worship, went against the grain of Islamic tenets and was repulsive to a Muslim.[184] Mus-

[177] Ibid., p. 35. [178] Ibid., p. 20. [179] Ibid., pp. 20–1.
[180] Ibid., pp. 41–2. [181] Ibid., p. 43. [182] Ibid., p. 29.
[183] Ibid., pp. 51–2. [184] Ibid., p. 54.

lims were also said to be placed at a disadvantage because Urdu, while allowed in courts officially was discouraged unofficially by officers.

Departmental examinations were held in Hindi in Bihar but not in Urdu; municipal committees in the Central Provinces did not entertain applications in Urdu. It was alleged that in one district in the CP which had been converted into a Compulsory Education area, the government had provided for expenditure with the express condition that the medium of instruction would be only Hindi.[185]

The Pirpur Report tried to 'expose' the highhandedness and hostility of Hindus as a community towards Muslims and alleged that Congress workers and officials either connived with Hindu mobs who tried to prevent Muslims from exercising their religious and cultural rights, or were simply incapable of protecting the rights of Muslims. One instance cited in the Report said that Muslim butchers at Badri village near Ballia had made arrangements to buy some two thousand cattle, when 'a large crowd of about a thousand well-armed Hindus attacked the butchers . . . and beat them mercilessly, thus rendering the butchers unfit to protect their cattle. The assaulters took away all the cattle forcibly from the butchers' possession'.[186] Again, in the village of Khairatia in Bihar, 'some trouble arose when the sugarcane of one Muslim peasant was being cut. Hindus assembled near the field and a crowd of many thousands attacked the Muslims, who were overpowered. They fled for their lives and some of them took shelter in their houses and some in a mosque. The Hindu rioters, who came from neighbouring villages, started looting and setting fire to the Muslim houses. Even the mosque was not spared by the Hindus who attacked the Muslims there with spears, *lathis*, and brick-bats. A number of Muslims were injured and many had spear wounds . . .'.[187]

Hindus were also accused of hindering processions on occasion of festivals celebrated by Muslims. Hindus placed obstacles in the way of Muslims carrying tazias.[188] Cow sacrifice was sometimes prevented on the festival of Bakrid;[189] Hindus would not let Muslims call *Azan*;[190] Hindus would play music before mosques and the Muslims, being in a very small minority, would have to yield.[191]

[185] Ibid., p. 40, 520. [186] Ibid., p. 68. [187] Ibid., pp. 46–7.
[188] Ibid., pp. 57, 63–4, 70, 72–3. [189] Ibid., p. 38.
[190] Ibid., p. 48. [191] Ibid., p. 63.

The government would give them no protection. In most of the cases cited in the Report, it was implied, if not definitely stated, that the number of Muslims killed or injured in communal riots exceeded that of the Hindus.[192]

Thus the Pirpur Report sought to embarrass Congress governments and also to instil in Muslims the fear that under 'Hindu' Raj they would always be a weak, powerless, and oppressed community.

The underlying cause behind the allegations made by the Muslim League against Congress governments was, as official British opinion quickly perceived, that it did not have effective political power. Administratively, it was felt that the League had little to complain of

> 'except that they do not have the general political influence, and the pull in petty local matters, that the supporters of the Ministry have. In essence the grievance is not a religious one, though it assumes an intensely communal form. It is political, and is due to the fact that the community is in opposition. It would largely cease to exist if the Muslim League had a share in the Government'.[193]

Official British opinion discounted the charges of atrocities and prejudice of Congress governments against Muslims. Linlithgow felt that 'proof of specific instances is not easily forthcoming . . .'.[194]

Sir Maurice Hallett, Governor of Bihar, said that he did not know of any case in which government or local officials had failed to take action against aggressors in communal riots. Muslims whom Hallett had met had 'admitted their inability to bring any charges of anti-Muslim prejudice against Government'.[195] It is worth remembering that in 1937, 58.69 per cent of ICS officers were British. In January 1940, the British held 64.8 per cent of the posts in the Indian Police Service.[196] It is difficult to believe that deliberate ill-treatment of Muslims would have gone on unnoticed and unrecorded by British officials in their confidential correspondence.

British officials infact supported the Congress view that the League was fomenting communal trouble in Congress-governed

[192] Ibid., pp. 71, 76, 77, 80.

[193] Haig to Linlithgow, 10 May 1939 and 3 June 1939, *HC*, vol. 6.

[194] Linlithgow to Zetland, 28 March 1939, *ZC*, vol. 17.

[195] Hallett to Linlithgow, 8 May 1939, *LC*, vol. 46.

[196] Home Establishments file no. 50/37, Home Establishments file no. 42/40.

provinces.[197] Sometimes issues of a very trivial nature could spark off a communal controversy, and, the case of Bihar showed that an indecisive government did not help matters. The Bihar ministry was reluctant to make any clear pronouncement on communal policy, which resulted in a piquant situation. The Muslim League in Bhagalpur took advantage of a suggestion in the provincial Legislative Assembly that custom should be the guiding principle regarding processions before mosques and the right to slaughter cows. A certain Hindu took out an idol in procession as he had done for many years. But he changed his residence and the procession was necessarily taken along a different route. There was therefore a departure from custom and the Muslims protested vigorously. The idol awaited the return journey while the Ministry 'are scratching their heads as to how they will deal with the situation.' The incident was trivial in itself but it was symptomatic of the desire of the Muslim League to embarrass the government at any cost. The indecisiveness of the Ministry created a near riot situation. The District Magistrate tried to mediate, but his influence was undermined by the circumstance that the Prime Minister himself had been listening to representations from both sides. The following year, the District Magistrate of Bhagalpur prohibited processions. This time, the Hindu Mahasabha protested and threatened satyagraha and the Prime Minister vacillated on the issue, for if the procession was allowed, the League would have a charge against the Ministry 'who are put in the difficult position of having to offend either Hindus or Muslims!'[198]

Opposition to the flag and Bande Mataram manifested itself soon after Congress ministries assumed office on September 1937. Congress leaders were quick to realize that the opposition was gaining strength, 'partly because of the thoughtless and inopportune action of our workers and sympathizers at certain places'.[199] But Congress governments usually dealt promptly with the situation. In Madras, the Prime Minister requested that the singing of Bande Mataram before assembly sessions be discontinued because of bad feeling stir-

[197] FRs for UP for July and September 1938, HP file nos. 18/7 and 18/9/38; FRs for Bihar for August and September 1938, HP file nos. 18/8 and 18/9/38.

[198] Stewart to Brabourne, 9 August 1938, 7 September 1938; *LC*, vol. 45, Hallett to Linlithgow, 5 August 1939, Ibid., vol. 46.

[199] Prasad to Patel, 28 September 1937, *RPC*, file II/37.

red up among Muslims.[200] By February 1938, agitation over the flag in Bihar was reported to be decreasing 'because Congress see clearly that it offends the Muslims and do not wish to press this issue.'[201] The official secret information report on Congress ministries had this to say on the flag and Bande Mataram at the end of 1938: 'Little is now heard of the exhibition of the Congress flag or the singing of Bande Mataram, except as a standing grievance of anti-Congress organizations'.[202] Congress ministries obviously moved fast to remove any causes of grievance.

Nevertheless, the Congress Working Committee was anxious to put the record straight. The Working Committee had already recommended in October 1937 that only the first two stanzas of the song Bande Mataram could be sung.[203] But in January 1939, the Committee decided, obviously in a defensive reaction to the Pirpur Report, that 'In regard to the Flag and to Bandemataram . . . we should avoid making this a matter of controversy as for (sic) as possible . . .'.[204]

The Congress Working Committee had also suggested that legal rights to cow slaughter as well as to music before mosques should be recognised and given effect to unless there was definite custom to the contrary. Nehru suggested that decisions on such matters should be taken after negotiations with the Muslim League, as 'it would be better than if a one-sided announcement was made. In a one-sided announcement that part which favoured one party would be accepted while the other party would be rejected'.[205]

British officials supported the Congress view that the Muslim League was often responsible for communal violence. 'Finding themselves unable to effect much by parliamentary methods, they are inevitably tempted to create unrest and disturbance outside the

[200] Erksine to Linlithgow, 7 March 1938, *EC*, vol. 13. See also FR for Madras for first half of March 1938, HP file no. 18/3/38.

[201] Hallett to Hubback, 8 February 1938, *LC*, vol. 34.

[202] *Quarterly Survey of Political and Constitutional Position of the British in India*, No. 6, p. 35, *LC*, vol. 142.

[203] Nehru to Jinnah, 6 April 1938, Pirzada, *Correspondence*, p. 119. The statement made by the CWC said that the first two stanzas were 'a living and inseparable part of our national movement . . . There is nothing in the stanzas to which any one can take exception.' *IAR*, 1937, vol. 2, p. 327.

[204] Draft Note by Gandhi on Hindu-Muslim Relations, AICC file no. G–34, 1939, pp. 65–9.

[205] Nehru to Pant, 16 January 1939, *NC*, vol. 79.

legislature, and there is no doubt that the Muslim League have set themselves quite deliberately to this policy.'[206] But Congress governments often hesitated to take action against the League for instigating communal violence—sometimes because of a seemingly intrinsic tendency to vacillate, as in the case of the Bihar government[207]—but more often because every effort on the part of governments to curb communalism 'is immediately represented as a breach of the elementary right of free speech and our Governments are fighting shy of strong measures.'[208] It was a forebearing Pant who informed Nehru in February 1938 that 'it will not be possible . . . to ignore their [the Muslim League's] activities of this type *any longer*.'[209] (Emphasis mine).

Congress leaders sought the cooperation of the League in resolving communal issues because they were aware that they did not enjoy much Muslim support, and because they recognized the psychological effect the League's propaganda could have on Muslims. This implies that they were anxious to conciliate, not the League, but the average Muslim voter. There is no evidence to suggest that any Congress leader between 1937 and 1939 was willing to accept the two major demands of the League—the recognition of its status as the 'sole' representative of Muslims, and the disbandment of the Congress Muslim Mass Contact Programme. The programme was started by Nehru, and many comments on it by other Congress leaders are not available, but there does not appear to be any evidence of disagreement over the aims of the programme within the Congress.[210]

There is, however, no doubt that the inception of the Programme contributed to an atmosphere of communal bitterness. It was because the success of the Programme would have spelt the defeat of the League that it roused Jinnah's ire. It was also natural that the campaign would stir some communal acrimony, as the League would turn to communal propaganda to counteract it.[211] But that

[206] Haig to Linlithgow, 23 October 1938, *HC*, vol. 2A.

[207] Hallett to Linlithgow, 7 April 1939, *LC*, vol. 46.

[208] AICC file no. G–32, 1938, p. 34.

[209] Pant to Nehru, 11 February 1938, *NC*, vol. 79.

[210] But see Gandhi's defence of the programme, Gandhi to Bashir Ahmad, 30 September 1937, *CWG*, vol. 66, p. 182.

[211] See, for example, FRs for Bihar and Bombay for first half of April 1937; Sind and CP for first half of May 1937; HP file nos. 18/4 and 18/5/37; FR for Sind for second half of May 1938, HP file no. 18/5/38.

did not mean that the Programme should never have been started. What was wrong with it was that it was carried out in a half hearted manner. It was 'totally unorganized. Except for the enrolment campaign of primary members, I do not think any other effort was made to come into direct contact with Muslims in large numbers'.[212] Consequently, it did not make much of a headway in any province. Instead, it left behind a residue of communal acrimony—the negative effect of the programme—without achieving the positive objective of winning Muslim mass support for the Congress.

The inception of the Muslim Mass Contact Programme had shown that the Congress recognized that it lacked a base among Muslims and considered it politically important to win their support. Why the programme was allowed to fizzle out by the summer of 1939, then, is something of a mystery. Why did the leadership not take more interest in the campaign? Was it because it was too involved in problems of party discipline and organization and the working of the Congress ministries? Was their implicit belief, that all Indians would eventually unite against the British, responsible for the lack of attention Congress leaders paid to the Muslim Mass Contact Programme? Whatever the reason, there can be no doubt that, in the long run, the failure of the campaign was an important factor in limiting the chances of the Congress in securing an undivided India.

The absence of prejudice against Muslims by Congress governments did not mean that communal elements were altogether absent from the organization. A Congress worker reported that an Arya Samaj preacher had become president of the Tehsil Congress Committee at Balrampur, and was advocating *shuddhi* and Hindu-Muslim unity simultaneously. Obviously it was felt that there would be 'great conflict, collision and mis-representation', if both things continued side by side.[213]

Communal prejudice and social reaction among Congressmen in Sind were reported to be alienating Muslims from the Congress in the province. Congress MLAs in Sind, who represented the trading and educated classes among the Hindus, 'cast away congress (sic) principles and programme (sic) to the winds, by obstructing and

[212] AICC file no. G-32, 1938, p. 15.

[213] Letter from Ambika Charan, 4 April 1937, AICC file no. P-20, p. 657.

sometimes even nipping in the bud legislation which aims at ameliorating (sic) the condition of Muslim masses in Sind who are mainly agriculturists and are weighed down by poverty and debts . . . As long as the congress (sic) is confined to the Urban Hindus, and acts as a cheap edition of the Hindu Mahasabha, there is no very bright future for congress (sic) amongst the downtrodden and ignorant muslim (sic) peasantry of Sind.'[214]

It was only in December 1938 that the Congress Working Committee passed a resolution defining the Muslim League and Hindu Mahasabha as communal organizations.[215] Congress workers themselves were often confused about the relationship between the Congress and the Mahasabha. The Bengal PCC reported that they were receiving enquiries from District Congress Committees if executives of Congress organizations could be members of the Hindu Mahasabha simultaneously. 'In our belief, Congress Organisation will suffer very much in prestige and hold over the masses, if Congress members be allowed to be members of the Hindu Mahasabha Organisations.[216] Prior to the passing of the resolution in December 1938, a Congress worker from Sylhet pointed that no specific organizations were mentioned as communal. 'If you think that the Hindu Mahasabha is such an organisation public opinion must assert itself and prevent the election of a member of Hindu Sabha to Congress Committee'.[217] There does not seem to be evidence of disciplinary action taken against communal elements within the Congress. They deepened its Hindu religious hues; and must have dampened Muslim enthusiasm for the organization.

The Congress attitude to tenancy legislation in Bengal and Bihar, somewhat conservative in contrast to its policy in the UP, also provided Muslim Leaguers with an opportunity to accuse the Congress of insincerity and communal prejudice. A supporter of the League wrote that Congressmen had opposed the Tenancy Bill in Bengal because 'most of the landlords there are Hindus and the peasants Muslims. But in the UP they insist on an ill-conceived and

[214] Report on Communal Riots in Sukkur town submitted to the Congress Working Committee by Abdul Qayyum, AICC file no. 1, 1939–1940, p. 18.

[215] *Bombay Chronicle*, 16 December 1939.

[216] Letter from Ashrafuddin Ahmad, Secretary, BPCC, to General Secretary, AICC, 16 August 1938, AICC file no. P-5, 1938, pp. 131–3.

[217] Letter from Acting Office Secretary to Secretary, Habiganj Sub-divisional Congress Committee, AICC file no. G-32, p. 33.

crooked tenancy law to persecute the landlords, no matter whether it would do real good to peasants or not, for the Muslims have some share in the land ownership . . . . But in Bihar, where Hindu landlords are strong, the Congress readily entered in a compromise with them over the tenancy question.'[218]

There seems little to substantiate these allegations. Local conditions and the overall—somewhat contradictory—attitude of the Congress to tenancy legislation were the main factors which determined the stand taken up by provincial Congress organizations. The UP tenancy bill of 1939 was not as radical as it has been made out to be,[219] and, prior to the introduction of the bill in the legislature, Congressmen were generally using their influence to induce tenants to pay up their rents and to maintain harmonious relations with zamindars.[220] The Bihar ministry was embarrassed by kisan agitation in the province, but the Bihar Tenancy Bill did not go 'as far as the demands of the Kisan Sabha.'[221] The Congress legislative party in Bengal remained 'neutral' in the debate on the Tenancy Amendment Bill which was introduced by the Huq ministry in October 1937—which was given a communal colouring in a province where the majority of cultivators were Muslims. Sarat Chandra Bose, leader of the Congress legislative party said that while the Congress did not look upon the rights of landlords as something which could not be touched, it discouraged any attempt on the part of a section of the people to describe another section as exploiters.[222]

In the NWFP, the Congress made the most of its opportunities to consolidate its position. Through intensive propaganda and a number of popular measures, the Congress had become, by January 1938, 'practically unassailable in the rural areas.' The Congress ministry introduced several measures which ended the monopoly

[218] Jamil-ud-din Ahmad, 'Is India One Nation?' (1941) quoted by K.N. Chaudhuri, 'Economic Problems and Indian Independence,' in Philips and Wainwright (eds.), *Partition of India*, pp. 308–9.

[219] G. Pandey, 'Rural Base for Congress 1920–1940' in D.A. Low (ed.) *Congress and the Raj* (London, 1977), pp. 217–18.

[220] FRs for UP for first half of September and second half of October 1937. HP file no. 18/9 and 18/10/37 respectively.

[221] Prasad to Nehru, 23 November 1937, *RPC*, file I/37; and Max Harcourt, 'Kisan Populism and Revolution in Rural India: the 1942 Disturbances in Bihar and East United Provinces,' in Low (ed.), *Congress and the Raj*, pp. 304ff. See also Patel to Prasad, 4 December 1937, *RPC*, file II/37.

[222] *IAR*, 1937, vol. 2, p. 142.

the Khans had enjoyed for centuries, by abolishing the posts of Naubati chaukidari and zaildari, and by throwing open to election the post of Lambardari.[223]

In the Punjab, the Congress remained neutral in the voting on the Alienation of Land (Third Amendment) Bill, which was introduced by the Unionist Ministry in June 1938. The bill sought to place agriculturist moneylenders under the same disabilities as non-agriculturists in respect of permanent acquisition of land in settlement of debts. Agriculturists of all communities supported the bill, while the Hindu non-agricultural and moneylending classes protested against it. The Congress Working Committee asked the Congress parliamentary party to support the measure and Azad reminded them of their duty to give full and unstinted support to all legislation likely to ameliorate the condition of the masses. Non-agriculturist members of the Congress were unhappy over these instructions, for the party, though realizing the necessity for not alienating the agriculturists, was at the same time loath to lose the support of the commercial and non-agriculturist classes who financed it.[224] The strategy of provincial Congress leaders was to accuse the Unionists of deliberately causing a split between agriculturists and non-agriculturists, a strategy which only led to the Congress losing further ground in the rural areas.[225]

If, by the beginning of 1939, it was clear that the Congress had yet to win the support of the Muslim masses, it was also evident that Jinnah had still to find a political vantage point. His parleys with the Congress in 1938 combined with attacks on Congress ministries kept him on the political horizon, but they also revealed the weakness of his position, the fact that his only weapon against the Congress was negative and somewhat unconstructive. The alliances with Huq and Sikander prevailed uneasily, as Huq flirted, off and on, with the Congress and the breakaway branch of the KPP.[226] Sikander's recognition of Jinnah's position as leader of Muslims at the all India level did not imply any unquestioning obedience to him. In July 1939, he was at odds with him over the question of Muslim

[223] NWFP Governor's Report dated 10 and 24 January 1938, *LC*, vol. 72. See also Summary of events in NWFP, March 1937–February 1946, *CC*, vol. 17.

[224] FR for Punjab for first half of July 1938 and supplement to FR, and FR for second half of July 1938, HP file no. 18/7/38.

[225] FR for Punjab for first half of August 1938; HP file no. 18/8/38.

[226] See, for example, Sen, *Muslim Politics*, p. 121.

League support to the British in the event of a war.[227] In Sind, Jinnah had failed, time and again, to persuade the ruling Azad Muslim Party to accept the communal policy of the League; to overthrow the ministry because provincial Muslim Leaguers remained unable to sink their differences against Allah Baksh.[228] Dominated by indolent and unpopular feudal landlords in the NWFP, the League earned the nickname, 'Motor League,' because its members reportedly spent most of their time driving to tea parties![229] Except in Bengal, where it had organized some district level branches to counteract the Muslim Mass Contact Programme of the Congress,[230] the constructive work of the League was negligible, and the few feeble and ineffective appeals to the Muslims of Lucknow to end the Shia-Sunni controversy were an example of its lack of real influence over Muslims.[231]

It is obvious, then, that the alienation of Muslims from the Congress had obviously not united them or made them into supporters of the League by 1939. The politicization of electorates since 1937 had not necessarily resulted in success for communal parties like the League. This observation is important if we are to avoid one of the pitfalls of the Whig interpretation of history—of judging the past from hindsight and concluding that anti-Congress feeling had made Muslims a nation by 1939.

[227] Haig to Linlithgow, 1 July 1939, *HC*, vol. 2A.

[228] See for example, FR for Sind for first half of October 1938, HP file no. 18/10/38; Graham to Linlithgow, 9 January 1939, L/P & J/5/254. See also Graham to Linlithgow, 2 March 1938, Ibid.

[229] Entry for 23 May 1938, Cunningham diaries, vol. 3, *CC*. See also Cunningham to Linlithgow, 26 May 1938, *LC*, vol. 72.

[230] Sen, *Muslim Politics*, pp. 123–5.

[231] See, for example, Jinnah to Ispahani, 20 April 1939, *Jinnah–Ispahani Correspondence*, pp. 49–50. Also *Quarterly Survey of the Political and Constitutional Position of the British in India*, no. 8, p. 32, *LC* vol. 143.

CHAPTER 2

India and the War

September 1939 to December 1941

On 3 September 1939, a new chapter in Indian politics opened. The Viceroy announced India's entry into the war without consulting political parties, legislatures or provincial ministries.[1] Linlithgow's overriding objective was to turn India into a war base, and to provide men and money;[2] and he regarded the problem of winning the cooperation of Indian parties for the war effort to be one of 'particular urgency'.[3] The Viceroy admitted that those in the Central Legislature as it stood did 'not necessarily' contain the men who were most representative of public opinion. His Executive Council would also have to be strengthened with more non-officials.[4] He attached the greatest importance to winning the support of Gandhi and Nehru, because of their popular appeal,[5] for the war effort. As late as May 1941 Linlithgow wrote home to Amery:

> '. . . I should myself regard it as unjustified in the light of all the teachings of history to try to proscribe or to ignore a great political party which represents unquestionably the spearhead of nationalism in this country . . . I have often wondered what is in the Mahatma's mind. Of course, he has been an intolerable nuisance since the beginning of the war. On the other hand, I do not believe that he wants our enemies to win this war . . . what he is really concerned to do is to maintain his nuisance, and his bargaining value at as high a level as possible, with a view to the post-war discussions . . . his desire is to keep the pot simmering but not boiling'.[6]

The other, more pressing, reason for seeking the cooperation of political parties for the war effort was to expand the numbers and to preserve the loyalty of the army, the ultimate bulwark of the

[1] Reginald Coupland, *The Indian Problem* (Oxford, 1944), p. 212.

[2] Linlithgow's report of his conversation with W. Philips, President Roosevelt's personal representative, 19 February 1943, *TOP*, vol. 3, p. 689.

[3] Linlithgow to Zetland, 31 August 1939, *ZC*, vol. 18.

[4] Linlithgow to Zetland, 5 September 1939, Ibid.

[5] Linlithgow to Zetland, 5 September and 4 October 1939, Ibid.

[6] Linlithgow to Amery, 15 May 1941, *LC*, vol. 10.

Empire. Hence the Viceroy began talks with Indian leaders to probe their terms for supporting the British. The attitude of Gandhi, who said that he contemplated the present struggle 'With an English heart,' 'could not have been better.' Throughout the talks, Linlithgow was 'profoundly moved' by Gandhi's sympathy for England; and he hoped that Gandhi would be able to 'keep things on the right line' at the CWC meeting on 14 September, especially on the matter of defence liaison.[7]

Linlithgow knew that Indian parties would require political concessions in return for their support of the war effort.[8] Jinnah hoped to extract from the Viceroy a promise that the British would jettison the idea of federation. The working of provincial autonomy had shown how 'Hindus' would behave if they were in a majority, and the Congress ministries should be turned out 'at once.'[9]

Linlithgow, however, saw no reason to give up the idea of federation and majority rule altogether. Jinnah's hold over the provincial Muslim Leagues was insecure; and his demand was probably a tactic to keep the Muslim League in tow, especially as Sikander Hyat Khan and Fazlul Huq had already promised the British unconditional support for the war effort against his wishes, and his disposition to bargain.[10] Jinnah's leadership was under fire from radicals in the League, Ispahani, for example, voiced 'their utmost regret and disappointment that you are gradually drifting more and more into the arms of the reactionaries and "jee hoozoors" [yes men].' Sikander had challenged the 'potency of the Muslim League . . . you as President . . . had chosen to keep silent . . . is it not time that you take stock of the whole situation and put your foot down with firmness?'[11]

As a 'public man who had to think of his followers,'[12] Jinnah had to tread a path which would preserve unity as well as his own authority within the League. He now placed his cards on the table. 'If . . . Britain wants to prosecute this war successfully, it must take Muslim India into its confidence through its accredited

[7] Linlithgow to Zetland, 5 September 1939 and Enclosure on his talks with Gandhi on 4 September 1939, *ZC*, vol. 18.

[8] Linlithgow to Zetland, 24 August 1939, Ibid.

[9] Linlithgow to Zetland, 5 September 1939, Ibid.

[10] Ibid.

[11] Ispahani to Jinnah, 12 December 1939, Zaidi, *Jinnah–Ispahani Correspondence*, p. 133. See also Raghunandan Saran to Nehru, 24 October 1939, *NC*, Vol. 84.

[12] Linlithgow to Zetland, 5 September 1939, *ZC*, vol. 18.

organization—the All-India Muslim League . . . Muslims want justice and fair play.'[13]

Coming as it did after a combative Congress resolution,[14] Jinnah's statement seemed to the Viceroy 'not on the whole unsatisfactory'.[15] While avoiding the impression of meddling in the politics of the Muslim community, Linlithgow's endeavour 'obviously must be to do all that I can to get *all* sections of the Muslim community into line behind us.'[16]

In the Congress Working Committee, Gandhi was alone in suggesting unconditional support for the British on a non-violent basis.[17] The Congress resolved on 14 September 1939, that the issue of war and peace 'must be decided by the Indian people, and no outside authority can impose this decision upon them, nor can the Indian people permit their resources to be exploited for imperialist ends.' The British government was invited 'to declare in unequivocal terms what their war aims are in regard to democracy and imperialism and the new world order that is envisaged; in particular, how these aims are going to apply to India and . . . be given effect to in the present.'[18]

In response to the Congress demand for a declaration of British war aims, Linlithgow thought the British should reiterate 'that we are not concerned with the form of government of particular countries; that what we are concerned to ensure and achieve is in the first place the restoration of good faith and of confidence in dealings between nations: in the second place the discharge of our treaty obligations.'[19] If the Congress was going to show itself 'entirely intransigent,' and if it became clear that Congress ministries would continue in office only 'at the price of promises or immediate concessions which you [Amery] and I are not in a position to make, it may appear expedient to call an all-parties conference, at which the

[13] *Times of India*, 9 September 1939.

[14] *IAR*, 1939, vol. 2, p. 261.

[15] Linlithgow to Haig, 8 September 1939, *LC*, vol. 102. See also Linlithgow to Zetland, 7 September 1939, Ibid, vol. 8.

[16] Linlithgow to Lumley, 9 September 1939, Ibid., vol. 53, and Linlithgow to Haig, 8 September 1939, Ibid., vol. 102.

[17] *Harijan*, 23 September 1939. See also Sitaramayya, *History of the Indian National Congress*, vol. 2, pp. 130–5.

[18] Congress Resolution on India and the War, J. Nehru, *The Unity of India* (New York, 1942), pp. 410–14.

[19] Linlithgow to Zetland, 18 September 1939, *ZC*, vol. 18.

hollowness of the Congress claim to speak for India would very soon be exposed.'[20] So, although Gandhi told him that what was needed was a declaration 'of a satisfying kind, rather than a great deal in the field of action,' the Viceroy told him that there was no prospect of amending the Act of 1935 at that stage. 'I added that it was not a question of fighting for democracy . . . to which I did not think that His Majesty's Government had ever committed themselves in the slightest degree'.[21] A consultative liaison group could be set up—and the British cabinet only agreed to this slight concession after Linlithgow had assured them that such a Committee would have no chance at all to entrench itself too deeply in the machinery of government.[22]

Nevertheless, Linlithgow still hoped to woo the Congress into cooperation with the war effort. They were after all the largest and most important party in British India and were responsible for the governments of nine provinces, and the British should be ready to turn to their advantage such readiness as the Congress Right might show to work with them. Linlithgow regarded the 'nuisance value of Congress, if they turn against us, as very substantial . . . Commander-in-Chief agrees with me, that they have it in their power in that event largely to cripple our capacity to exert our maximum strength in the war'. So it was worthwhile to take some risk to secure the support of the Congress.[23]

In the light of the Congress attitude, meanwhile, the Muslim League resolution of 18 September had given the Viceroy what he badly needed to resist Congress demands. The League offered its support for the war effort if the Viceroy would take its leaders into confidence and accept the League as 'the only organisation that can speak on behalf of Muslim India.'[24] In contrast to Congress, the League was not interested in an independent, united and democratic India: it resolved that such a system was 'totally unsuited to the genius of the peoples of this country which is composed of various nationalities and does not constitute a national state.'[25]

[20] Linlithgow to Zetland, 21 September 1939, Ibid.

[21] Linlithgow to Zetland, 27 September 1939; Enclosure containing note of interview between Viceroy and Gandhi on 26 September 1939, *LC*, vol. 8. See also Enclosure to Linlithgow to Zetland, 4 October 1939, Ibid.

[22] CAB 67/1, W.P. (G) (39) 24 Secretary of State to Viceroy, 27 September 1939.

[23] Viceroy to Secretary of State, (T) 11 October 1939, *ZC*, vol. 26.

[24] *National Herald*, 19 September 1939.

[25] *National Herald*, 20 September 1939.

If the League's resolution was aimed at frustrating a possible settlement between the Congress and the British, it succeeded. Zetland decided that the British could not meet Congress demands, and, in the present situation, they should avoid offering them any concession which might antagonize the League.[26]

Although most Congress leaders were put off by the Muslim League resolution, in an attempt to draw the League into a united nationalist front, they offered an impartial enquiry into Muslim grievances against their ministries. Jinnah's rejection of this olive branch seemed to some Congress leaders to have 'practically barred the door' to any settlement.[27] Nevertheless, mindful of the need for unity among Indian parties at this time, Nehru and Azad still hoped to bring Jinnah to terms, and were willing to discuss any Congress-League differences with him.[28] At the Nehru-Jinnah talks between 16 and 18 October 1939, it was obvious that the real difference between the two men lay in their attitude to the British. Jinnah wanted the Congress to give up its anti-imperialist policy. According to Nehru, 'On no account did he [Jinnah] countenance any action on our part which might lead to a conflict with British Government (sic) . . . under the circumstances he felt that unless this matter was cleared up, other important questions did not arise'.[29]

Meanwhile, Linlithgow was frustrated both with the political deadlock and with the British government's failure to define their political objectives—'that is, if H.M.G. know what their political objectives are.'[30] He knew that the statement which he had been authorized to issue would not satisfy the Congress.[31] The Viceroy stated that, for the time being, the British would not define their war aims, but they would be willing to consult with representatives of different communities, parties and interests in India and with the Indian princes to discuss constitutional reforms for India after the war. The Viceroy added that representatives of minorities had urged most strongly on him the necessity of a clear assurance that full weight would be given to their views and interests in any modifica-

[26] Memorandum by Zetland on India and the War dated 25 September 1939, War Cabinet W.P. (G) (39) 21, *ZC*, vol. 26.

[27] Prasad to Azad, 13 October 1939, *RPC*, file no. XIV/40.

[28] Nehru to Prasad, 16 and 17 October 1939, Ibid., file no. 3–C/39.

[29] Nehru to Zakir Husain, 25 November 1939, *NC*, vol. 104.

[30] Viceroy to Secretary of State, (T), 11 October 1939, *ZC*, vol. 26.

[31] Linlithgow to Prasad, 16 October 1939, *RPC*, file no. 2–P/39. See also Linlithgow to Zetland, 16 October 1939, *LC*, vol. 8.

tions that might be contemplated. This assurance the Viceroy readily gave.[32]

The statement fell far short of Congress demands, and there was little hope of winning the party's cooperation in the war effort. Rajendra Prasad regretted that 'a great opportunity has been missed.'[33]

Jinnah hastened to make political capital out of the Viceroy's statement, exaggerating the strength of his position. The MLWC claimed that the British Government had 'emphatically repudiated the unfounded claim of the Congress that they alone represent all India . . .'. Referring to Linlithgow's assurance that the British would not ignore representatives of minorities, the resolution noted with satisfaction, though, as British officials acknowledged,[34] not very accurately, 'that his (sic) Majesty's Government recognise the fact that the All-India Muslim League alone truly represents the Muslims of India and can speak on their behalf . . .'. Accordingly, the Working Committee empowered Jinnah, as President of the League, to assure Britain of Muslim support and cooperation during the war.[35]

Linlithgow was relieved at the Muslim League resolution, while noting that it would be wrong to assume 'that the present Moslem attitude will long persist. Their platform is essentially anti-national and anti-democratic, and I feel sure their younger leaders will soon grow restive about a policy so utterly sterile. I therefore do not regard Moslem support as something upon which, by itself, we can safely afford to build any long term policy.' Linlithgow's feelings about the Congress remained ambivalent. 'It would be much easier to deal with the situation that confronts us had the Congress claims not been pitched so high.'[36]

A few days later, after the League had resolved that the 'entire problem of India's future constitution . . . be considered "de novo",'[37] Linlithgow concluded that the safeguards for Muslims which were demanded by the League were 'quite incompatible'

[32] *National Herald*, 18 October 1939.

[33] Prasad to Linlithgow, 18 October 1939, *RPC*, file no. 2–P/39.

[34] (This assumption seems a large one). *Quarterly Survey of the Political and Constitutional Position of the British in India*, no. 7, p. 25, *LC*, vol. 143.

[35] *National Herald*, 23 October 1939.

[36] Viceroy to Secretary of State (T), 24 October 1939, *ZC*, vol. 26. See also Linlithgow to Zetland, 22 October 1939, Ibid., vol. 18.

[37] *National Herald*, 26 October 1939.

with any relaxation of British control over India.[38] Congress leaders accused the British of using Congress–League differences as an excuse to avoid political advance.[39] Zetland's speech in the House of Lords on 18 October had been a pointer to British policy in the days to come.[40] Linlithgow later agreed that the policy of the League could be criticized as 'the sole, or most important' obstacle to the achievement of Indian independence,[41] while Jinnah himself admitted that his attitude was exposing him to a very formidable indictment—that he was a supporter of imperialism.[42]

Samuel Hoare's speech in the House of Commons on 28 October ensured that the political stalemate would persist. Partly conciliatory, partly admonitory, he pointed to the absence of unity amongst Indians themselves as the main obstacle to Dominion Status. The Congress, he insisted, should join the Viceroy's consultative committee. The alternative was non-cooperation, which would lead to civil disobedience, to breaches of law and order and repression.[43] For the Congress, Rajendra Prasad concluded that Hoare's speech 'has not carried anything further . . . there does not seem to be any intention of parting with the power (sic) at present to any extent and making definite promise (sic) of doing so at the end of the war.' There was thus 'no point of contact.'[44] As a result, on 30 October 1939, the CWC ordered the Congress ministries to resign.

The Congress decision to withdraw from office deprived Jinnah and the League of their chief weapon of attack against it—the Muslim grievances against Congress ministries. On the other hand, Linlithgow was now all the more dependent on the League as a counterpoise to the Congress. Dismayed by the Congress attitude to the war effort, the Viceroy shaped his policy in an attempt to attract both the Congress and the League into his Council, while discouraging them from uniting against the British.[45] On 1 November, at a meeting with Jinnah, Prasad and Gandhi, he placed a veto on political advance in Jinnah's hands by stipulating that

[38] Viceroy to Secretary of State, (T), 22 October 1939, *ZC*, vol. 26.
[39] *National Herald*, 26 October 1939.
[40] *Times of India*, 20 October 1939.
[41] Linlithgow to Zetland, 28 November 1939, *LC*, vol. 13.
[42] Linlithgow to Zetland, 16 January 1940, Ibid., vol. 9.
[43] *Times of India*, 30 October 1939.
[44] Prasad to B. Shiva Rao, 28 October 1939, *RPC* file no. 2–P/39.
[45] CAB 67/2 W.P. (G) (39) 53. Viceroy to Secretary of State, 22 October 1939.

there could be no agreement about the centre unless the two parties came to an agreement about the provinces.[46] No such agreement was possible in November 1939. The Congress would not contemplate any coalition with Jinnah unless he clarified his position on the Viceroy's broadcast of 18 October.[47]

Congress leaders, of course, were dismayed that Linlithgow was encouraging the pretensions of the League to put off the question of independence, but decided that there was little use in talking further to Jinnah. While he could rely on the British so much, the Congress could do nothing to satisfy him. Jinnah would exploit the situation to ask for even more than the British were willing to give or guarantee. Therefore, Congress leaders inferred, there would be no limit to his demands.

Linlithgow was gratified at Jinnah's refusal to support the Congress demand for a declaration of British war aims. Summing up the British position, the Viceroy observed that had the British been confronted with a joint demand, 'the strain upon me and upon H.M.G. would have been very great indeed.' At the same time, Linlithgow was aware of the intrinsic weakness of Jinnah's political position. 'I thought . . . I could claim to have vested interest in his position, and I had been asking myself how far that position was intrinsically sound. But I was bound to confess that I did not like it.' The 'eroding effect of nationalism' on Jinnah's platform was likely to be swift and serious.[48] Jinnah was also unreliable, and Linlithgow had feared 'a *volte face* of the most drastic character at the shortest notice' during their discussions with Gandhi. Jinnah's demands were exorbitant, and there was no case for abandoning federation and the principle of majority rule altogether. But the wise course would be to give him brief and reassuring replies, 'and to give even fuller weight than we may have done in the past in such public statements as you and I may have to make on Indian policy generally'.[49] Apparently, the Viceroy did not think much of the chances of Muslim political communalism standing up against Congress nationalism at the end of 1939.

[46] Note of interview between Viceroy, Prasad, Gandhi and Jinnah on 1 November 1939; enclosed in Linlithgow to Zetland, 2 November 1939, *LC*, vol. 8.

[47] Ibid.

[48] Note of interview between Linlithgow and Jinnah on 4 November 1939; Enclosure no. 2 of Linlithgow to Zetland, 6 November 1939, *LC*, vol. 8.

[49] Linlithgow to Zetland, 5 November 1939, Ibid.

Jinnah's refusal to support the Congress demand for independence had indeed weakened his position. With the Congress out of the way, the League had to find a new course of action. Jinnah could not openly support the British, for he would not have been able to carry the League with him. The Congress would not discuss provincial matters with him except on the basis of a British declaration, which was not forthcoming. So Jinnah would have to wait for political developments.

So Jinnah adopted a strategy to keep anti-Congress feeling high. He called on Muslims to observe 22 December as 'the day of deliverance and thanksgiving as a mark of relief that the Congress Governments have at last ceased to function.'[50] The call surprised many of his own party, for Muslims in the NWFP and Bengal thought that he had fallen back on a low form of politicking.[51] Deliverance Day itself passed off quietly in most places, and 'fell very flat' in the Muslim majority provinces of Sind and the NWFP;[52] but naturally it infuriated Congress leaders. 'There is a limit even to political falsehood and indecency but all limits have been passed', wrote Nehru. 'I do not see how I can even meet Jinnah now.'[53]

In December 1939, Huq published a series of articles in the League press,[54] and in January 1940, the Bihar Muslim League brought out a report on the grievances of Muslims in Bihar under Congress ministries,[55] on lines similar to those of the Pirpur Report of 1938. In reply the Congress suggested an inquiry into the charges by a federal judge, which Jinnah refused. An impartial inquiry perhaps would have deprived the allegations of their propaganda value for the League. Instead he asked for a Royal Commission to investigate the charges, knowing that the Congress would not agree,

[50] Quoted in Bolitho, *Jinnah Creator of Pakistan*, p. 124.

[51] Entries for 12 and 16 December 1939, Cunningham Diaries, vol. 3, *CC*. See also Ispahani to Jinnah, 12 December 1939, Zaidi, *Jinnah-Ispahani Correspondence*, p. 132.

[52] FRs for Punjab, UP, CP, Sind and NWFP for second half of December 1939, HP file no. 18/12/39. See also NWFP Governor's Report date 23 December 1939, *LC*, vol. 74.

[53] Nehru to Mahadev Desai, 9 December 1939, *NC*, vol. 17.

[54] Published as *Muslim Sufferings Under Congress Rule*. A copy is available in L/I/628.

[55] *All-India Muslim League (Bihar Province) Publicity Committee: Report . . . on some Grievances of the Muslims 1938–9*, President S.M. Shareef. (Shareef Report) (Patna, 1940).

as it would have implied acquiescence in British intervention in Indian affairs.[56]

The Viceroy saw little substance in Jinnah's charges, but, as he had commented earlier, 'the existence of the atmosphere is the thing that matters and the thing to which we have to give weight in formulating our policy and reaching our conclusions.'[57] British officials maintained a deliberate silence about their opinion of the League's exaggerated charges against Congress ministries, while Sir Hugh O'Neill, Under Secretary of State for India, announced in the Commons that no inquiry would be held into the allegations as no purpose would be served by it. Jinnah replied that O'Neill's statement had imposed 'an additional task upon us.' The charges against Congress ministries must be investigated in order to prevent a recurrence in future.[58] By repeating his demand for an enquiry, Jinnah, with some help from the British, kept alive 'Muslim sufferings' under Congress rule.

Evidently Jinnah did not want a settlement with Congress. When Linlithgow asked him if he would be able to settle with Congress if the British assured him that no constitutional departure would be made without the approval of the League, he replied, ' "But what have you to lose if no agreement is reached?" '[59] And so the political *impasse* continued. The British had no intention of giving way to Congress demands, and noted the disparity between the personal friendliness of Congress leaders and their politically tough attitude.[60] Both Linlithgow and Whitehall stood firm. The Act of 1935 had been passed not to terminate the Empire but to preserve it. The War Cabinet turned down Zetland's proposal for any concessions to Congress, insisting that talk of 'independence within the Empire' should be avoided in favour of 'autonomous communities within the Empire.' Such terminology was less likely to imply the right of secession from the Empire. So long as the Congress and League remained divided, the Viceroy could mark time and wait until the pieces on the political chess-board had taken their place.[61]

[56] *Bombay Chronicle*, 16 December 1939.
[57] Linlithgow to Zetland, 28 November 1939, *LC*, vol. 13.
[58] *National Herald*, 26 and 29 January 1940.
[59] Linlithgow to Zetland, 16 January 1940, *LC*, vol. 9.
[60] *Quarterly Survey of the Political and Constitutional Position of the British in India*, no. 9, p. 25.
[61] See R.J. Moore, *Churchill Cripps and India, 1939–45*, (Oxford, 1979), p. 26. See, for example, Linlithgow to Zetland, 18 December 1939, *LC*, vol. 8.

While the British ruled by ordinance, introduced press censorship, and rounded up Congressmen in many places, the Congress Working Committee, meeting at Patna on 1 March 1940, discussed the possibility of civil disobedience as soon as organization permitted and circumstances demanded. The Ramgarh Congress on 20 March reaffirmed the Patna resolution. Freedom could not exist within the orbit of British rule, and the Congress could not be a party to the war without British guarantees for a Constituent Assembly based on adult suffrage and independence. For Congress, there could be no solution to the communal problem except through the Constituent Assembly, where the rights of minorities would be protected by agreement between the representatives of various communities.[62]

The political stalemate was also worrying Jinnah. His platform of blank negation was wearing out, for the Congress resolutions at Patna and Ramgarh were passed in spite of League hostility and its intensification of communal tension over the last three months. Even Linlithgow was tiring of Jinnah's tactics and had advised him to formulate constructive suggestions for a political settlement. Jinnah sulked at the British refusal to break with Gandhi,[63] and warned Linlithgow 'not to sell the pass behind their [League's] backs.[64] In Bengal, Huq was engaged in one of his intermittent flirtations with the Congress;[65] and in the NWFP, the possibility of an intercommunal ministry appeared imminent.[66] Muslim Leaguers themselves were urging Jinnah to define the party's goals;[67] some even suggested a Congress–League pact.[68] There was, then, not much sign of a solid Muslim political front in the early months of 1940.

Against this background, on 23 March 1940, the Muslim League passed its celebrated 'Pakistan' resolution at Lahore. It declared that no constitutional plan would be acceptable to Muslims unless

> 'geographically contiguous units are demarcated into regions which should be so constituted, with such territorial readjustments as may be necessary, that the areas in which the Muslims are numerically in a

[62] *IAR*, 1940, vol. 1, p. 218.
[63] Viceroy to Secretary of State, (T), 6 February 1940, *LC*, vol. 19.
[64] Linlithgow to Zetland, (T), 16 March 1940, *LC*, vol. 74.
[65] Herbert to Linlithgow, 2/3 January and 6 February 1940, Ibid., vol. 40.
[66] Entry for 13 February 1940, Cunningham Diaries, vol. 4, CC.
[67] *National Herald*, 20 February 1940.
[68] *National Herald*, 26 February 1940.

majority, as in the North-Western and Eastern zones of India, should be grouped to constitute Independent States in which the constituent units shall be autonomous and sovereign.'[69]

Although this was the first time that any Muslim party had adopted 'Pakistan' for a policy, the idea was not entirely new. The notion of a Muslim homeland in north-west and north-east India was made possible, not by the fact that the majority of Indian Muslims lived in the Muslim provinces—indeed, more than 60 per cent lived in the Muslim minority provinces—but because of what has been described as an 'accident of geography'[70]: that there happened to be four provinces in which Muslims were in a majority. Without these Muslim majority areas, communalism would have existed in India but it seems inconceivable that any section of Muslims would have been able to demand any kind of "homeland." The Aga Khan and Muhammad Iqbal were among the first to moot the idea of a Muslim homeland, and the term "Pakistan" was coined by Chaudhury Rahmat Ali, a student at Cambridge, in 1933. In the summer of 1939, Sikander Hyat Khan had published a scheme for the loosest of federations, with regional or zonal legislatures to deal with common subjects. In January 1940, Dr. Abdul Latif of Hyderabad had outlined a plan for a minimal federation of homogeneous cultural zones.[71] In March 1939, Khaliquzzaman had discussed the possibility of partition with Zetland[72] and in September Jinnah had suggested it to Linlithgow as a political alternative to federation.[73] In February 1940, Aurangzeb Khan, provincial League leader in the NWFP, told Cunningham that the League proposed to press for a Muslim homeland in the northwest and northeast of India in direct units with the Crown.[74] On 4 March, Jinnah told Edward Benthall, Finance Member in the Viceroy's Executive, that Muslims would not be safe without partition,[75] and twelve days later, he told Linlithgow that if the British could not resolve the political deadlock,

[69] Pirzada, *Documents*, p. 341.

[70] S.R. Mehrotra, 'The Congress and the Partition of India,' in Philips and Wainwright (eds.), *Partition of India*, p. 201.

[71] For these partition schemes see Gwyer and Appadorai, *Speeches and Documents on the Indian Constitution*, vol. 2, pp. 435–65.

[72] Khaliquzzaman, *Pathway to Pakistan*, pp. 205–8.

[73] Note of interview between Linlithgow and Jinnah on 4 September 1939; Enclosure 2, Linlithgow to Zetland, 5 September 1939, *ZC*, vol. 18.

[74] Entry for 13 February 1940, Cunningham Diaries, vol. 4, *CC*.

[75] Entry for 4 March 1940, Benthall Diaries, *Benthall Collection*.

the League would have no option but to fall back on some form of partition.[76]

That Jinnah envisaged a sovereign Pakistan was clear from his assertion at Lahore, that 'The problem in India is not of an inter-communal character, but manifestly of an international one and must be treated as such.'[77] By international, as Professor Mansergh points out, he meant literally as between nations.[78] The demand for a sovereign Pakistan answered both Linlithgow's criticism that he was unconstructive, and the indictment that he was not supporting the Congress demand because he was on the imperial side. It has often been argued that Jinnah's call for a sovereign Pakistan was simply a ploy to secure the League a vantage point at the centre. But even if the demand was mere tactics, the tactics must have been aimed at achieving something or preventing something. Prevention would surely be of a Congress–British agreement bypassing the Muslim League. In that case, Jinnah, as we have seen, preferred the prevalence of the differences between them and the maintenance of the status quo, that is, the continuation of the Raj. On the other hand, if he wanted to achieve something, why not a sovereign Pakistan? The League's weak position in the provinces need not have put him off from making the demand; he might get more popular support for an idea which promised Muslims salvation from imagined 'Hindu' domination. The League's poor position in the Muslim majority provinces probably introduced the element of calculation in the demand. A man of Jinnah's political shrewdness and dialectical skill might have calculated that, from political expediency, the British would not reject the possibility of Pakistan, because the very existence of the idea would help them to repudiate the Congress demand for independence.

Jinnah calculated correctly. On 23 March 1940, Linlithgow wrote that the British should mark time. To the Viceroy, the Lahore resolution was the answer to Patna and Ramgarh, showing 'how deep is the gulf and how little the prospect of these two parties getting together in the present circumstances.'[79] On 9 April, the War

[76] Viceroy to Secretary of State, (T), 16 March 1940, *LC*, vol. 19.

[77] Pirzada, *Documents*, p. 337.

[78] Mansergh, *Prelude to Partition*, p. 27.

[79] Linlithgow to Lumley, 23 March 1940, *LC*, vol. 54, and Linlithgow to Herbert, 28 March 1940, R/3/2/14. See also Viceroy to Secretary of State, (T), 6 April 1940, *LC*, vol. 19.

Cabinet decided that the Lahore resolution had 'complicated' the situation, and that it was difficult for the Viceroy to announce any positive policy.[80] On 18 April, Zetland stated in the House of Lords that agreement among Indian communities was essential if the vision of a united India was to become a reality, and added that the British could not force a constitution on the Muslims.[81] This statement could only be interpreted as an indication that partition would henceforth be one of the options to be kept open by the British in India. Indeed, on 8 April, Linlithgow had cautioned Zetland against overemphasizing the unacceptability of the Pakistan scheme—'it would be politically unfortunate'—and it 'might be pressed' after the war.[82]

Many Muslim politicians, as Linlithgow himself observed, were 'unhappy' about the Lahore resolution.[83] No Muslim minister in Sind favoured it;[84] and Allah Baksh, the erstwhile Premier of Sind, described it as 'harmful and fantastic.'[85] The interest the resolution aroused in the NWFP can be gauged from the fact that neither Cunningham nor the Chief Secretary mentioned it in their reports in March or April 1940. In Bengal, Fazlul Huq, who moved the resolution at Lahore, was talking, only a month later, of working for a united India.[86]

These reactions of Muslim politicians from the Muslim majority provinces suggest that the call for Pakistan was not an expression of the political aspirations of a solid Muslim communal nationality from below, but those of Jinnah and his all India Committee from above. Nevertheless, the evidence does leave open the possibility that from Jinnah's point of view the demand for Pakistan was required as a tactic to gain more cooperation from, and control over, Muslim provincial politicians, whether within or without the League, by appealing to and arousing Muslim communal sentiment.

The sharp reactions of Congress, Hindu Mahasabha and Sikh leaders to the Pakistan resolution, along with the calculated silence

[80] War Cabinet W.P. (G) (40) 96, Memorandum by Zetland, 9 April 1940, *ZC*, vol. 26.

[81] *Times of India*, 20 April 1940.

[82] Viceroy to Secretary of State, (T), 8 April 1940, *LC*, vol. 19.

[83] Viceroy to Secretary of State, (T), 6 April 1940, *LC*, vol. 19.

[84] Graham to Linlithgow, 9 April 1940, L/P&J/5/256.

[85] *Tribune*, 28 April 1940.

[86] *Tribune*, 29 April 1940.

of the British on the subject, gave more substance to the demand for Pakistan than perhaps it deserved. Rajagopalachari described the two-nation theory as 'a mischievous concept . . . that threatens to lead India into destruction.'[87] Hindu Mahasabha leaders conjured up—prophetically—visions of civil war;[88] Satyamurti accused Jinnah of wanting on a smaller scale what Hitler wanted in Europe.[89] Nehru declared that the Congress would not have anything to do with the 'mad scheme' of the Muslim League and ruled out the possibility of any settlement or negotiations.[90] Gandhi expressed the emotion of Indian nationalism with an idealism which was defined by his understanding of his religion: 'I am proud of being a Hindu, but I have never gone to anybody as a Hindu to secure Hindu-Muslim unity. My Hinduism demands no pacts.'[91] 'Partition means a patent untruth. My whole soul rebels against the idea that Hinduism and Islam represent two antagonistic cultures and doctrines. To assent to such a doctrine is for me a denial of God. For I believe with my whole soul that the God of the Quran is also the God of Gita . . . I must rebel against the idea that millions who were Hindus the other day changed their nationality on adopting Islam as their religion.'[92]

And so the Lahore resolution, until now the dream of theorists, was put forward by an important political organization as a serious aim, and it altered the complexion of Indian politics. Its practicability for the time being was irrelevant, and it was given some substance by the sharp reactions of its opponents. It hoisted the banner of Muslim separation, at least partly because the British chose to ignore nationalist Muslim opinion, and dealt only with Jinnah 'on the Muslim side'.[93]

Its political ramifications on the provincial as well as all India level ensured that the Pakistan resolution could not be ignored. It stirred the politics of the Punjab partly because it gave Jinnah a foothold in the province and partly because of the uncertain future it held out for the Sikhs, who were a minority in every district of the province which was their homeland. Behind his silence on the Lahore resolution lay Sikander's political debt to Jinnah. On 28 February, his Unionist ministry had banned the carrying of arms

[87] *Bombay Chronicle*, 27 March 1940. [88] *Tribune*, 25 March 1940.
[89] *Tribune*, 26 March 1940. [90] *Tribune*, 14 April 1940.
[91] *Harijan*, 30 March 1940. [92] *Harijan*, 13 April 1940.
[93] Linlithgow to Amery, 14 May 1940, *LC*, vol. 9.

under the Defence of India Act and the police had fired on the Khaksars, a semi-military organization of Muslims, who had defied the ban. On the eve of the Muslim League session at Lahore, Sikander's Muslim opponents in the Unionist party demanded an enquiry into the police firing and urged removal of the ban on the Khaksars. Banners proclaiming "Sikander murdabad" [death to Sikander] were hoisted near the entrance to the hall where the session was to be held. Sikander was indebted to Jinnah for shelving discussion of the issue at the open session of the League: Jinnah thus avoided a clash between a government headed by a Muslim and a Muslim organization, safeguarded the position of the Punjab ministry, but also maintained the unity of the League in a very difficult situation, and increased his influence over Leaguers in the Punjab.[94]

So Sikander was safe for the time being, but he was in no position to oppose the Pakistan resolution, although he knew that it would place his intercommunal coalition under a strain. The first sign of restiveness within the coalition came from Sikander's Sikh colleagues, the Khalsa Nationalist Party. The exact nature of Pakistan had been left undefined at Lahore. The Lahore resolution promised that 'adequate, effective and mandatory safeguards should be specifically provided in the constitution for minorities . . . for the protection of their religious, cultural, economic, political, administrative and other rights and interests in consultation with them'[95], without spelling out the least idea of what would be considered adequate and effective. As the League had dismissed similar assurances to Muslims, Tara Singh could well argue that if Muslims could not trust the Hindu majority they should also presume that the Sikhs could not trust the Muslim majority in the Punjab.[96] If, as the Raja of Mahmudabad had suggested at Lahore, Pakistan was to be an Islamic state, based on the *Sharia*,[97] the Sikhs had reason to be alarmed.

After giving up all hope of agreement with the League, the majority of the CWC persuaded Gandhi that the Congress must embark on civil disobedience. Action was necessary to avoid demoralization in Congress ranks; the problem of civil disobedience against a back-

[94] *Quarterly Survey of the Political and Constitutional Position of the British in India*, no. 11, pp. 11–12 and 26; Craik to Linlithgow, 31 March 1940 and 8 April 1940, *LC*, vol. 89.

[95] Pirzada, *Documents*, p. 341.

[96] *Times of India*, 25 March 1940.

[97] Pirzada, *Documents*, p. 342.

ground of communal tension had been known even at the time of the passing of Patna and Ramgarh resolutions.[98]

By the end of April 1940, the British felt prepared to cope with civil disobedience. Reginald Maxwell, the Home Member, however, advised Linlithgow to resolve the political stalemate, otherwise even moderate opinion would veer round to the Congress.[99] Linlithgow remained satisfied with the Congress–League rift. Jinnah would continue to blow hot and cold, but he would not obstruct any constitutional initiative made by the British, and they could look in general for the help of the Muslim League.[100]

So Linlithgow was understandably dismayed when neither the Congress nor League allowed their members to join the War Committees and the Civic Guards, the formation of which he announced on 5 June. War Committees would be set up in every district to organize people and to disseminate official information. The Civic Guards were organized from volunteers to help the regular police maintain order.[101] Both the Congress and League, however, decided to set up their own organizations for civil defence, and the Viceroy considered yet again the possibility of making a move 'at the right moment' which would bring the two parties into the Executive Council.[102] With the fall of France on 27 June 1940, Linlithgow confessed that he was willing to reconsider his attitude about not appearing to take sides, if the League was willing to enter the Executive Council and the Congress remained intransigent.[103] Jinnah was anxious 'above all things' to get into the administration, but refused to lift the ban on Muslim Leaguers serving in the War Committees—they would only be allowed to go into civil defence organizations set up by the government if and when his party came into the Executive Council.[104]

There were good reasons for the Viceroy to want the Congress and the League—or at least the latter—in his Council at this time. The German invasions of Holland and Belgium on 10 May, and the

[98] *IAR*, 1940, vol. 1, pp. 228ff. See also AICC file no. G-32, 1940.

[99] Maxwell to Laithwaite, 25 April 1940, HP file no. 3/13/40, p. 3.

[100] See, for example, Viceroy to Secretary of State, (T), 28 June and 1 July 1940, *LC*, vol. 19.

[101] *Times of India*, 6 June 1940.

[102] Viceroy to Secretary of State, (T), 10 June 1940, *LC*, vol. 19.

[103] Linlithgow to Amery, 27 June 1940, Ibid., vol. 9.

[104] Viceroy to Secretary of State, (T), 28 June 1940, Ibid., vol. 19.

British withdrawal from Dunkirk on 27 May, exposed Britain to a possible German attack. England faced the Axis singlehanded, and this fact was at least partly responsible for a changed role for India in the Imperial defence machine. India was of vital importance because of her resources, her manpower and the economic potential east of Suez. On 21 May Defence Plan of India "A" was issued by the Commander-in-Chief, ordering the immediate expansion of the Indian Army by six divisions;[105] on 24 May the development of aircraft production in India, so far refused, was recommended by the Government of India;[106] and on 7 June, Linlithgow launched his plan for pooling the resources and production of member countries of the British Empire in the Indian Ocean with India as its 'natural' centre,[107] a plan which was to result in the creation of the "Eastern Group Supply Council." On 27 June, Parliament passed the India and Burma Emergency Provisions Act providing 'in the event of a complete breakdown of communications with the United Kingdom' for the Governor General to take over the powers normally exercised by the Secretary of State. 'I am quite clear that the point has been reached in the prosecution of the war at which it is unsound and unsatisfactory and likely to prove increasingly difficult in terms of public reaction, that we should continue at the Centre to handle matters through an entirely bureaucratic government,' wrote Linlithgow to Amery on 1 July.[108]

In these circumstances, the CWC made another offer on 3 July. If the British would acknowledge that the complete independence of India was the only solution to the political deadlock, the Congress would join a provisional National Government, formed of representatives of all parties. Only such a government, Congress claimed, would be able to organize effectively the material and moral resources of India for defence.[109] The Working Committee disagreed with Gandhi's emphasis on non-violent cooperation. 'We know that arms and ammunitions have not been able to save the freedom

[105] Memorandum by Amery for War Cabinet, W.P. (G) (40) 137 and 139, 23 and 24 May 1940, CAB 67/7. See also S.N. Prasad, *Expansion of the Armed Forces and Defence Organisation 1939–45* (Calcutta, 1956), pp. 58ff.

[106] Private Secretary to Viceroy to Private Secretary to Secretary of State, 24 May 1940, L/E/8/1711.

[107] Linlithgow to Amery, 30 May, 1940, *LC*, vol. 9.

[108] Linlithgow to Amery, (T), 1 July 1940, Ibid., vol. 19.

[109] See AICC file no. G-32/KW-1, Part I, 1940, pp. 31–43.

of France, Holland, Belgium and Norway but we also know that human nature . . . is not prepared to give up force . . . Mahatma Gandhi has to give the message of non-violence to the world and, therefore, it is his duty to propagate it, but we have to consider our position as the representatives of the Indian Nation meeting in the Indian National Congress. The Indian National Congress is a political organization pledged to win the political independence of the country. It is not an institution for organizing world peace.' Gandhi would go his own way, but the Congress would co-ordinate its activities with him whenever possible.[110]

The British Cabinet, however, frowned on the Viceroy's proposal for a British constitutional initiative, especially as the Congress and League had yet to reconcile their differences.[111] An indignant Churchill, seeing the correspondence between the Viceroy and the Secretary of State for the first time,[112] rejected Linlithgow's suggestion that the cabinet promise in advance to frame at the conclusion of the war, a constitution to which representatives of the principal Indian parties would agree. It was also quite impossible to pledge in advance the attitude of a future parliament, and to fix a date for India to achieve Dominion Status. The cabinet agreed merely to an enlarged Executive Council and the setting up of a War Advisory Committee.[113]

This was the background to the "August Offer", which the Congress turned down even as it was published in the press. There was no suggestion of a National Government and therefore no scope for further discussion.[114] Even Rajagopalachari, who had framed the Poona Congress resolution for a National Government, was one of the first to reject the Offer.[115]

The League was apparently satisfied with the British stipulation in the August Offer of consultation with the minorities in any future constitutional discussions, and its assurance that they would not transfer their 'responsibilities' to any government whose au-

[110] *IAR*, 1940, vol. 2, pp. 193–4.

[111] Viceroy to Prime Minister, (T), 18 July 1940 and Prime Minister to Viceroy, (T), 16 July 1940, PREM 4/47/1.

[112] Prime Minister to Viceroy, 26 July 1940, Ibid.

[113] Prime Minister to Viceroy, 28 July 1940, Ibid.

[114] See Linlithgow to Azad, 4 August 1940 and Azad to Linlithgow, (T), 8 and 10 August 1940; AICC file no. G-1, Part 1, 1940-1941.

[115] *IAR*, 1940, vol. 2, pp. 196ff.

thority 'is directly denied by large and powerful elements in India's national life.' This meant that the British would ignore the Congress demand for independence. The demand for a sovereign Pakistan had served at least one of Jinnah's aims: to ensure that the League was not ignored in any settlement between the Congress and the British. Not surprisingly, the MLWC now allowed Leaguers to join war committees. Probably this also signified a concession to loyalists like Sikander and Huq, who had earlier defied Jinnah's orders banning Leaguers from serving on war committees. But the British had not accepted Pakistan; nor had they accepted the League's claim to be treated as an equal of the Congress in any constitutional discussions. So the League rejected the August Offer on the ground that it had not been offered 'equal partnership' at the centre and in the provinces in return for cooperation with the war effort. The logic of the League's claim to parity and recognition by the British as the 'sole' representative of Muslims demonstrated the seriousness of Jinnah's call for a sovereign Muslim state. Concession of parity by the British would mean their acceptance of the Muslim claim to nationhood, the League the equal of the Congress, with an equal claim to the spoils of a transfer of power. Conversely, if the British accepted the contention that Muslims were a nation, they must accord them parity. This logic rationalized Jinnah's persuasion of his working committee to reject the August Offer. The majority of the MLWC wanted to accept it, but deferred to Jinnah's warning that full cooperation would mean that the entire burden of responsibility for protecting the Indian empire, crushing the Congress, supplying men and money and running the administration would fall on the League. If the Congress decided to cooperate, the British would reject the Pakistan scheme. So he counselled patience with a view to extracting as many concessions as possible.[116] That Jinnah's word prevailed points to his ability to get his way, responsible in no small measure for is hold over the all-India Muslim League.

'It is lamentable that we should have to await in this way on Jinnah's vanity, but it cannot of course be helped,' wrote Linlithgow to Amery on 5 September. His demand that the League should be taken into full and equal partnership with the British in the running of the country was absurd. At the same time, it was important to

[116] This account is based on FR for Bombay for first half of September 1940, HP file no. 18/9/40; and Pirzada, *Documents*, p. 403.

hold the League together, 'and in those circumstances there is nothing for it but to be patient with Jinnah.'[117] But there was no response from Jinnah, who dashed Linlithgow's hopes of his full cooperation, and by October, the offer had been put into cold storage.[118]

With the Congress embarking on its individual civil disobedience campaign, and with no further British initiative, Jinnah found the political stalemate worrying, perhaps because there was nothing for him to reject and so keep himself in the limelight, especially at a time when the League was in trouble in the Muslim majority provinces. The call for Pakistan seems to have done little to strengthen his control over provincial Leaguers. In Sind, the League's coalition ministry headed by Mir Bunde Ali Khan broke up when Allah Baksh and two Hindu ministers resigned; and the League was out of office in March 1941.[119]

In the Punjab, Sikander had defied Jinnah's ban on Muslim Leaguers joining War Committees, while his personal antipathy to Pakistan and the need to reassure his Hindu and Sikh colleagues had brought him out against Pakistan in February 1941. Unity alone could bring freedom, declared Sikander. The Punjab had no use for Pakistan or any separatist scheme. His ministry announced plans to promote communal harmony by organizing lectures on the subject, subsidizing newspapers sympathetic to the idea, and organizing common birthday celebrations for the founders of different religions.[120] He and other Muslim Unionists stayed away from Jinnah's meetings in Lahore on 1 and 2 March;[121] and he also did not attend the Muslim League Conference in Madras in April 1941.[122] Embarrassed by Jinnah's continued advocacy of Pakistan, Sikander proposed to resign from the MLWC; but the idea did not suit Linlithgow. He instructed Henry Craik, Governor of the Punjab, to persuade Sikander discreetly not to resign from the Working Committee, for two significant reasons. First, Muslim Leaguers in the

[117] Linlithgow to Amery, 5 September 1940, *LC*, vol. 9.

[118] Linlithgow to Amery, 8 October 1940, Ibid.

[119] Graham to Linlithgow, 3 March 1941, Ibid., vol. 97.

[120] *Times of India*, 4 February, 5 March 1941.

[121] Craik to Linlithgow, 4 March 1941, *LC*, vol. 90. FR for Punjab for first half of March 1941, HP file no. 18/3/41.

[122] Extract from FR of Central Intelligence Officer, Madras, dated 22 April 1941, HP file no. 4/8/41.

Punjab who were opposed to Sikander might try to overthrow his Unionist ministry on the Pakistan issue. Linlithgow wanted Sikander to stay on as Prime Minister of the Punjab, because of his successful organization of the provincial war effort. If Sikander were hounded out by extreme Muslim elements, it 'would be a bad thing from the Punjab point of view.[123] Secondly, the Viceroy did not want a split in the Muslim League. He had taken great pains to get Sikander to drop his negotiations with the Congress in the summer of 1940.[124] In March 1941, when the individual civil disobedience campaign was in progress, a split in the League could only encourage the Congress. In Linlithgow's policy, it was 'very important' to maintain the League a 'a solid political entity,' able to speak on behalf of Muslim opinion in India. Jinnah was 'the one man' who had succeeded in unifying the Muslims over the last forty years and whose control over them appeared at the moment to be effective.[125] Sikander eventually decided not to resign from the MLWC, as this might have lost him the support of some Muslim Unionists in favour of Pakistan. Linlithgow was satisfied. For, as he confessed later, 'I do not want to be left with only one side in this business organized'.[126] In this instance also, Jinnah's call for Pakistan had divided him from the most influential Muslim leader in the Punjab, though it had attracted the support of others whom Sikander feared. Ironically, however, though Sikander needed Jinnah, and to a lesser extent Jinnah needed Sikander, the Viceroy needed them both; and it was he in this case who worked most effectively to preserve unity within the Muslim League.

The deep division between Jinnah and provincial Leaguers was illustrated again in June 1941, when the Viceroy invited Sikander, Huq and Saadullah, among others, to serve on the National Defence Council. He intended to secure their acceptance before Jinnah got wind of the invitations. Once they had entered the NDC, he doubted whether Jinnah would quarrel with them.[127] The Muslim Prime Ministers agreed to serve on the NDC. Jinnah said nothing

[123] Viceroy to Governor of Punjab, (T), 1 March 1941, *LC*, vol. 90. See also Linlithgow to Amery, 1 March 1941, Ibid., vol. 10.

[124] P. Moon, 'May God Be With You Always,' *The Round Table*, July 1971, p. 418.

[125] Linlithgow to Amery, 15 May 1941, *LC*, vol. 10.

[126] Linlithgow to Amery, 8 September 1941, Ibid., vol. 10.

[127] Linlithgow to Reid, 19 June 1941, Ibid., vol. 34.

until he found out that the Viceroy had made the tactical error of inviting the provincial Premiers not as Premiers but as representatives of the Muslim community. Then Jinnah claimed that the invitations should have been issued through the League as it was the 'sole' representative of Muslims.'[128]

Jinnah drew the attention of the League Prime Ministers to his circular of June 1940, which barred Muslim Leaguers from joining war committees. At first, the Premiers stood up to him. Saadullah, Prime Minister of Assam, made it clear to Jinnah that he was already on provincial war committees and his government was committed to the prosecution of the war.[129] He threatened Jinnah that if he had to resign from NDC or from the League, it would be the end of his ministry and a setback to the League in Assam.[130] But he took shelter behind Sikander. Sikander wavered but felt that his position would remain secure in the Punjab even if he fell out with Jinnah. According to Linlithgow,

> 'Jinnah sent for Sikander at Bombay and told him that he had decisive evidence that I had invited him to serve as a Muslim representative and not qua Prime Minister. There seems to have followed an amusing scene; for Sikander asked to be shown the evidence, and Jinnah, after a great deal of searching around the room and turning up papers, expressed his regret that he could not lay his hand on it. Sikander holding his ground, Miss Jinnah was called to pursue the search, but she was equally unsuccessful. Sikander was still holding his ground, the missing document was produced and Sikander was told that this was the answer and that he had better go away and think about it. Later in the evening two members of the League (quite obviously on Jinnah's instructions) called on him to say that they had seen Lumley's letter and that Sikander must give way.'[131]

At the meeting of the Muslim League Council next morning, Sikander told someone present who said to him ' "you seem to be in the position of an accused" ', ' "I am not an accused, I am a convict!" ' (sic).[132] On 25 August, he resigned from the NDC.

Saadullah returned to Assam and submitted his resignation from the NDC, while Huq struggled to maintain his Premiership in Ben-

[128] Lumley to Jinnah, 20 July 1941 and Jinnah to Lumley, 21 July 1941, Ibid., vol. 55. See also Linlithgow to Amery, 30 August 1941, Ibid., vol. 10.

[129] Reid to Linlithgow, 29 July 1941, Ibid., vol. 34.

[130] Reid to Linlithgow, Ibid.

[131] Linlithgow to Amery, 30 August 1941, *LC*, vol. 10.

[132] Linlithgow to Amery, 1 September 1941, Ibid.

gal. His alliance with the League in 1937 had been made at the expense of the support of radicals in the KPP, who deserted him when he joined hands with their old adversaries. The League's support enabled him to maintain his Premiership, but it had also meant that he was in a minority in the Bengal Provincial League.[133] A political maverick, Huq was restive with League attempts to dictate to him, and had, on more than one occasion, roused their ire because of his flirtation with the Congress and the Mahasabha. In September 1939, he had come out in support of the war effort, which had further estranged him from many provincial Muslim Leaguers, and, in June 1940, he had defied Jinnah's directive that Leaguers must not join War Committees.

Jinnah had not taken disciplinary action against Huq because he had been joined by other provincial Leaguers, including Nazimuddin and Suhrawardy, who said they would not support any action against Huq.[134] Wanting to avoid a split in the League, Jinnah did nothing.[135]

Ispahani and his friends called on Jinnah to take action against Huq when he joined the NDC in August 1941.[136] Huq then came out with a lengthy manifesto attacking Jinnah:

> '. . . Principles of democracy and autonomy in All India Muslim League are being subordinated to arbitrary wishes of a single individual who seeks to rule as omnipotent authority over destiny of 33 millions in Bengal who occupy key position in Indian Muslim Politics'.

At the same time, he played safe and announced his resignation from the NDC![137]

Even as Huq's enemies in the provincial league organized mass demonstrations against him in several towns,[138] Jinnah made up his mind to remove Huq from the MLWC. Huq's attack on his authority could not be ignored. But he did not want to take action against him unless he was certain that the provincial League would support it. On 26 September 1941, he wrote to Ispahani:

[133] Sen, *Muslim Politics*, p. 98.
[134] Governor of Bengal to Viceroy, (T), 31 July 1941, *LC*, vol. 41.
[135] Zaidi, Introduction to *Jinnah–Ispahani Correspondence*, p. 38.
[136] Ispahani to Jinnah, 6 September 1941, *Jinnah–Ispahani Correspondence*, pp. 176–7.
[137] Huq to Liaqat Ali Khan, 8 September 1941, HP file no. 17/4/41.
[138] Herbert to Linlithgow, 21 September and 1 October 1941, *LC*, vol. 41.

'In my opinion he is a source of danger to the vital interests of not only the Musalmans of Bengal but of the whole of India. It is humiliating for the Musalmans to acknowledge a man of this type to be one of their leaders. The whole world is laughing at this issue. It is entirely up to you all in Bengal to stand united and put an end to this agony.'[139]

Jinnah was anxious to avoid what Herbert, the Governor of Bengal described as 'the onus of splitting the Bengal Muslims' being put on him.[140]

Provincial Leaguers, including Nazimuddin and Suhrawardy, were keen to avoid a break with Huq, and on 20 October 1941, the Bengal League passed a motion of confidence in him.[141] On 16 November Jinnah accepted Huq's explanation for joining the NDC although Huq had not withdrawn the letter attacking him. Ispahani and his friends were now spoiling for a fight with Huq and withdrew support from his ministry. They were joined by Nazimuddin and Suhrawardy, who had been given, interestingly enough, the tacit assurance by the governor that they would be asked to form a ministry in case Huq lost his majority in the legislature.[142]

But as Pearl Harbour fell, and allied fortunes reached their lowest ebb, Herbert seems to have had second thoughts. He was apprehensive that a League ministry which excluded Hindus would not be able to inspire support for the war effort amongst a sizeable section of the population in Bengal. Moreover, there was no guarantee that the League would work wholeheartedly for the war effort.[143] So he decided to allow Huq to form a ministry with the breakaway Bose Congress group and the Mahasabha. This gave Jinnah and the MLWC an opportunity to accuse Huq of betraying Muslims, and Huq was expelled from the League in December 1941.

These episodes illustrated first, that the Viceroy's need to maintain the League as a counterpoise to the Congress at the all India level did not necessarily mean that he or provincial officials wanted it in power in Muslim majority provinces. Linlithgow himself, as we have seen, did not want the League in power in the Punjab because

[139] Jinnah to Ispahani, 26 September 1941, Zaidi, *Jinnah–Ispahani Correspondence*, p. 188.

[140] Herbert to Linlithgow, 21 October 1941, L/P & J/5/134.

[141] Zaidi, Introduction to *Jinnah-Ispahani Correspondence*, p. 41.

[142] Copy of letter from Nazimuddin to Jinnah, 14 December 1941, HP file no. 232/41.

[143] Governor of Bengal to Viceroy, (T), 9 December 1941, R/3/1/30.

he feared that they would throw a spanner in the successful organization of the war effort in the province. Thus the Viceroy himself could follow different policies towards the League at the all India and provincial levels.

Secondly, it was clear that Jinnah could ultimately emerge the winner in any trial of strength with provincial Leaguers at the all India level, and could threaten them at the provincial level: nevertheless, his direct influence on Muslim provincial politics depended on tactical opportunities of exploiting rivalry between factions.

It was also obvious that it mattered less to Linlithgow that Jinnah was not cooperating fully with the war effort than that he was opposing the Congress. The Viceroy was surprised and dismayed that Jinnah could put up 'as stiff a show' against the League Prime Ministers on the NDC issue,[144] but saw no point in calling what he regarded as Jinnah's bluff. The League was the only counterpoise to the Congress at the all India level. There was no platform at this level on the Muslim side in opposition to Jinnah. Saadullah and Haroon were too small on the all India level, Huq was emotionally uncertain, and Sikander had no backbone. 'I am not averse to a little tiger shooting', concluded the Viceroy, 'but I attach a good deal of importance to my companions being staunch before I embark on sport of that kind.'[145]

[144] Linlithgow to Herbert, 25 August 1941, R/3/2/46.
[145] Linlithgow to Amery, 1 September 1941, *LC*, vol. 10.

CHAPTER 3

Provincial and All India Politics: Currents and Cross-Currents—December 1941 to April 1945

The Cripps Mission and Its Aftermath

The attack on Pearl Harbour on 6 December 1941 inspired the British to consider a fresh political initiative in India to attract a greater measure of popular support for the war effort. Pressure came from India, the USA, China and the UK,[1] and Whitehall was confronted with the task of showing its allies that it was making constitutional moves to end the political deadlock in India. Whitehall could not have been heartened by reports from some provinces that anti-British feeling was becoming more widespread.[2] But neither Whitehall nor Linlithgow were interested in offering the political advance which Congress demanded at Bardoli at the end of 1941.

Frustrated by the political *impasse*, the Congress Right discussed the possibility of returning to office in November 1941. Rajagopalachari and Bhulabhai Desai, who had no confidence in *satyagraha*, wanted the Congress to resume parliamentary activities. But they did not want Gandhi to leave the Congress or to abstain from supporting their suggestions, as they would then have 'real trouble' in controlling their 'leftist colleagues.'[3] Rajagopalachari wanted the Congress to give the government an inkling of the party's desire to return to office and to cooperate with the war effort so that the government could make an offer.[4] Nehru, however, was impatient with the talk of negotiations with the British. 'With whom are we going to negotiate—with an Empire which is crumbling to dust?'[5] Gandhi

[1] M.S. Venkataramani and G. Srivastava, *Quit India: The American Response to the 1942 Struggle* (New Delhi, 1979), pp. 72 and 33–61.

[2] See, for example, Lumley to Linlithgow, 7 February 1942, *TOP*, vol. 1, p. 130; and Hallett to Linlithgow, 10 February 1942, Ibid., p. 147.

[3] Sapru to B. Shiva Rao, 13 November 1941, *BSRC*.

[4] G.D. Birla to P. Thakurdas, 8 November 1941, *PTC*, file no. 239, p. 179.

[5] Shiva Rao to Sapru, 26 January 1942, *BSRC*.

was not prepared to budge an inch from the stand he had taken. 'The Congress represents the spirit of resistance of a certain pattern.'[6] He was confident that he had Nehru's support and with this could defeat any proposition that the Congress should return to office.[7] Rajagopalachari, however, was prepared to have it out with Nehru. When Shiva Rao told him that Nehru, being 'a man of strong convictions,' would turn down any move that was intended to get the Congress into office again, Rajagopalachari 'corrected me over the word "convictions" and said I had better use "strong opinions."'[8] At Bardoli, Rajagopalachari persuaded the Congress Working Committee to set aside Gandhi and to ignore Nehru and to offer the cooperation of a free India in defence of the country on a national basis. Civil disobedience seemed to him to have served its purpose; the people were exhausted and unless the Congress did something definite in this crisis its cause would suffer. Wisdom lay in making as much political progress as possible during the war.

British officials failed to perceive the sincerity of the desire of the Congress Right to cooperate with the war effort and to return to office. Roger Lumley, the Governor of Bombay, for example, regarded Bardoli as an attempt by the Congress Right to paper over the cracks in the party. The Congress had not softened its stand. Bardoli was merely intended to make it appear realistic and generous. If the British failed to respond, '"arrogant imperialism"' would again have banged on the door. Bardoli made nothing easier for the British: they could not expect anything from the Congress except 'interminable manoeuvring for position and hard bargaining.'[9] Amery surmised that it was 'nonsense' to say that Bardoli meant that the Congress had 'opened the door to co-operation, the need for our meeting them half-way by some initiative, and all the rest of it.'[10] Linlithgow thought it 'important not to let ourselves be hypnotised by Rajagopalachariar and his appearance of reasonableness and plausibility.' He was endeavouring to concentrate the spotlight on himself and to obscure 'the very significant dissident strains' that had emerged in the discussions at the AICC.[11]

[6] Gandhi to Jayakar, 9 November 1941, *MRJC*, file no. 276, p. 369.

[7] Note from D. Pilditch to R. Tottenham, 19 November 1941, HP file no. 4/8/41, p. 47.

[8] Sapru to Jayakar, 11 December 1941, *TBSC*, vol. 10.

[9] Lumley to Linlithgow, 1 January 1942, *TOP*, vol. 1, pp. 2–3.

[10] Amery to Linlithgow, 5 January 1942, Ibid., p. 9.

[11] Linlithgow to Amery, (T), 21 January 1942, Ibid., p. 45.

Jinnah and the Muslim League, ever fearful that the British would respond to the overtures of the Congress Right, reminded them that the League could not be ignored,[12] and assured them of the League's opposition to the Bardoli resolution.[13]

The British smugly concluded that Jinnah's stand precluded the possibility of any surrender to the Congress.[14] The War Cabinet simply wanted to sit pat. Churchill argued that bringing a hostile political element into the defence machine would paralyse action,[15] conveniently forgetting that the Congress was not hostile to the war effort as such, but to their exclusion from any responsibility for it. Merely picking and choosing friendly Indians would do 'no serious harm,' but would 'not in any way' meet the political demands. The Indian liberals, though plausible, 'have never been able to deliver the goods. The Indian troops are fighting splendidly, but their allegiance is to the King Emperor.'[16] Amery had convinced himself that 'there is no further interim constitutional advance that we can make.'[17] The Viceroy made no bones about what he stood for.

> 'India and Burma have no natural association with the Empire,' [he wrote to Amery] 'from which they are alien by race, history and religion, and for which as such neither of them have any natural affection, and both are in the Empire because they are conquered countries which had been brought there by force, kept there by our controls, and which hitherto it has suited to remain under our protection.'

So the British must not relinquish power 'beyond a certain point.'[18] There could not have been a better summing up of British intentions in India at this time.

How much power were the British prepared to part with? Pressure from the USA, the Congress Right, and, at the beginning of February 1942 from Attlee, the Lord Privy Seal, induced Churchill to propound 'the great scheme.' It left the crucial executive and legislative position in India untouched, while it gave the proposed Defence of India Council 'some interesting sugar plums' in the shape of democratic representation in it and at the Peace Conference. It would fulfil British pledges to bring Indian parties together on the

[12] Muslim League Nagpur Resolution, 27 December 1941, Ibid., pp. 884–6.
[13] Lumley to Linlithgow, 15 January 1942, Ibid., pp. 26–9.
[14] Lumley to Linlithgow, 1 January 1942, Ibid., p. 3.
[15] Churchill to Attlee, (T), 7 January 1942, Ibid., p. 14.
[16] Ibid. [17] Memorandum by Amery, 28 January 1942, Ibid., p. 90.
[18] Linlithgow to Amery, (T), 21 January 1942, Ibid., p. 49.

constitutional issue by offering to accept this body as the future constitution-making body. Neither the Congress nor the League were expected to accept the proposals. The Congress would turn it down as it did not offer India immediate self-government, while Jinnah would be suspicious of any body in which Muslims were represented in proportion to population and in which he might not be actual leader of Muslims. But the failure of the effort would not discredit the War Cabinet; it would show 'our goodwill and only expose the unreasonableness of Indian parties.'[19] However, the scheme was eventually put into cold storage because Linlithgow strongly opposed giving the proposed Defence of India Council any constitution-making powers. Communal rivalries, he argued, would throw defence into disarray and would interfere with the conduct of the war, gravely damage 'our power of resistance to the Japanese invasion.'[20]

A draft declaration by Whitehall remained necessary, if only to convince its allies of its liberal intentions in India. So any talk of transferring power to Indians would be qualified by the requirement that the Congress and League must agree. The British would not coerce minorities into a political system against their will.[21] Even the possibility of accepting "Pakistan" was considered, inspite of Linlithgow's confession that he had no idea of the popularity of the idea of Pakistan; and the strength of the League had not yet been tested. He did not know what Jinnah meant by it and he would not ask him to define it because he was sure that Jinnah would come up 'with something pretty woolly and general.' He did not think that there was anything to justify the demand for Pakistan in terms of the League's allegations against Congress ministries.

Jinnah had made clear in his presidential address to the League in April 1941 that Pakistan would have 'the status of an independent nation and an independent State in this Subcontinent.'[22] He emphasized his definition of Pakistan when he told British officials that he 'preferred to talk of a co-national or a coalition government, rather than a national government.'[23] But Muslim Leaguers the Reforms Commissioner had met—and they included Nazimuddin, Ismail

[19] Amery to Linlithgow, 8 February 1942, Ibid., pp. 137–9.

[20] Linlithgow to Amery, 13 and 16 February 1942, (T), Ibid., pp. 166–8 and 178 respectively.

[21] Speech by Amery on 4 February 1942, Ibid., p. 230, fn. 5.

[22] Pirzada, *Documents*, p. 362.

[23] Lumley to Linlithgow, 15 January 1942, *TOP*, vol. 1, p. 29.

Khan and Abdul Matin—'interpreted Pakistan as consistent with a federation of India for common purposes like defence, provided the Hindu–Muslim elements therein stood on equal terms.'[24] Abdul Hamid Khan, who chaired the League's session in Madras in April 1941, had defined Pakistan as 'the establishment of independent and separate Muslim States with a confederating outlook,' a vision which would 'not run counter to the idea of India's political unity, nor does it mean the vivisection of India, since the basis of Pakistan has existed all the time in this country.'[25] From the NWFP, Cunningham reported that educated Muslims wanted safeguards for their community, but that it was 'very difficult to get any constructively helpful ideas out of them.'[26] From Sind, Dow reported that most people who called themselves Muslim Leaguers knew or cared very little about the League's policy or affairs, and are 'actuated almost entirely by opposition to Allah Baksh and his Hindu supporters. There are hardly more than half a dozen Muslim Leaguers in Sind who have any contacts with Leaguers outside the province.'[27] The view of many educated Muslims in the Punjab that independence must not place them at the mercy of Hindus[28] gave credence to Hodson's observation that one of the reasons Muslims he had met would not repudiate Pakistan was that they did not want to impair Muslim solidarity. Their fear of 'Hindu' domination did not, however, necessarily mean that they favoured the creation of a sovereign Pakistan. The idea of Hindus and Muslims as two nations, even within a federation, had emotional appeal for Muslims, even if its content had not been very consciously thought out, because it put both communities on an equal footing—*nations* negotiated as equals. "Safeguards" defined their status as *minorities*; safeguards would improve but not alter their position as a minority, 'a Cinderella with trade-union rights and a radio in the kitchen but still below stairs.' The two-nation theory therefore transmuted the ideology of "minorities", and may well, as Hodson discerned, have been more fundamental to the present thought of educated Muslims than the Pakistan theory, which transmuted the ideology of "safeguards."[29]

[24] Annexure to Linlithgow to Amery, 23–7 January 1942, Ibid., p. 66.
[25] Pirzada, *Documents*, p. 356.
[26] Cunningham to Linlithgow, 22 March 1942, *TOP*, vol. 1, p. 457.
[27] Dow to Linlithgow, 22 March 1942, Ibid., p. 459.
[28] Glancy to Linlithgow, (T), 4 March 1942, Ibid., p. 321.
[29] Annexure to Linlithgow to Amery, 23–7 January 1942, Ibid., pp. 66–7.

The fall of Rangoon on 21 February, and that of Singapore on 8 March 1942, spurred Whitehall to make a show of working for political change in India. But the British, Churchill informed Roosevelt, could not renege on their obligations to the Muslims or the Princes.[30] Amery admitted that it could be argued that the League was being given a blackmailing veto on political advance.[31] But this charge could be averted. The British would say that no province could be coerced into joining the federation. That would meet Jinnah 'in principle.' On the other hand, the Congress would feel that the British were not holding back freedom, and would be given a strong incentive to settle with the Muslim majority provinces.[32]

The draft declaration Cripps brought to India envisaged the granting of Dominion Status to India, leaving the Dominion free to remain in or to secede from the Commonwealth. Elections to provincial legislatures would be held after the war. The Lower Houses would then act as a single electoral college and elect the constitution-making body by proportional representation. The constitution framed by it would be accepted by the British subject to the right of any province that was unwilling to accept the new constitution to secede from the Union. The British government would be prepared to agree to a new constitution framed by the seceding provinces.[33]

Jinnah pointed out to Cripps that in a Constituent Assembly elected by proportional representation, Muslims would have only 25 per cent of the votes, and would not be able to vote against joining the Union. Cripps assured him that if less than 60 per cent of the provincial legislature voted in favour of accession, the minority would have the right to call for a plebiscite of the adult male population of the province, the verdict of which would be implemented by the British government.[34] Thus a simple majority vote in a plebiscite could turn the balance in favour of Pakistan.

According to Cripps, Jinnah was 'rather surprised' in the distance the British offer went to meet the Pakistan case and did not raise any serious objection to it.[35] But the provision for provinces to opt out of the federation does not seem to have encouraged the League to

[30] Churchill to Roosevelt, 4 March 1942, Ibid., pp. 309–10.

[31] Amery to Churchill, 25 February 1942, Ibid., p. 240.

[32] Amery to Linlithgow, (T), 22 February 1942, Ibid., p. 223.

[33] Draft Declaration, Ibid., pp. 314–15.

[34] Note by Cripps on interview with Jinnah on 25 March 1942, Ibid., pp. 480–81. See also Cripps to Azad, 2 April 1942, Ibid., p. 610.

[35] Note by Cripps on interview with Jinnah on 25 March 1942, Ibid., pp. 480–81.

settle with the Congress. It is worth noting that, after Cripps had discussed his formula with Jinnah, a proposal by Sikander Hyat Khan for a Congress–League *rapprochement* was brushed aside at a MLWC meeting.[36] By giving the provinces the right to opt out of the federation, Whitehall was creating the sort of political climate that must have confirmed Jinnah's belief that as the British held power, they would transfer or confer it: so why should he go out of his way to reach a settlement with the Congress?[37]

The Cripps formula thus made provision for partition before the transfer of power took place. In one stroke, the British overthrew the act of 1935 as a basis for a post-war constitutional settlement. Cripps' visit to India also made clear, for the first time, that the British envisaged that the main parties involved in the transfer of power would be the Congress and the Muslim League: the principle of partition had in fact been incorporated into the Cripps proposals in recognition of the League's demand for Pakistan.

These points were confirmed by the clarification given by Cripps to Sikh leaders, that the position of the Sikhs in the new constitution would be decided by agreement between the Congress and the League: that Sikh fears about their position would not stop the British from agreeing to a constitution which had been accepted by those two parties. Cripps tried to console the Sikhs by telling them that the Congress, in order to enlarge its majority in the Constituent Assembly, would try to win over the Sikhs by making the most ample provision for them in the new constitution, which might even entail the sub-division of the Punjab into two provinces or the setting up within the province, of a semi-autonomous district for the Sikhs on the Soviet model. Similarly, although the Muslims would be able to obtain a narrow majority in a plebiscite to secede from the Union, they would be anxious to increase that majority as much as possible, both in order to make certain of a majority and also to have a favourable atmosphere for setting up the second new Dominion. Cripps 'promised' Akali leaders that he would mention to Jinnah their demand for a special vote for Sikhs to decide whether they would join the first or second union.[38] There is no evidence in

[36] Note by D. Pilditch, Intelligence Bureau, Home Department, dated 28 March 1942, HP file no. 221/42, p. 18.

[37] K.B. Sayeed, *Pakistan: The Formative Phase*, p. 187.

[38] Note by Cripps on interviews with a number of Sikhs, 27 March 1942, *TOP*, vol. 1, pp. 496–7, and with the Sikh delegation, 31 March 1942, Ibid., p. 581.

Cripps' own notes that he did in fact raise the point with Jinnah; nor did it ever come up for discussion in the War Cabinet. But it was obvious that Cripps—and Whitehall and Linlithgow—thought that Jinnah was the man who counted in coming to a decision about the Punjab, and that his role in the transfer of power was already being taken for granted by them.

'One permanent effect', to quote R.F. Mudie, Chief Secretary to the UP government, 'of the British Government's offer will probably be an increase in estrangement between the two major communities. Pakistan has advanced one stage further.'[39] Communal tension was indeed intensified in many provinces, as communal organizations began to organize local defence volunteers to safeguard their communities, ostensibly for purposes of defence. The UP League Defence Committee had 'for its sole object' the defence of Muslims against attacks by Hindus.[40] In Bihar, the committee appointed by the League to organize a Muslim Protection Scheme urged Muslims to organize to oppose Hindu aggression in the event of a deterioration in the war situation. Muslim League Defence Committees weaned away Muslims from non-party defence committees set up by the Congress.[41] In the Punjab, the Sikhs were relieved at the failure of the Cripps Mission. But Glancy feared internal unrest, as Muslims and Sikhs became increasingly suspicious of one another.[42] The Akalis, League, Hindu Mahasabha, RSS, and Khaksars all had plans to raise volunteer communal organizations. The Akalis talked of plans to arm the Sikh community and to organize them on a semi-military basis for self-preservation. The Congress deprecated the formation of a communal volunteer corps and stressed the need for Indians to unite against British imperialism. But faction fights within the provincial Congress kept its influence at a low ebb.[43] From the NWFP, Cunningham reported that Hindus had been 'thoroughly alarmed' by the conditional offer of Pakistan, and 'I have heard more talk than usual lately of the necessity for Hindus to establish themselves on a strong footing in the Army. Indeed, Hindu and Sikh officers have been heard talking in terms of complete independence and Hindu *raj* in India.' Muslims

[39] FR for UP for first half of April 1942, HP file no. 18/4/42.
[40] FR for UP for second half of April 1942, Ibid.
[41] FR for Bihar for second half of April 1942, Ibid.
[42] Glancy to Linlithgow, 1 May 1942, *TOP*, vol. 2, p. 7.
[43] FR for Punjab for second half of April 1942, HP file no. 18/4/42.

believed that their interests were identical with those of the British, and they had some idea of the British coming to a separate agreement with the League. Hindus also hinted apprehensively at this.[44]

Sikh fears were not eased by Rajagopalachari's formula to end the Congress–League deadlock. There was frustration in Congress circles with the failure of the Cripps mission, and Gandhi renewed talk of civil disobedience. Almost singlehandedly, Rajagopalachari, believing that an end to Congress–League differences was the necessary precursor to any constitutional settlement, pushed through the Congress legislative party in Madras two resolutions, one in favour of conceding Pakistan and the other calling on the provincial Congress to enter office again. He resigned from the Congress Working Committee to introduce the first resolution at the AICC session in Allahabad on 23 April. The AICC turned down the resolution by 120 votes to 15,[45] and Gandhi chided Rajagopalachari. 'He yields the right of secession now to buy unity in the hope of keeping away the Japanese. I consider the vivisection of India to be a sin . . . '[46] If Rajagopalachari really thought the League was interested in settling differences with the Congress, 'Why don't you go now to Q A and discuss the whole thing with him.?'[47] But despite Rajagopalachari's defeat in the AICC, the acceptance of the principle of Pakistan by a leading Congressman kept it in the air and intensified communal tension.

The Rajagopalachari scheme came as a shock to the Sikhs, who felt that further reliance on the Congess was useless. Sikh leaders fell back on a counter demand for changes in the boundaries of the Punjab which would provide for Sikh autonomy between Delhi and Lahore.[48] Let down, as they saw it, by the Congress, in spite of their support to the organization since 1920, the Akalis now sought to improve relations with the British, who controlled India, and the Unionist Muslims, who headed the Punjab ministry. Interested in maintaining their position in the army, and persuaded by an Indian

[44] Cunningham to Linlithgow, 23 April 1942, *TOP*, vol. 1, p. 833.

[45] P. Sitaramayya, *History of the Indian National Congress 1935–1947*, vol. 2, p. 336.

[46] *Harijan*, 24 May 1942, See also *Harijan*, 31 May 1942 and 7 June 1942.

[47] Gandhi to Rajagopalachari, 3 June 1942, *MGC*, Serial no. 2087. Gandhi often referred to Jinnah as "QA"—the abbreviation for "Qaid-i-Azam"—as Jinnah was often called.

[48] Weekly Summary no. 28, 15 May 1942, L/WS/1/1433, p. 33.

Army officer, Major Short, a section of the Sikh leadership now sought to improve their relationship with Sikander and the Muslim Unionists as the best way of safeguarding their position in the Punjab. Their dislike of Pakistan made some Muslim Unionists receptive to the idea of strengthening their coalition with Akali support.

Division of the Punjab was opposed to the interests of all three communities in the province. 'At first sight the distribution of population in the Punjab as it then existed might appear not unfavourable to partition.' The western districts were predominantly Muslim, the eastern predominantly non-Muslim; and it might therefore have seemed 'easy and natural' to divide the province into two roughly equal parts by a line drawn between Amritsar and Lahore. But the population of the Punjab was so intermingled that, wherever the line was drawn, 'large numbers of all three communities would find themselves on the wrong side of it'. The Lahore division, for example, had a Muslim majority, but it included a great part of the Sikh "Holy Land" and economic interests which were largely non-Muslim. Partition would destroy the Punjab economically. British Punjab was what Sir Evan Jenkins described as 'an artificial creation of Irrigation Engineers', consisting of a large network of canals, which had enabled large areas of desert to be converted into flourishing colonies, and on which the prosperity of the province rested. A line drawn between Amritsar and Lahore would mean that the non-Muslim state would inherit the colony districts which were the joint creation of all Punjabis over half a century.[49]

Pakistan according to the conception of extremist Muslims included the whole of the Punjab. For the Sikhs, division would leave two million of them, with all their colony lands as well as some important Sikh shrines, on the Pakistan side. 'To a small community of only six million such a division might well be fatal.' The prospect of a disruption of the Punjab, which the demand for Pakistan seemed to portend, made natural the coming together of Unionists and Akalis. Even if, at worst, the latter were compelled to translate into reality their nominal adherence to the idea of Pakistan, a Unionist–Akali alliance was likely to prevent the division of the province between two sovereign states and lead to an offer to the Sikhs of special rights and privileges.[50] This was the logic behind the

[49] This paragraph is based on Moon, *Divide and Quit*, pp. 34–5, and enclosure to Jenkins to Wavell, 7 March 1947, *TOP*, vol. 9, pp. 880–1.

[50] Moon, *Divide and Quit*, pp. 35–7.

Sikander–Baldev pact of June 1942. The terms of the pact included the extension of facilities for the provision of *jhatka* meat to all government institutions where separate kitchens could be provided; the introduction, as soon as possible, of *Gurmukhi* as a second language in schools where an adequate number of students desired it, and the establishment of a convention that in matters which exclusively concerned a particular community the members of that community alone would exercise voting power in the Assembly, and the maintenance of Sikh representation in the provincial services at 20 per cent. Sikh claims for representation in the Executive Council would be supported by the Unionists.[51]

Though most sections of Sikhs were satisfied with the Sikander–Baldev pact, it left unanswered what was for them the crucial question of their future political status. With the British incorporating the principle of partition in the Cripps plan, and with a section of the Congress apparently accepting it as well, Pakistan loomed threateningly on the political horizons of the Sikhs. So far, the Sikhs had not received any assurances about their future from either the British, Congress or League—all three seemed to treat them as if they were of little or no political consequence. In Sikh eyes, the demand for Pakistan would remain 'a demand for civil war', as Tara Singh put it.[52]

Sikander's alliance with a section of the Sikhs, as well as his own discomfiture with the Pakistan theory, induced him to outline in July 1942 a proposal which would satisfy the political aspirations of the Sikhs and Muslims and also show up the impractability of Pakistan. In the absence of a majority of three-quarters of the members of the Punjab Legislative Assembly voting in favour of either accession or non-accession to the Indian federation, the Muslim community should by means of a referendum be given an opportunity to decide on non-accession, and that, if they so decided, the non-Muslim population should by a similar referendum be accorded the right to cut themselves adrift from the province as constituted at present. If it actually came to the point of deciding to cut themselves adrift, this would mean, assuming that the unit covered was a district, that

[51] FR for Punjab for first half of June 1942, HP file no. 18/6/42. '*Jhatka*' can be translated literally as 'a sudden jerk'. Thus *Jhatka* meat would mean that the head of the animal must be cut off with a single stroke; the meat of such an animal alone is lawful for Sikhs.

[52] *IAR*, 1942, vol. 2, pp. 299–300.

Ambala division and a large part of Jullundur division and also Amritsar district would cease to belong to the Punjab. If a smaller unit such as a *tehsil* was taken, at least a very large part of the areas mentioned and possibly certain others would disappear from the province.[53]

According to Glancy, Sikander's position was that he had succeeded in bringing about a *rapprochement* with the Sikhs; he had in mind proposals to placate the urban population over the Sales Tax Act;[54] and the 'only other remaining menace which he fears as being likely to impede the war effort in the Punjab is the Pakistan controversy.' He felt his formula would lay it to rest until the war was over. If the Viceroy had no objection, Sikander would consult Muslim Unionists and Sikh members of the coalition, and then put the formula before the party as a whole. If the reactions were favourable, the provincial assembly would be invited to pass a resolution endorsing the scheme.[55]

Both Glancy and Linlithgow doubted that the plan would show up the weakness of the Pakistan theory. It would also offend Jinnah. With the Congress threatening 'total rebellion', Linlithgow had no desire to offend him. The British could not stop any individual from making assumptions about their future policy. But the formal position would be that Glancy could not encourage his Prime Minister 'to promote a plan which makes unjustifiable assumptions as to the future policy of His Majesty's Government,' and it was 'equally not possible' for the Governor to tell his Prime Minister not to propose such a plan, '*outside the provincial sphere though it may be*.' Glancy could only give Sikander 'friendly advice' to save him from error.[56] Sikander's weakness was that he would not do anything without the permission of the British; so he shelved his proposals, while Pakistan disturbed the atmosphere of the Punjab so long as the possibility of its realization existed.

[53] Glancy to Linlithgow, 10 July 1942, *LC*, vol. 91.

[54] The Sales Tax Act, IV of 1941, imposed a levy on annual turnover in excess of Rs. 5,000 per annum. The measure aroused strong opposition from shopkeepers, and in February 1942, it was amended, so that the Punjab General Sales Tax Amendment Act, III of 1942, raised the exemption limit from Rs. 5,000 to Rs. 10,000 per annum.

[55] Glancy to Linlithgow, 10 July 1942, *LC*, vol. 91.

[56] Linlithgow to Glancy, 17 July 1942, Ibid. (Emphasis mine)

The Quit India Movement—August 1942–March 1943

On the all India front, British officials sensed the frustration among most sections of Indian political opinion—barring the Sikhs and the Mahasabha—with the failure of the Cripps Mission;[57] and Linlithgow favoured the inclusion of more non-officials in the Executive Council to relieve the atmosphere of bitterness.[58] For the moment, however, he was satisfied that the Congress lacked direction; that it was 'now in a more difficult position than they had even been in; we had reduced them to pulp and destroyed the national spirit'.[59] But his complacency was shortlived. By the middle of May 1942, reports of preparations for a mass movement were coming in from many provinces[60] and Linlithgow showed signs of discomfiture at the 'indecently outspoken' tone of Gandhi's writings in *Harijan*.[61] The Congress Working Committee resolution of 13 July[62] left no doubt about the intentions of its leadership. 'There is no room- . . . for withdrawal, for negotiation', explained Gandhi, 'either they recognize India's independence or they don't . . . . There is no question of one more chance. After all it is an open rebellion.'[63]

Jinnah's reaction was predictable. He accused the Congress of aiming to establishing Hindu *raj* 'under the aegis of the British bayonet, thereby placing the Muslims and other minorities at the mercy of the Congress *raj*.'[64] Jinnah's perennial fear was that the British would be pressurized by the Congress into accepting its terms, leaving the League in the cold.[65]

For all that he was not surprised by Jinnah's interpretation of the Congress resolution, Gandhi was, nevertheless, emotionally wounded by it. 'How can you expect me to approach QA after his performance,' he wrote to Rajagopalachari. 'Will he not be right in showing me the door if I dared to go to him. I should certainly re-

[57] See, for example, Lumley to Linlithgow, 1 May 1942; Twynam to Linlithgow, 1 May 1942; Stewart to Linlithgow, 3 May 1942; Hallett to Linlithgow, 4 May 1942; Clow to Linlithgow, 9 May 1942, *TOP*, vol. 2, pp. 2, 3, 19, 25, 55 respectively.

[58] Linlithgow to Governors, 30 April 1942, *TOP*, vol. 2, p. 1.

[59] Linlithgow to Amery, 25 May 1942, Ibid., p. 123. See also Amery to Linlithgow, 27 May 1942, Ibid., p. 141.

[60] FRs for Bengal, Bihar, UP, CP, Bombay—from April to July 1942, HP file nos. 18/4 to 18/7/42.

[61] Linlithgow to Amery, 18 May 1942, *TOP*, vol. 2, p. 102.

[62] Quoted in Sitaramayya, *Indian National Congress*, vol. 2, pp. 340–2.

[63] *Statesman*, 15 July 1942. [64] *Statesman*, 1 August 1942.

[65] See, for example, *Statesman*, 3 July 1942.

fuse to see a person whom I thoroughly distrust and discredit. Supposing he is great and good enough to see me, what am I to say to him?'[66] He did not think Jinnah wanted a settlement with the Congress. Otherwise, why had he not accepted Azad's offer that representatives of the Congress and the League 'should put their heads together and never part until they have reached a settlement. Is there any flaw or want of sincerity in this offer?'[67]

The British cabinet reacted to the Congress resolution with indignation. 'What I feel', wrote Amery, 'is that Congress has definitely shown its hand as claiming to be an authority parallel to the Government of India and entitled to tell the public to defy the authority of the latter'. The challenge must be taken up. If the War Cabinet hesitated, Amery had 'no doubt that they will not be able to stand up to the two of us together . . . This is a time when a fire brigade cannot wait to ring up headquarters, but must turn the hose on the flames at once'.[68]

But Amery need not have worried. The war cabinet authorized Linlithgow to take decisive action whenever it seemed necessary.[69] The Government of India would strike when the AICC ratified the resolution.[70] Yet Linlithgow would have preferred public opinion to counteract Gandhi and the Congress.[71] Governors, however, had no success in persuading influential provincial politicians to speak out against the Congress. Fazlul Huq airily told Herbert that he did not think civil disobedience would succeed in Bengal; that the League and the Mahasabha would be enough to deal with it. He was reluctant to issue any statement or to carry out any propaganda against Gandhi, on the ground that his present relations with Jinnah made it difficult to identify himself with statements which Jinnah had issued.[72] Jogendra Singh, who had recently joined the Executive Council, was not expected to be 'as outspoken as one would like',

[66] Gandhi to Rajagopalachari, 1 August 1942, *MGC*, Serial no. 2093.

[67] *Harijan*, 26 July 1942.

[68] Amery to Linlithgow, 13 July 1942, *TOP*, vol. 2, pp. 380–1.

[69] War Cabinet W.M. (42) 91st Conclusions, Minutes 8–9, 13 July 1942, Ibid, p. 378.

[70] Government of India Home Department to Secretary of State, 3 August 1942, Ibid., pp. 535–6.

[71] See, for example, Linlithgow to Lumley, (T), 16 July 1942; and Linlithgow to Herbert, (T), 16 July 1942; Linlithgow to Glancy, 16 July 1942, Ibid., pp. 395–6, 396, 398 respectively.

[72] Herbert to Linlithgow, 23 July 1942, Ibid., pp. 439–40.

for he took his cue from the Akalis, who, sailing as usual in two boats, were represented in the Unionist ministry and in the Viceroy's Executive but had not severed their connection with the Congress.[73]

Even as they discussed the administrative measures to be taken in the event of a civil disobedience movement, British officials were sceptical whether Gandhi would really launch one. There had been very few signs of preparations for a no-tax or no-rent movement, or of interference with civil and military establishments. 'Lack of any real eagerness' for this latest assault on the British *raj* by Congress was very noticeable throughout the country, noted intelligence officials. This, coupled with 'the apparent lack of preparation', cast 'an air of unreality' over the whole movement, and raised doubts as to whether it was not all 'a piece of bluff on the part of Gandhi'.[74]

Only a month later, Linlithgow informed Churchill: 'I am engaged here in meeting by far the most serious rebellion since that of 1857, the gravity and extent of which we have so far concealed from the world for reasons of military security'.[75] The British reacted to the ratification of the Congress Working Committee resolution by the AICC on 8 August by arresting Congress leaders on the morning of 9 August, in the expectation that the arrests would finish off any contemplated movement.[76] They were, therefore, understandably taken aback when, three days later, the leaderless and unorganized supporters of the Congress rose in revolt in various parts of the country. Intelligence sources held that the disturbances 'represent the spontaneous reaction to the arrest of popular leaders . . . there is no indication of any real coordination of effort.' There was nothing new which had not been tried in previous campaigns, 'except perhaps that the sense of frustration leading to racial animosity ismore marked'.[77]

The events of 1942 showed the depth of the national will. In August and September, the British used 57 batallions to crush the rebellion, twenty-four of which had to be withdrawn from field formations under training.[78] The administration broke down com-

[73] Glancy to Linlithgow, 18 July 1942, Ibid., p. 409.

[74] Weekly Summary no. 39, 31 July 1942, L/WS/1/1433, p. 63.

[75] Linlithgow to Churchill, 31 August 1942, *TOP*, vol. 2, p. 853.

[76] Government of India Home Department to Secretary of State, 3 August 1942, Ibid., p. 536.

[77] Weekly Summary no. 41, 14 August 1942, L/WS/1/1433, p. 71.

[78] John Connell, *Wavell: Supreme Commander* (London, 1969), p. 230.

pletely in most of North-Central Bihar and Eastern UP, and the Fortnightly Reports from Bihar for August could not be sent to Delhi because of a breakdown of communications.[79] Railways were blocked or dismantled, telegraph wires were cut, certain railway stations in Orissa could not be declared protected areas because forces were not available to protect them.[80] The Whipping Act was revived in Bombay, and a concerned war cabinet was told that it would be used very sparingly; that the introduction of whipping, 'which might better be termed corporal punishment, is a minor detail in a serious situation.'[81]

By the beginning of 1943, the movement was suppressed, but the administration did not come out of it unscathed. The British knew that Indians did not identify with the war effort, and it was difficult to cultivate a spirit of war-mindedness among the masses 'when the spirit of self-sacrifice and personal identification with the war effort is weak among the educated classes, and even among members of the European business community and some officials.'[82] Nor was it 'particularly bracing', as Herbert wrote, 'for sorely-tried police officers to read in the Press that Jawaharlal Nehru and his friends are extremely well and enjoying a game of Badminton.'[83]

The long-term problem was the British intention to leave India 'at no very remote date'. Indian officials were opportunistic: they had remained staunch during the Quit India movement, but they looked to their future rulers, 'whoever they may be,' and shared with 'a large part of the human race a desire to be on the winning side.'[84] In Bihar, for example, where the movement resulted in a major administrative breakdown, government officials 'as a class' did not relish being cited as opponents of the Congress. They claimed to be, as was the British Civil Service, outside politics. 'No doubt the exponents of this view are looking to the future when Congress adminis-

[79] FR for UP for the first half of August 1942, HP file no. 18/8/42. See also Max Harcourt, 'Kisan populism and revolution in rural India', in D.A. Low (ed.) *Congress and the Raj*, p. 316.

[80] Minutes of Home Department Meeting held at 3 p.m. on 28 August 1942 in Additional Secretary's room, HP file no. 3/17/42, p. 22.

[81] Lumley to Linlithgow, 14 August 1942, *TOP*, vol. 2, p. 700.

[82] Some reflections on official propaganda, by H.V. Hodson, Reforms Commissioner, dated 26 August 1942; Reforms Office file no. 143/42-R.

[83] Herbert to Linlithgow, 8 October 1942, L/P&J/5/149.

[84] Maxwell to Laithwaite, 24 October 1942; *TOP*, vol. 3, pp. 156–8.

trations will again be in power.'[85] Hindu officials, in any case, had Congress sympathies; while Muslim officials thought that Pakistan held out good prospects for them.[86] The uncertain loyalties of Indian officials were already beginning to stir the foundations of the Raj.

Jinnah described the movement as 'a most dangerous mass movement' intended to force Congress demands "at the point of the bayonet," which, if conceded, would mean the sacrifice of all other interests, particularly those of Moslem in India'. He appealed to Muslims 'to keep completely aloof' from the movement, and to the Hindu public 'to stop this internecine civil war before it is too late.'[87]

Provincial Muslim Leaguers followed Jinnah's lead,[88] even as the Muslim League Working Committee made another overture to the British. The League would negotiate 'with any party on a footing of equality' to set up a provisional Government of India in order to mobilize the resources of the country for the defence of India. 'If the Muslim masses are to be roused to intensify the war effort it is only possible provided they are assured that it will lead to the realization of Pakistan.' The League called on the British, 'without further delay,' to make an 'unequivocal' declaration guaranteeing the right of self-determination with a pledge to abide by the verdict of a plebiscite of Muslims.[89] Jinnah declared that the words "any party" in the resolution meant any recognized party 'which is able to deliver the goods', and called on the British to give the League half the seats in the Executive Council.[90]

Jinnah and provincial Muslim Leaguers concentrated on using their influence to keep Muslims away from the Quit India movement. The League devoted much attention to getting Muslims exempted from collective fines imposed on villagers in areas where sabotage had taken place.[91] In the NWFP, however, many Muslims appeared willing to follow the Congress lead, and anti-Congress propaganda had to be built up 'by pretty intensive propaganda' by

[85] Stewart to Linlithgow, 19 September 1942, L/P&J/5/178.

[86] Note by Conran Smith dated 19 October 1942, *TOP*, vol. 3, pp. 160–1.

[87] *Statesman*, 10 August 1942.

[88] E.g. *Morning News*, 15 August 1942, *Eastern Times*, 17 August 1942.

[89] *Statesman*, 21 August 1942.

[90] *Morning News*, 21 August 1942.

[91] *Morning News*, 1, 8 September 1942.

ulema organized by British officials.[92] But there was evidence of Muslim complicity in Baramati town in Bombay;[93] in the CP and Berar Muslims were generally exempted from collective fines but individual liability was enforced.[94] The League and its followers held aloof from the movement in Bihar—but so did the Mahasabha—but there were cases of arrests of Muslims because of participation in lawlessness.[95] Muslims, 'like other people, for instance the big landholders of Bihar, generally took no part in opposition to Hindu law-breaking.'[96] In Bengal, Herbert was apprehensive of an 'increasing lack of support for Government in this all-important question of law and order, and even in the war effort, in quarters where we generally expect it.

> 'At a recent meeting of the Provincial League Working Committee, the view was advanced that the "neutrality" towards the war effort forced upon the League by the attitude of the British Government might be regarded as an asset to Muslims in the event of a successful Japanese invasion! . . . I am concerned at the grave possibility of our losing throughout India the support of even those whom we have hitherto regarded, if not as our friends, as the enemies of our enemies.'[97]

In Bihar and Assam, Muslims protested against their being included in collective responsibility schemes for safeguarding communications.[98] Muslim League circles in Patna were agitated over the question of lighting restrictions as they affected arrangements for Moharrum processions.[99] Assam officials were concerned that 'protest has been aroused among non-Muslims at the use of assistance to check subversive activity, rather than Muslims protesting at the serious hardship which had been caused by that activity.'[100] Muslims joined in prayers for Gandhi's life when he

[92] Cunningham to Linlithgow, 28 September 1942, *TOP*, vol. 3, p. 56. On organization of ulema by NWFP government since August 1939, see *CC*, vol. 19.

[93] FR for Bombay for the first half of September 1942, HP file no. 18/9/42.

[94] FR for CP and Berar for the first half of September, Ibid.

[95] FR for Bihar for the first half of September, Ibid.

[96] *Quarterly Survey of the Political and Constitutional Position of the British in India*, no. 21, *LC*, vol. 145.

[97] Herbert to Linlithgow, 6 November 1942, *TOP*, vol. 3, p. 211.

[98] FR for Bihar for the first half of November and December and FR for Assam for the first half of October 1942. HP file nos. 18/10, 18/11 and 18/12/42.

[99] FR for Bihar for the first half of January 1943. HP file no. 18/1/43.

[100] FR for Assam for the second half of November 1942 and Clow to Linlithgow, 17 November 1942, HP file no. 18/11/42.

undertook his fast in February 1943 'until Mr. Jinnah's statement in reply to the invitation to attend the All-Parties Conference came and stopped them from joining in'![101]

One of the most remarkable features of the Quit India movement is the absence of any communal incident or disorder. In report after report, notes Hutchins, the entry under 'Communal' was the single phrase, '"Nothing to Report."'[102] If the aloofness of the Muslim community at large was one of the most noticeable characteristics of the movement, 'the almost complete absence of Hindu aggression against Muslims remains a remarkable fact.'[103] On the question of fines, there was no doubt that 'Muslims . . . held aloof from any acts of commission,' but there were many cases in which 'they did not do all they could in their power to help the authorities and were thereby equally guilty of acts of omission with other communities.'[104] Reports from provinces indicate that officials had difficulty in obtaining evidence against saboteurs, either because of sympathy with the Congress or apathy.[105] In the sources consulted, except for two instances in the Midnapore district in Bengal,[106] I have not come across a single instance of Muslims giving evidence against saboteurs, most of whom, presumably, were Hindus. So, if the Quit India movement demonstrated for the first time since 1937 that the Congress did not have a hold over Muslims, except perhaps in the NWFP, the absence of reports of Muslim cooperation with British officials in tracking down saboteurs and rebels suggests that they collaborated with neither the Congress nor the British.

The Akali reaction to the Quit India movement was to allow a limited number of followers to offer token civil disobedience while Tara Singh exhorted his followers to support the British. The Akali Conference at Vahilla Kalhan in Lyallpur district on 26 and 27 September 1942 passed a resolution which called for the independence of India and an end to the political deadlock. The resolution represented a compromise between the Kartar Singh faction who

[101] FR for Bihar for the second half of February 1943. HP file no. 18/2/43.

[102] F. Hutchins, *Spontaneous Revolution* (Harvard, 1971), p. 228.

[103] *Quarterly Survey of the Political and Constitutional Position of the British in India*, no. 21, *LC*, vol. 145.

[104] P.D. Barran to R. Tottenham, 6 November 1942, HP file no. 3/46/42, p. 9.

[105] E.g. FR for Bombay for the first half of December 1942; FR for Bengal for the first half of January 1943; FR for Bihar for the second half of February 1943, HP file nos. 18/12/42, 18/1 and 18/2/43.

[106] FR for Bengal for the first half of September 1942, HP file no. 18/9/42.

wished to avoid any reference to the Congress and the pro-Congress faction who wanted the Dal to pledge unequivocal support for the Congress.[107] The Akalis wished to maintain the position of the Sikhs in the Army; and they thought that the best way of doing so was to support the British. They were also aware of the political advantage of being associated with the Punjab government and at the Centre. So Tara Singh's conception of the role of a leader was, in the words of Glancy, 'a resolute refusal to give a lead in any definite direction.' The attitude was understandable in view of Sikh fears of their future, for they could not rely on anyone. The British had not granted them any favours unconditionally. 'We have taken steps to point out to him and his friends that any continuance of this form of response to the favours which the Sikhs have received from Government must make it increasingly difficult for those who sympathise with the community to espouse their cause.'[108]

The Muslim League Ministries and Jinnah—August 1942 to March 1945

With the Congress and its sympathizers engaged in civil disobedience on a scale which had shaken the very foundations of Empire, Linlithgow advised Governors to explore the possibilities of forming non-Congress ministries in their provinces, in view of their 'propaganda value.'[109] The basic principle, then, behind the reconstruction of ministries in Assam, Sind, NWFP and Bengal, was that, wherever possible, a counterpoise to the Congress should be built up in the provinces. To the extent that British policy resulted in the formation of League ministries in the Muslim majority provinces, they were responsible for the enhanced stature of the League, and the growth of the idea of Pakistan.

How much control did Jinnah exercise over provincial League ministries, and what evidence was there of support for a sovereign Pakistan in the Muslim majority provinces? These are among the questions which we shall try to answer.

The arrests of Congress MLAs in Assam led to the fall of the coalition ministry which had existed since 1937, and Mohammad

[107] FR for Punjab for the second half of September 1942, Ibid.
[108] Glancy to Linlithgow, 21 August 1942, L/P&J/245.
[109] Linlithgow to Amery, (T), 16 August 1942, *TOP*, vol. 2, p. 731.

Saadullah formed a new coalition with other parties represented in the legislature.[110] In Sind, Allah Baksh was dismissed by Dow, on instructions from Linlithgow, because he had renounced his titles. Linlithgow had earlier been critical of the half-hearted manner in which Allah Baksh's ministry was carrying out the war effort, and the renunciation of his titles, which the Viceroy regarded as being inconsistent with his oath of office, gave Linlithgow an opportunity to dispose of him.[111] The way was now open for G.H. Hidayatullah to form a ministry.

Provincial Leaguers decided to join Hidayatullah's ministry against the wishes of Jinnah, who urged them not to enter a government in which they were not the dominant element. The provincial League passed a resolution asking Jinnah to abstain from giving instructions on provincial matters of which he did not know much, and supported the decision of the League Assembly party to join the ministry.[112] A new turn was given to ministerial politics when Hidayatullah decided to join the League. He stated that his Hindu colleagues were being pressurized by the Congress, and in view of this and in the interests of his community, he had decided to join the League. Hidayatullah's decision surprised everyone, including provincial Leaguers, who had not been told of his intentions.[113] The rationale behind his joining the League could have been his apprehension that Hindu ministers and their supporters might eventually walk out on him: in that event, he could best assure his future prospects of retaining the Premiership by lining up with the League.

The League extended its organization in Sind while it held power. By March 1943, nearly 30,000 members had been enrolled in the Thar Pakkar district alone.[114] Whether this was done by the provincial League of its own accord or under instructions from the all-India body, is not known. It is possible that the provincial League took the initiative itself to strengthen its base against its Muslim opponents in Allah Baksh's Azad Muslim Party. For, if both parties resorted to communal propaganda, as they did during the by-

[110] FR for Assam for the first half of September 1942, HP file no. 18/9/42.

[111] Viceroy to Governor of Sind, (T), 26 September 1942, *LC*, vol. 98.

[112] Dow to Linlithgow, 22 October 1942, L/P&J/5/258. See also *Eastern Times*, 25 October and 10 November 1942.

[113] Dow to Linlithgow, 5 November 1942, L/P&J/5/258.

[114] FR for Sind for first half of March 1943, HP file no. 18/3/43.

election in Shikarpur,[115] the party which had the broader political base would be more likely to consolidate its position in the province.

In the NWFP, divisions in the provincial League had discouraged Cunningham from installing a League ministry. The detention of eight of the twenty-one Congress legislators had reduced the party's majority in the assembly, but Cunningham turned down a suggestion from Feroze Khan Noon, a member of the Viceroy's Council, that the League could win the support of non-Congress MLAs. 'The balance between the Congress and the non-Congress in the assembly is so delicate that this would almost certainly mean a defeat for the ministry', he informed Linlithgow on 28 September 1942.[116] It was not until April 1943 that the League was able to form a ministry. Aurangzeb Khan wanted to form an intercommunal ministry, and solicited the support of the Akalis and the Mahasabha. The Akalis debated whether their interests would be served better by cooperation with the League or by joining 'nationalist' elements in the opposition. A statement by V.D. Savarkar, the Mahasabha leader, that where the formation of a Muslim League ministry was inevitable, Hindus and Sikhs might enter into a coalition with the League to further their interests,[117] coupled with the refusal of Khan Saheb to guarantee a seat for the Akalis in a future Congress ministry, induced Ajit Singh to accept a portfolio in Aurangzeb's cabinet. The Akalis joined the coalition on the understanding that the question of Pakistan would not be raised during the tenure of the ministry.[118] The Mahasabha withdrew from the coalition following Aurangzeb's refusal to concede the speakership of the House to Mehr Chand Khanna; and Aurangzeb's ministry came to be known as the League–Akali coalition. The ministry never acquired the support of more than 19 of the 43 members in the Assembly.[119]

Bengal provided an illustration of a Muslim League ministry being brought into power almost solely by the inclination and action of the governor. Since the start of the Quit India movement, Herbert had expressed dissatisfaction with the conduct of the Huq

[115] Dow to Wavell, 3 November and 22 November 1943, L/P&J/5/260.
[116] Cunningham to Linlithgow, 28 September 1942, *TOP*, vol. 3, pp. 55–6.
[117] FR for NWFP for first half of May 1943, HP file no. 18/3/43.
[118] A.K. Gupta, *Northwest Frontier Province and the Freedom Struggle, 1932–1947* (New Delhi, 1979), p. 133–4. [119] Ibid., p. 135.

ministry in all matters relating to the war effort. His coalition with the Bose section of the Congress produced, in Herbert's opinion, a situation 'in which local officers are deterred from exercising firmness and initiative in dealing with disturbances.' Herbert thought that the dismissal of the ministry was 'increasingly called for consideration'.[120] It was not that Herbert had any great faith in the advantages of a League ministry. This alternative would be 'little better, as its main concern would be to find more and better jobs for Muslims'.[121] The circumstances of Huq's dismissal in April 1943 are best explained by Herbert himself. The Governor thought that the ministry was already tottering, that it could only maintain itself 'by pandering to the wishes of those whose votes kept it in existence'. A motion of no-confidence was to be moved in the assembly on 29 March. 'I felt, perhaps wrongly,' that yet another debate on such a motion resulting in the fall of the Ministry would further embitter the relations between parties to an extent which would make negotiations for a Ministry of all the parties quite impossible. 'If, on the other hand, Huq wanted to scrape through the session . . . he would have continued his tricks . . . . Further, it would . . . have been exceedingly difficult for me to dismiss Huq despite his numerous acts of misconduct.'

Huq had announced publicly several times that he would resign if such an action would facilitate the formation of an all-parties ministry. Herbert felt that 'Huq's promise to resign, openly expressed in the Assembly, was an opportunity not to be neglected; and I must admit that I urged him pretty firmly to honour it, though "compulsion" is quite unfair description'.[122]

Huq did not intend to resign when he came to see Herbert on 28 March,

> 'but . . . at some stage in the interview he decided that it might be to his advantage to do so if he subsequently played his cards well. This . . . he succeeded in doing. He signed a draft letter of resignation prepared, not for his signature, but merely as a model, so that he could say that he was "framed" by the Governor; he undertook to see the Budget through the next day, thus allaying my mind until it was too late; and he asked for the announcement of his resignation to be postponed in order that he might spring it himself, wreck the budget and claim universal sympathy'.[123]

[120] Herbert to Linlithgow, 8 October 1942, L/P&J/5/149.
[121] Herbert to Linlithgow, 11 January 1943, Ibid.
[122] Herbert to Linlithgow, 7 April 1943, L/P&J/5/150. [123] Ibid.

When the House met on the 29th, Huq stated that he had been made to resign by the Governor. The speaker then announced that the ministry did not exist and adjourned the assembly for a fortnight. On the 31st, Herbert proclaimed Section 93. 'I do feel that I have (shall I say?) blundered into the right solution in spite of all the political disadvantages,' concluded Herbert.[124]

Section 93 was proclaimed while Huq still had a majority. He had won a division by 10 votes only on the previous day. But they were the votes of the Congress. 'The position was that he was in the hands of the party in sympathy with the disturbances which are prejudicing our war effort'.[125]

Linlithgow was 'uneasy' at the manner of Huq's dismissal, and also at the prospects of a Muslim League ministry in Bengal. The criticism in the press had been embarrassing to the government, and 'Jinnah if he wants to' might try to make the formation of any administration impossible 'save on his own terms which might be quite unpalatable so far as we are concerned.'[126] The Viceroy had no alternative but to approve of Section 93, but he informed Herbert that he would not approve of any League ministry unless it was supported by a 'suitable majority' in the legislature. 'Nor should you commit yourself to commission Nazimuddin in light (sic) of his investigations to form a Ministry without prior reference to me.'[127] Clearly, Linlithgow had little faith in Herbert's ability to handle the ministerial crisis in Bengal. In his view, it was a mistake to put Huq in a position to suggest that his resignation was based on a letter, the draft of which had been prepared in Government House. He could not, he wrote to Amery, 'imagine a greater folly'.[128]

Nazimuddin formed a ministry with the support of the 25 Europeans in the Bengal legislature, who had, until now, always supported Huq. They openly said that they would oppose any new Huq ministry because they were 'disgusted' with his misgovernment and corruption. The new ministry contained no Muslim who was not a member of the Muslim League. Nazimuddin failed to get the support of the Congress Bose group, which had supported Huq,

[124] Ibid. [125] Governor of Bengal to Viceroy, (T), 31 March 1943, *LC*, vol. 43.

[126] Viceroy to Governor of Bengal, (T), 30 March 1943, R/3/2/84.

[127] Viceroy to Governor of Bengal, (T), 31 March 1943, Ibid.

[128] Linlithgow to Amery, 2 April 1943, *TOP*, vol. 3, p. 875; and Linlithgow to Herbert, 11 April 1943, R/3/2/46.

and the Mahasabha. Nazimuddin promised to 'take every possible measure to advance the war effort.'[129]

Nazimuddin's expression of support for the war effort was probably made against Jinnah's wishes.[130] Yet Jinnah would not, or could not take any action against Nazimuddin, presumably because he did not want to fritter away the prestige the League had acquired by forming a ministry in Bengal. There does not seem to be much evidence of Jinnah's increasing control over the League ministries. It was not until December 1943 that Jinnah appointed a Committee of Action, consisting of 5 to 7 members, 'to prepare and organize the Muslims all over India to meet all contingencies, resist the imposition of an all-India Federation or any other constitution for the United India, and prepare them for the coming struggle for the achievement of Pakistan'. The Committee of Action would control and direct the activities of the provincial Leagues.[131]

How much control was actually exercised by the Committee of Action is difficult to say. When the Committee visited the NWFP in June 1944, it was surprised and dismayed to find that no organizational work had been attempted in the province.[132] This suggests that contacts between the Committee and the provincial League were almost non-existent; and that the provincial League had not carried out the Committee's instructions, assuming that they had been given.

Jinnah himself does not appear to have been very interested in provincial politics. Ispahani wanted him to advise Nazimuddin on the selection of personnel for his ministry in April 1943.[133] But much to Ispahani's disappointment, Jinnah expressed his preference

> 'that Sir Nazimuddin and you people there should settle the personnel of the Ministry, and I hope that you will do it in a manner which will be most creditable to the Party, the Bengal Muslims and Muslim India as a whole . . . I, therefore, think that I should not go to Calcutta, nor is it really necessary.'[134]

[129] Herbert to Linlithgow, 19 April 1943, *LC*, vol. 53; see also FR for Bengal for second half of April 1943, HP file no. 18/4/43.

[130] Jinnah to Ispahani, 9 April 1943, *Jinnah–Ispahani Correspondence*, p. 347.

[131] K.B. Sayeed, *Pakistan: The Formative Phase*, p. 190.

[132] NWFP Governor's Report dated 24 June 1944, *CC*, vol. 16.

[133] Ispahani to Jinnah, 13 April 1943, and 15 April 1943; Zaidi (ed.) *Jinnah–Ispahani Correspondence*, pp. 353 and 355.

[134] Jinnah to Ispahani, 15 April 1943, Ibid., p. 357.

Again, Jinnah turned down an appeal by Muslim Leaguers in the Punjab to visit the province and to sort out their problems with the Unionists. He merely expressed the hope that if the ministry and the League would work together 'these little ripples that you see on the surface will disappear'.[135] Jinnah did exert himself—albeit unsuccessfully—in Sind in February 1945. A dispute arose between G.M. Syed, President of the provincial Muslim League and Hidayatullah, and Syed withdrew support and supported a cut motion against the ministry. Jinnah pointed out to him that only the Hindus would benefit from the quarrel between two Muslim leaders.[136] Hidayatullah was now ready to take in Maula Baksh, brother of Allah Baksh, into his ministry and to coalesce with his Azad Muslim party. Jinnah's efforts to persuade Hidayatullah to drop Maula Baksh were of no avail. Hidayatullah regarded as interference by Jinnah the suggestion that he should either get Baksh to sign the League's pledge or drop him. Hidayatullah was still a member of the League, but he defied a directive from the provincial League to drop Baksh.[137] Dependent on Maula Baksh, he now accepted a suggestion by him that he release Congress MLAs. The Congress legislative party agreed to support Hidayatullah in return for the release of their MLAs. For the time being then, the League was out of power in Sind, having been replaced by the Azad Muslim party and the Congress. It also lost prestige as it lost two by-elections in the province to the Azad Muslim party in March.[138] The events of February and March 1945 clearly demonstrated that Jinnah's hold over the Sind League was extremely uncertain; and that when openly defied, he could do very little unless he was sure of his following in the provincial League.

Jinnah's apparent lack of interest in the provincial politics of the Punjab and Bengal in 1943, as compared with his attempts to interfere in Sind in 1942 and in 1945, suggests that his primary aim was to maintain his position and prestige as leader of all Muslims at the all-India level. Coalitions with non-League Muslims in the pro-

[135] Jinnah to Amjad Ali, 8 May 1943, S. Jafri (ed.) *Qaid-e-Azam Jinnah's Correspondence with Punjab Muslim Leaders* (Lahore, 1977), p. 14.

[136] *Statesman*, 13, 22, 25 February, 1 March 1945.

[137] *Statesman*, 9 and 12 March 1945, 15 March and 27 March 1945. See also Wavell to Amery, 21 February 1945, *TOP*, vol. 5, p. 286, and Memorandum by Amery, 5 April 1945, Ibid., pp. 830–2.

[138] See for example, Dow to Wavell, 22 January 1945, L/P&J/5/261.

vinces would detract from the League's claim to represent *all* Muslims, and this could be why he tried to put his foot down whenever Leaguers attempted to line up with non-League Muslims. In the CP, for example, he would not allow the provincial League leader to enter into a coalition with any non-League Muslims, and Rauf Shah seems to have given way tohim.[139] Where the League had not coalesced with non-League Muslims, as in the NWFP and Bengal, he does not seem to have paid much attention to provincial Leagues.

The Unionist–League Tussle––November 1942 to June 1944

It was in the Punjab that Jinnah launched a unique campaign to establish a League ministry in a province. His visit to the Punjab in November 1942 rippled the surface of Punjab politics, disturbing the Unionist coalition by his advocacy of Pakistan and his reference to the Sikhs as a 'sub-nationality'. The main points made by him in his speeches were that the League had made enormous strides in recent years towards attaining the goal of Pakistan; the Quit India movement aimed at establishing Hindu domination over India; the British should acknowledge the right of Muslims to self-determination and promise to give effect to the verdict of a Muslim plebiscite. He ridiculed the view that 'sub-national' groups should be given the same right of self-determination as the Muslims. The 'Hindu-Muslim question is an all India one, but the Muslim-Sikh question is between Pakistan and the Sikhs.' This statement created the impression that he was opposed to the Sikander formula; an impression which was not wholly dispelled by his subsequent assertion that he had no knowledge of this formula and had never referred to it.[140]

Embarrassed by Jinnah's statement, yet afraid to risk his position among Muslim Unionists by an open rupture with Jinnah, Sikander proclaimed that he saw eye to eye with the 'champion of Pakistan'—thus shaking the foundations of his alliance with Baldev Singh and widening the communal cleavage in the Punjab.[141] The Sikhs, whose political horizons were essentially provincial, were

[139] Twynam to Linlithgow, 12/14 July 1943, *LC*, vol. 64.

[140] FR for Punjab for second half of November 1942, HP file no. 18/11/42. See also *Morning News*, 17 November 1942.

[141] Glancy to Linlithgow, 28 November 1942, *LC*, vol. 91.

caught between their wish to confine discussion on the communal problem to 'local men' and the uncomfortable knowledge that the League, 'by including the Punjab within the scheme of things for Pakistan, has made our problem an all India one.' Pakistan would mean the annihilation of the Sikhs.[142] Simultaneously, the Akalis negotiated with Jinnah, leading Hindus to accuse them of deserting the Hindu-Sikh front against Pakistan. The negotiations with Jinnah broke down because of Jinnah's unwillingness to agree to a readjustment of the provincial boundaries, while the Akalis made it clear that the Sikhs were not prepared to live under Muslim rule unconditionally. The failure of the negotiations between the Sikhs and Jinnah led to recriminations within the Unionist coalition, with the Sikhs accusing Sikander of not honouring his pact with Baldev Singh and of Muslim bias.[143]

It is interesting to look at the extent of support for the League in the Punjab at this time. Punjab officials noted that Jinnah's meetings had attracted large audiences of between ten to thirty thousand persons and had given the Pakistan movement a fillip, but doubted whether the effect of his visit to the province would be lasting. The League's influence in the Punjab was mainly confined to the urban classes; few of the provincial leaders commanded any widespread support; much of the interest attached to reports of current political speeches was artificially stimulated by the press and died down as soon as another topic presented itself for discussion. Jinnah voiced the determination of Muslims not to submit to the rule of the Hindu majority at the *all-India* level, but in the Punjab, most Muslims were with the Unionists.[144]

These comments were corroborated by the *Eastern Times*, a paper sympathetic to the League in the Punjab. An editorial lamented that the number of persons on the rolls of the League was very small, and that no sustained effort had been made to remedy the situation. Jinnah's meeting at Lahore was described as 'a badly managed affair'. Some volunteers seemed more interested 'in watching the *tamasha* (fun) than in doing their job', and it was obvious that they were never trained for any such work. This was because the Lahore City Muslim League was itself a non-entity, and had made no effort to organize primary Leagues in the city. 'And how has the

[142] *Tribune*, 10 December 1942.
[143] *Tribune*, 17 December 1942.
[144] FR for Punjab for second half of November 1942, HP file no. 18/11/42.

City Muslim League come into existence without Primary Leagues? The Lahore City Muslim League is a clique, whose main purpose seems to be to enable certain men to pose as President, Vice-President, etc., and remain in the public eye'. The city League had presented a purse of Rs. 3000 to Jinnah; a city like Lahore 'could have easily presented ten times that sum.'[145]

The death of Sikander Hyat Khan in December 1942 was a blow to his party and to the British, who acknowledged that they owed the success of the war effort in the Punjab to him.[146] Sikander had maintained political stability in the province—Punjab was probably the only Muslim majority province which had escaped internecine conflicts and frequent changes of ministries since the outbreak of the war. Jinnah failed in his attempt to have a say in the selection of a new leader of the Unionist party, and therefore, of the Punjab. Khizar Hyat Khan Tiwana, son of Sir Umar Hyat Tiwana, was one of the biggest landowners in the Punjab. His loyalty to the British dated from 1919, when he had lent 150 horses to the British to control the non-cooperation movement in Amritsar. He had served in the ministries of Fazli Husain and Sikander, and he was chosen as the new leader of the Unionists. A motion of confidence, moved by Chhotu Ram, the Revenue Minister, at the meeting of the Unionist party, was seconded by Mamdot, president of the Punjab Muslim League. Earlier, Muslim Unionists had unanimously passed a vote of confidence in Khizar.[147]

Linlithgow doubted Khizar's ability to stand up to Jinnah, but he thought that Glancy, who had become Governor of the Punjab in 1942, was 'now well in the saddle' and in a position to give him a great deal of assistance.[148] The Viceroy was probably implying that Jinnah should not be allowed to disturb the war effort in the Punjab. Linlithgow did not make clear whether he would have encouraged Khizar to break with Jinnah, if necessary, thus reversing his policy of using influence with Sikander in 1941—especially as the Congress leaders were now in jail and the Quit India movement had been brought under control; and the need for Muslim unity, under Jinnah's leadership, may not have appeared so urgent. Linlithgow had regarded Jinnah as unreliable and uncooperative as the Con-

[145] *Eastern Times*, 29 November 1942.
[146] Linlithgow to Amery, 28 December 1942, *TOP*, vol. 3, p. 431.
[147] *Statesman*, 24 January 1943.
[148] Linlithgow to Amery, 11 January 1943, *LC*, vol. 12.

gress in the matter of supporting the war effort, and was apprehensive that Jinnah, always out to extract the most favourable political bargain—in this case from the British—might hamper the war effort in the Punjab if he managed to tighten his hold over the Unionist ministry, or actually establish a Muslim League ministry in the province. Linlithgow feared that the break up of the tenuous alliance between the Muslim and non-Muslim ministers would lead to purely communal politics in the Punjab, which in turn would create instability in the province. The Sikhs already appeared nervous; non-Muslim officials might be anxious. Therefore, Glancy must make it clear that he would use his special powers to prevent the fall of the Unionist ministry.[149]

Somewhat on the defensive against Jinnah, Khizar managed, nevertheless, to hold his own. At a meeting of the all-India Muslim League in Delhi in March 1943, Khizar acknowledged the general leadership of Jinnah and affirmed his adherence to the Sikander–Jinnah pact, but a resolution advocating more active interference by the League in the Punjab was withdrawn. Khizar, however, failed to prevent the setting up of a separate League party in the Punjab—he said it already existed under the terms of the Sikander–Jinnah pact—and promised, however vaguely, that he would work for the uplift of the League in the province in accordance with the terms of the pact. But Khizar would remain leader of the provincial League.[150]

On the warpath with Khizar, Jinnah now alleged that Glancy had violated constitutional procedure by failing to consult the Muslim League before taking steps for the appointment of a Prime Minister and was 'disagreeably surprised' when Khizar drew his attention to the Governor's Instrument of Instructions.[151]

The tussle between the League and Khizar continued. Mamdot and Jinnah told Khizar that the Unionist ministry should be redesignated 'Muslim League coalition.' Khizar retorted that he intended to abide by the Sikander–Jinnah pact and to maintain the name 'Unionist'. He pointed out that he himself had been elected to the assembly on the Unionist ticket. Jinnah was 'much incensed'. But he realized that he could not go further as he did not have a majority in the provincial assembly. So he instructed Mamdot to come to a satisfactory agreement with Khizar. The weakness of Jin-

[149] Linlithgow to Glancy, 1 February 1943, Ibid., vol. 92.

[150] *Statesman*, 5 and 8 March 1943; and *Tribune*, 8 March 1943.

[151] Glancy to Linlithgow, 14 March 1943, *TOP*, vol. 3, p. 809.

nah's position on Unionist–League relations in the Punjab was also illustrated by his failure to force a decision that the constitution of the provincial League should be determined by the all-India Muslim League so as to remove any inconsistency with the constitution of the all-India body.[152]

It was Wavell's appreciative reference in February 1944 to the geographical unity of India, and his praise for the 'conspicuous success' which had characterized the working of the intercommunal Unionist ministry which roused Jinnah's ire against Khizar.

> 'On the main problem of Indian unity', said Wavell, 'the difference between the Hindu and Muslim, I can only say this. You cannot alter geography. From the point of view of defence, of relations with the outside world, of many internal and external economic problems, India is a natural unit . . . That two communities and even two nations can make arrangements to live together in spite of differing cultures or religions, history provides many examples . . . . Coalition government by Indians for Indians is not an impossible ideal. It is being carried out at the Centre without friction; it has been carried on for nearly seven years with conspicuous success in the Punjab. Thanks to the leadership of men of good sense, goodwill, and good courage, the affairs of that Province have prospered with the minimum of communal friction; they have administered their Province in the interests of the Province, but also with regard to the interests of India and of the war effort of the United Nations, to which the Punjab has made so striking a contribution.'[153]

Ministerial circles in the Punjab welcomed Wavell's reference to the harmonious working of the Unionist majority—they thought it would strengthen their position for the future. Jinnah now showed his displeasure with Wavell. He summoned Mamdot to Delhi on the eve of the budget session of the Central assembly. In the assembly itself, the League joined the Congress in defeating cut motions on the railway budget. Liaqat Ali Khan was cheered by Congress benches when he stated that Britain was fighting the war for interests other than India's.[154]

The League's war with the Unionists was now under way. Daultana, then General Secretary of the Punjab Muslim League, outlined an ambitious mass contact programme to mobilize Muslims against the British and the Hindus.[155] In discussions with Muslim Leaguers,

[152] *Statesman*, 29 March 1943.
[153] *Legislative Assembly Debates*, 1944, vol. 1, pp. 342–3.
[154] *Statesman*, 21 and 28 February 1944.
[155] *Statesman*, 20 March 1944.

Jinnah reportedly emphasized that the Unionist party should be liquidated.[156] Leaguers alleged that Muslim Unionist ministers were ignoring the interests of their community, whose position in every department of the provincial government was deplorable. The creed of the Unionist party was Dominion Status and a united, democratic federal constitution 'for India as a whole.' Its policies reflected the interests of only one class—the zamindars—whereas the League was 'the people's party and the custodian and trustee of all interests and classes that constitute the Muslim nation.' Its 'fundamental and basic principles' were therefore 'quite different' from those of the Unionist Party.[157]

Jinnah returned to Lahore in April 1944. He was preaching Pakistan as the panacea for all ills, but avoided any reasoned explanation 'of where it begins and ends and what benefits it will confer. He might make an ideal leader of a Demolition Squad', mused Glancy, 'but anything in the way of constructive suggestion seems foreign to his nature'. His attempts to woo Chhotu Ram and Baldev Singh had met with little success. Many rural Muslim MLAs resented his dictatorial attitude and went so far as to threaten resignation from the League.[158]

Khizar, however, was assailed by grave misgivings, according to Glancy. He had told Glancy that 'he is thinking seriously of giving way to Jinnah's demand'.

> 'He says that the Unionist Party exists only in name, it has no funds and practically nothing in the way of organization, and its disappearance would cause little regret . . . He believes that there will be only two parties of any importance in India in the near future—the Congress and the Muslim League: if he defies Jinnah and persuades his staunch adherents to adopt this course, he fears that in a comparatively short time they will all be relegated to political oblivion.'

Khizar kept 'harping on the bitter experiences' of what occurred after World War I: 'those in the Punjab who had fought for the Empire found themselves ousted by traitors and non-cooperators while the British Government stood by and acquiesced.' Khizar wanted an "order" from Glancy that he should stand up to Jinnah in the interests of the war effort: 'tell him that I consider it to be his duty as a loyal subject to act in the manner suggested.' Glancy told

156 *Statesman*, 23 March 1944.
157 *Statesman*, 5 April 1944.
158 Glancy to Wavell, 6 April 1944, L/P&J/5/247.

Khizar that he could not issue any such "order": he could only tell him 'as a friend' that 'he will have no peace hereafter, nor will he be serving the interests of the Province or of India or of Muslims or of the Empire if he gives way to Jinnah and places himself in his power'.[159]

Wavell favoured the encouragement given by Glancy to Khizar to stand up to Jinnah.[160] Wanting to help Khizar, Glancy discerned that he could take action against one of his ministers, Shaukat Hyat Khan, the son of Sikander, who appeared to be flirting with the League. Shaukat, observed Glancy, 'by his betrayal of his leader and his colleagues . . . has richly earned his removal.' But it would be better to avoid removing him on political grounds and there were other reasons which entitled him to dismissal. Shaukat had dismissed a lady inspectress of schools ostensibly for corruption but actually because she reportedly offended one of his subordinates. Eight different charges, mainly concerned with corruption, were made against her. Not one was proved. At the cabinet meeting Glancy intervened and dismissed Shaukat on the ground that his colleagues had lost confidence in him. Glancy admitted that 'I do not altogether like this course of action, but larger issues are at stake—the tranquility of the Province and the continuance of the war effort'.[161]

Shaukat's dismissal from the Unionist ministry added a new element to the Unionist–League rift for Shaukat claimed that he resigned a week before his dismissal on this issue. His ejection became an all India issue at the Sialkot session of the League in May 1944, when Jinnah demanded an explanation from Khizar and Glancy, and alleged not altogether unjustifiably, that Shaukat had been dismissed for his sympathy with the League. At Sialkot, Jinnah denied that there had ever been a pact between him and Sikander. There was, he said, only 'a record of what Sikander had said he would carry out.' Khizar's attitude was childish, and Jinnah wanted 'to kill the very name "Unionist" and see its funeral.'[162]

Hindu and Sikh Unionist ministers, joining the fray, refused to

[159] Glancy to Wavell, 14 April 1944, *TOP*, vol. 4, pp. 880–2.

[160] Wavell to Glancy, 15 April 1944, Ibid., p. 882, and Wavell to Amery, 18 April 1944, Ibid., p. 898.

[161] Glancy to Wavell, 24 April 1944, Ibid., pp. 922–5.

[162] *Statesman*, 30 April and 1 May 1944. See also FR for Punjab for second half of April 1944, HP file no. 18/4/44.

accept a League coalition and suggested that it could only be part of an all-India settlement. Jinnah described their proposal as 'preposterous'. Choosing to misinterpret their suggestion, he stated that an all-India understanding could not be achieved 'with only 3 non-Muslim Ministers in the Punjab.' Together they represented only 20 out of 175 MLAs in the provincial assembly. There could be no settlement with them on Pakistan, which was an all-India question.[163] While reaffirming his faith in Pakistan—Muslim right to self-determination—Khizar said that he could not accept a demand involving the all-India League's interference in provincial affairs. If he did so he would be guilty of a breach of promise to the other communities represented in his coalition.[164] Earlier, Khizar had defended his dual adherence to a communal party like the League and the intercommunal Unionist party, but Jinnah had argued that 'for a Muslim to adhere to the Unionist Party as well as to the Muslim League was like keeping a mistress in addition to a wife. To this Khizar adroitly responded that being a Muslim himself he was entitled to have two wives, if he wished to do so.'[165]

It was against this background that the Muslim League Committee of Action charged Khizar with having acted in contravention of the constitution and rules of the League, rendering him liable to expulsion. It was evident from his statement of 27 April that he did not either approve or believe in the formation and organization of communal parties, while the aim of the all-India Muslim League 'is to organize and consolidate the position of the Muslims as a separate nation both inside and outside the legislatures under the control, discipline and supervision of the All-India Muslim League and its provincial branches.' Khizar's rejection of the League's authority in provincial matters was 'fundamentally in opposition' to the rules and constitution of the League. His first allegiance was evidently to the Unionist party and 'allegiance to the League, if at all, is only a secondary one.' It was the declared policy of the all-India Muslim League that 'a member of the Muslim League organization cannot owe allegiance or belong to any political party except the Muslim League.'[166]

Denying the existence of the Sikander-Jinnah pact once more, the

[163] *Statesman*, 2 and 3 May 1944.
[164] *Statesman*, 28 April 1944.
[165] Glancy to Wavell, 21 April 1944, *TOP*, vol. 4, pp. 906–7.
[166] *Statesman*, 5 May 1944.

League's Working Committee declared that the Unionist label 'was a pretence for keeping down the Mussalmans and making them subservient to the dominant Hindu group'.[167] And so a communal rationale was given to Khizar's expulsion from the League, even as 26 Muslim Unionists joined the Punjab provincial Muslim League. The League now announced that its organization would be strengthened and extended. Five organizing secretaries would be appointed in each of the five divisions of the Punjab.[168] Divisional workers would complete a tour of the province by the end of June. In July they would hold large meetings at *tehsil* headquarters followed by district conferences at short intervals. 'At this stage we will need speakers of all India fame.'[169] One League worker reported to Jinnah that he visited mosques at prayer time on Fridays and explained the programme of the League to Muslims. 'Three times a week I lead a deputation to leading wards and mohallas in the city and enrol members in large numbers.'[170]

That the majority of Muslim Unionists remained with Khizar in May 1944 indicated that the extreme form of Pakistan defined by Jinnah held little appeal for them. The League's lack of support in the Punjab legislature was also evident from a province-wide campaign it started in December 1944 to enrol new recruits for the legislative party.[171] Why even some Muslim Unionists went along with the League in 1944 is hard to gauge. In some cases, the deserters appear to have been individuals who, for one reason or other, were disenchanted with the Unionist ministry.[172] Mamdot's personal wealth may have made provincial Leaguers eager to have him on their side: for his part, as a rather simple and not very strong character, he may have been lured by the possibility of holding the Presidentship of the Punjab League or enticed by promises of power in the future.[173] Other Unionists may have simply responded to the call of Pakistan.

[167] *Statesman*, 29 May 1944.

[168] FR for Punjab for second half of November 1944, HP file no. 18/11/44.

[169] Daultana to Jinnah, 31 May 1944, *Qaid-e-Azam Jinnah's Correspondence with Punjab Muslim Leaders*, p. 249.

[170] Rashid Ali Khan to Jinnah, 4 July 1944, Ibid., p. 336.

[171] *Civil and Military Gazette*, 31 December 1944.

[172] As suggested by Glancy to Wavell, 6 April 1944, L/P&J/5/247.

[173] This was suggested by Mr. Henry Taylor, then D.C. Ferozepur. Interview with author on 23 February 1981.

There is little sound evidence that most Leaguers were thinking of a sovereign Pakistan in 1944. Ispahani could only tell Casey that the Muslims did not want to be under Hindu domination. Muslim writers in Bengal thought East Pakistan would promote Bengali language and culture.

> 'Religion and culture are not the same thing. Religion transgresses the geographical boundary but "tamaddun" (culture) cannot go beyond the geographical boundary . . . Here only lies the difference between Purba-Pakistan and Pakistan. For this reason the people of Purba-Pakistan are a different nation from the people of the other provinces of India and from the "religious brothers" of Pakistan.'[174]

Nazimuddin, then heading the League ministry in Bengal, thought that East Pakistan should include Bengal (less the Burdwan division), all of Assam, and a part of Purnea district in north-west Bengal. A centre that had always been controlled by Bombay, UP and Madras had worked against the interests of Bengal. It was for this reason, together with the intolerance towards Muslims that the Congress governments had displayed, that Bengal Leaguers found attractive the idea of a sovereign state in northeast India separated from the rest of India. Apparently Nazimuddin was thinking of an independent East Bengal.[175] On another occasion, Nazimuddin told Twynam, the governor of the CP, that the League insisted on the principle of self-determination, but that this principle would not necessarily involve complete severance from Hindustan.[176] The manifesto brought out by the Bengal provincial League in 1944 emphasized the link between Pakistan and East Bengal. It did not say that Pakistan would be an Islamic state, but it looked forward to a revival of the law of the *Shariat* and the culture of East Bengal. It defined the League's objectives to establish equal opportunities for all, irrespective of creed, caste or class; the right to education, the nationalization of the jute industry and the elimination of 'vested interests.'[177]

The manifesto of the Punjab Muslim League[178] promised to safeguard the religious, cultural and spiritual traditions of Muslims. It

[174] Quoted in Sen, *Muslim Politics*, p. 179. I have corrected some grammatical errors in Sen's (?) translation of the passage.

[175] Casey to Wavell, 11 September 1944, *TOP*, vol. 5, pp. 29–30.

[176] Twynam to Wavell, 9 October 1944, Ibid., p. 95.

[177] Sen, *Muslim Politics*, pp. 184–5.

[178] *Civil and Military Gazette*, 8 November 1944.

was intended to appeal to the small landed proprietor, who formed the bulk of the agrarian classes in the Punjab. Agricultural development would be based on the welfare of smaller zamindars, peasants and landless agriculturalists. Agricultural debts would be wiped out; and cheap credit facilities provided by the state. Taxation would be increased on big landlords. Non-Muslim minorities would be allowed to organize education in accordance with their religious and cultural traditions.

But the minorities would not have been lured into Pakistan by the League's hymn of hate against them, especially against Hindus. The Zamindar League was described as 'a substitute for the *Shudhi* movement';[179] League propaganda took the line that Islam was in danger. Another theme of the speeches delivered was that Pakistan would mean the revival of the Caliphate.[180] Pakistan, then, clearly meant all things to all Muslims.

It is interesting that, while the League held power in the NWFP from 1943–1945, the provincial legislature, in which almost 75 per cent of the seats were reserved for Muslims,[181] never passed a resolution in favour of Pakistan. As for the Muslim minority provinces, most Leaguers appear to have thought of Pakistan as a bargaining point, and an indication of Muslim opposition to Hindu raj. Most of them would have been satisfied with 50:50 representation for the Congress and the League at the centre and coalitions in the provinces.[182] The dislike or fear of Hindu domination of Muslims, did not, therefore, necessarily mean that they wanted a sovereign Pakistan.

Congress and the League—March 1943 to March 1945

Of the Pakistan of Jinnah's conception there had never been any doubt. In March 1943 he urged Leaguers to 'remove from your mind any idea of some form of loose federation. There is no such thing as loose federation. When there is a central government and provincial governments, they [Central Government] will go on

[179] *Civil and Military Gazette*, 23 November 1944. On the revival of the *Zamindara League*, see editorial, 'The Zamindara League', *Eastern Times*, 7 November 1944.

[180] *Civil and Military Gazette*, 3 December 1944.

[181] A.K. Gupta, *NWFP Legislature in the Freedom Struggle*, p. 146.

[182] Note by Porter (undated), R/3/2/54. The note was probably written around the end of November 1944.

tightening, tightening and tightening until you are pulverized with regard to your powers as units.'[183] The League's muscular reaction to Wavell's reference to the geographical unity of India was actuated by the party's apprehension that the British would renege on Cripps's offer of self-determination for minorities. The League wanted an advance on that offer. Khaliquzzaman's thesis in April 1944 was that the Congress would, eventually, accept any British award, even if it were made without their consent—they had done so in 1909, 1932 and 1935. 'That is what Jinnah is playing for.' Therefore Jinnah would no longer accept the Cripps offer with its provision for a preliminary National Government at the centre. The League's reliance on the British was underlined by Khaliquzzaman's assertion that British rule must be 'retained for many years'; once they declared for Pakistan, administrative problems would be raised and the 'unreality' of the Congress demand for independence exposed.[184] The inference is that the League could not publicly ask for the retention of the Raj for fear of exposing itself to Congress charges of servility to the British. But both its political conservatism and the Muslim fears of Hindu domination that it represented; the desire and expectation that a sovereign Pakistan would be created under the British aegis and guaranteed by them were inextricably interwoven, and although their separate threads can be picked out, their combination would render impossible any agreement with the Congress on the basis of a united independent India. So it is not surprising that Jinnah negotiated with Gandhi on the basis of a sovereign Pakistan in September 1944.

Gandhi and Rajagopalachari helped to restore Jinnah's prestige at the all-India level by political initiatives which conceded the principle of Pakistan. The origins of the Gandhi–Jinnah talks in July 1944 lay in a formula which was presented by Rajagopalachari to Gandhi in March 1943, when Gandhi was still under detention. The formula reflected Rajagopalachari's belief that an agreement with Jinnah was a necessary precursor to the establishment of a National Government at the centre, no matter how obdurate Jinnah might be. 'I could easily give a grand fight to Jinnah now and demolish him in his own organization', he wrote to Devdas Gandhi on 29 November 1942, 'but even Hercules is no match for two. Had the British Government not been there, the whole thing would have been different.

[183] Pirzada, *Documents*, p. 427.

[184] Enclosure to Mudie to Jenkins, 14 April 1944, *TOP*, vol. 4, pp. 878–9.

We should clench our teeth and choose our opponent.'[185] Rajagopalachari argued that 'Pakistan is not so dreadful.' The Punjab and Bengal were already under Pakistan. His proposals aimed at bringing a majority of Hindus in these two provinces under one Hindu fold and only contiguous districts of those provinces in which Muslims were in a majority would be given the right of self-determination. His formula would not throw the Sikhs to the wolves. They would be better off in a free India and a strong force on the side of the Hindus.[186]

In April 1944, Rajagopalachari presented his formula to Jinnah in the hope that it would bring about 'a final settlement of the most unfortunate impasse we are in.'[187] Jinnah replied that he could not accept the formula, but he would place it before his Working Committee. This would have served no purpose, so Rajagopalachari ended the correspondence on 8 July.[188]

Gandhi put forward the formula to Jinnah after his release from prison in May 1944. The terms of the formula were as follows. When the war ended, a commission would demarcate the "contiguous districts" in North West and East India having an absolute majority. In the areas thus demarcated, a plebiscite of the adult population would be taken. If the majority voted for a separate sovereign state, it would be given effect to, but border districts would have the option to join one of the new states. In the event of separation, mutual agreements would be entered into for safeguarding defence, commerce and communications. These terms would be binding when the British transferred full power to India.[189]

The formula clearly conceded the principle of Pakistan, and embodied Rajagopalachari's belief that this would satisfy the Muslims and that they would, in time, cease to want Pakistan.[190] Provincial Muslim Leaguers and Muslim League papers were jubilant that Gandhi had accepted Pakistan in principle.[191] Congressmen were

[185] Rajagopalachari to Devdas Gandhi, 29 November 1942, *MGC*, serial no. 2032.

[186] *Statesman*, 13 January 1943.

[187] Rajagopalachari to Jinnah, 8 April 1944, *IAR*, 1944, vol. 2, p. 129.

[188] Jinnah to Rajagopalachari, 2 July 1944, Ibid., p. 130; and Rajagopalachari to Jinnah, 4 July 1944, Ibid.

[189] See Jinnah to Gandhi, 10 September 1944; Gandhi to Jinnah, 11 September 1944, Ibid, pp. 135–7.

[190] See Wavell to Amery, 11 July 1944, *TOP*, vol. 4, pp. 1077–9.

[191] E.g. *Eastern Times*, 10 July 1944, FRs for Punjab for second half of July and first half of August 1944, HP file nos. 18/7 and 18/8/44.

surprised and did not know what to make of Gandhi's attitude.[192] The Sikhs, the Mahasabha and the Unionists were alarmed that the success of the Gandhi–Jinnah parleys would prejudice their position in the Punjab.[193]

The Rajagopalachari formula was probably an attempt to get Jinnah out into the open about Pakistan. Until then, the only attempt at a definition of Pakistan had been made in the Lahore resolution of 1940, and it was considered even by the British to be an obscure definition.[194]

It is unlikely that Gandhi ever thought that Jinnah would accept the formula. For, as Jinnah pointed out, demarcation of boundaries on the lines suggested would relegate 11 districts in the Punjab and the same number in Bengal to Hindustan. Karachi and Dacca would be the only ports left to Pakistan. Gandhi had also not said how the new constitution would be framed and the provisional government formed.[195]

Gandhi replied that the constitution would be framed by the provisional government or an authority set up by it after the British withdrawal. The independence contemplated was 'of the whole of India as it stands.' The Boundary Commission would also be appointed by the provisional government. Absolute majority meant a clear majority over non-Muslim elements in the Muslim majority province. Power would be transferred by the British to the provisional government.[196]

For Jinnah, however, 'the only solution of India's problem was to accept the division of India into Pakistan and Hindustan.'[197] He said it was clear that Gandhi did not accept that Muslims were a separate nation, and that they had the inherent right of self-determination; he did not accept that 'they alone are entitled to exercise this right of theirs for self-determination.'[198]

Gandhi rejoined that Muslims could not be a separate nation 'by reason of acceptance of Islam. Will the two nations become one if

[192] FRs for UP, Bombay, Bengal and Punjab for second half of July and first half of August 1944, HP file nos. 18/7 and 18/8/44.

[193] FRs for Punjab for July 1944, HP file no. 18/7/44.

[194] Note by Jenkins, 23 July 1945, R/3/1/105.

[195] Jinnah to Gandhi, 10 September 1944.

[196] Gandhi to Jinnah, 15 September 1944, *IAR*, 1944, vol. 2, p. 141.

[197] Jinnah to Gandhi, 11 September 1944, Ibid., p. 137.

[198] Jinnah to Gandhi, 25 September 1944, Ibid., p. 147.

the whole of India accepted Islam?' The majority of Muslims in India, were, after all, converts to Islam.[199]

Gandhi later said that the outlines of any scheme of interim government were never discussed by him and Jinnah. His impression was that Jinnah wanted 'two independent sovereign states with no connection between them except by treaty'. Gandhi accepted a division of India 'as between members of the same family and therefore reserving for partnership things of common interest. But Qaid-e-Azam would have nothing short of the two nations theory and therefore complete dissolution amounting to full sovereignty in the first instance. It was just here that we split.'[200]

Jinnah had pointed to the unrepresentative character of Gandhi at the start of the negotiations. British officials wondered why he went to talk to Gandhi in the first place.[201] According to Gandhi, he declared Gandhi to be unrepresentative, but 'he insisted . . . that if I first accepted the Pakistan of his conception, he could then discuss other things with me even though I was but an individual.'[202]

Wavell could not believe that Jinnah, as 'a highly intelligent man, is sincere about the "two nations theory".' His refusal to answer the awkward questions raised by Gandhi showed that he had not thought out the implications of Pakistan, or that he would not disclose them.[203] Sir Evan Jenkins, then Private Secretary to the Viceroy, later observed that the Gandhi–Jinnah talks clarified the Lahore resolution only to the extent of showing that, in Jinnah's mind, Pakistan 'consists initially of Sind, Baluchistan, the NWFP and Punjab, Bengal and Assam; and that the question of their sovereignty is to be decided by Muslims resident in them without reference to wishes of other inhabitants.' This was 'not really a definition' of Pakistan in any case. 'Does Jinnah . . . really mean that, because in Eastern and parts of Central Bengal the Muslims are in an absolute majority, a Muslim vote alone is to transfer Calcutta to a Muslim sovereign state?'[204]

The breakdown of the Gandhi–Jinnah talks pleased only the Un-

[199] Gandhi to Jinnah, 15 September 1944, Ibid., p. 140.
[200] Gandhi to Sapru, 26 February 1945, *TBSC*, vol. 6.
[201] *Quarterly Survey of the Political and Constitutional Position of the British in India*, no. 29, L/WS/1/1433.
[202] Gandhi to Sapru, 26 February 1945, *TBSC*, vol. 6.
[203] Wavell to Amery, 3 October 1944, *TOP*, vol. 5, p. 75.
[204] Note by Jenkins, 23 July 1945, R/3/1/105, pp. 34–5.

ionists, the Sikhs and the Mahasabha. Provincial Leaguers were disappointed, but pleased at Gandhi's concession of the principle of Pakistan.[205] Gandhi himself may not have expected anything from the talks, for he went 'in hope but without expectation. So if I return empty handed, I shall not be disappointed.'[206] But by inviting Jinnah soon after the latter's failure to bring the Unionists to heel, and by letting Jinnah thus occupy in the talks 'the dominating position of one who spurns what is offered him and of whom favours are sought', Gandhi helped Jinnah to recover the prestige he had lost in the Punjab.[207]

On the all-India front, it was Wavell who was now considering a political initiative. Since August 1942, the British had concentrated on suppressing the Quit India movement, and there had been no inclination, either by Whitehall or Linlithgow, to make any move in India. Since his arrival in India in October 1943, Wavell had pleaded with Whitehall for 'a change of spirit' on the British side; a declaration by the British government that it had a definite intention to give India self-government as soon as possible.[208] Churchill, however, appeared to be the main stumbling-block in the way of political advance in India. According to Amery, he 'passionately' hoped that any solution involving the fulfilment of British pledges 'can somehow still be prevented.' Whenever the question of India cropped up in the Cabinet, ministers would be 'over borne by the Prime Minister's vehemence.'[209] Wavell himself favoured a settlement with the Congress Right and an understanding with the League. The Right were restive with Gandhi's obstructionist policies, and if Rajagopalachari was offered a seat in the government, the Right could be weaned away from Gandhi. Some 'inclination of the ear' to the League's demands might prove the 'shortest way of bringing about a more reasonable frame of mind in the Congress High Command, and so paving the way towards ending the deadlock.' Once Gandhi understood that the British would not be frightened out of the principle of self-determination for the Muslim

[205] FR for Punjab for first half of October 1944, HP file no. 18/10/44.

[206] Gandhi to Sapru, 8 September 1944, *TBSC*, vol. 6.

[207] *Quarterly Survey of the Political and Constitutional Position of the British in India*, no. 29, L/WS/1/1433.

[208] See, for example, Wavell to Amery, (T), 26 October 1944, *TOP*, vol. 5, pp. 68–9, and 140.

[209] Amery to Wavell, 16 August 1944, *TOP*, vol. 4, p. 1206.

areas, a more reasonable approach could be expected from the Congress. Such a policy has its long-term implications as well. The Cripps offer envisaged not only a settlement between the League and the Congress 'but also the negotiation of a treaty between H.M.G. and the proposed Constituent Assembly' which would make provision for the safeguarding of Britain's interests as a world power and for a winding up of British control on terms 'which will be just and equitable'. If the Congress remained in its present frame of mind, it would oppose all proposals for treaty provisions essential to British interests and world security 'as incompatible with the word "Independence".'

Wavell welcomed the news that the Congress Right was interested in an agreement with Jinnah and hoped to form a national government.[210] K.M. Munshi, ex-Premier of Bombay, suggested to Jenkins the establishment of a centre to discuss constitutional details.[211] Reports that Liaqat Ali Khan was keen to come to an agreement gave heart to the Congress Right. Gandhi would not discourage them. Writing with his approval, Syed Mahmud, a Congress Muslim from Bihar, asked Bhulabhai Desai, leader of the Congress in the Central Assembly, to meet Liaqat.[212]

Desai met Wavell on 15 November 1944, and told him that the British should take the initiative, which need not include any constitutional change during the war. This fitted in with Wavell's own ideas, and he wanted to visit London to discuss the prospects of a British move with the cabinet. But the war cabinet did not respond,[213] and a frustrated Wavell wrote at the end of his first year in office: 'I have found H.M.G.'s attitude to India negligent, hostile and contemptuous to a degree I had not anticipated, or I think I might have done more.'[214]

Encouraged by his talks with Wavell, Desai met Liaqat Ali Khan who said that a Congress–League coalition at the centre was not only desirable but possible. Later, Desai gathered from him that he had mentioned the matter to Jinnah.[215] In the first week of January

[210] See Wavell's appreciation of the Indian Political Situation, February 1944, Ibid., pp. 884–93.

[211] Wavell to Amery, 15 November 1944, *TOP*, vol. 5, p. 206.

[212] Syed Mahmud to Desai, 18 November 1944, *Syed Mahmud Collection.*

[213] Wavell to Amery, 23 November 1944, *TOP*, vol. 5, enclosure: pp. 230–1. See, for example, Amery to Wavell, 14 December 1944, Ibid., p. 303.

[214] Wavell, *Journal*, entry for 20 October 1944, p. 93.

[215] Pyarelal, *Mahatma Gandhi, the Last Phase*, vol. 1, p. 103.

1945, Desai met Gandhi at Sevagram. Gandhi was against a return to office by the Congress, but he knew that many Congressmen desired it. So he encouraged Desai to go ahead.[216] The British and the public never ascertained whether Desai's proposals had the support of Gandhi. There is, however, a copy of the proposals in Desai's handwriting, with alterations in Gandhi's handwriting in pencil—in the papers of Desai.[217]

Desai hoped that a successful coalition at the centre with the League might induce them to give up Pakistan. The terms of the Desai–Liaqat pact were that the Congress and the League would join the interim government at the centre. Each party would have 40 per cent of the seats, and 20 per cent would be reserved for minorities. The government would work under the act of 1935, though the Viceroy should not use his powers to enforce a measure not passed by the legislature. The first task of the interim government would be to release the arrested members of the Congress Working Committee. If the coalition was formed at the centre, the next step would be to form coalitions in the provinces.[218] A copy of the Desai–Liaqat Pact, carrying the initials of the two leaders, is also in the Desai papers.

The release of the Congress Working Committee was not made a preliminary condition of the signing of the pact, as Desai explained to Wavell, because the Working Committee would wreck the negotiations, but once the coalition government had started functioning at the centre and in the provinces the Committee would accept the *fait accompli*.[219] But Gandhi always doubted the *bona fides* of Jinnah and Liaqat. Their public denial of any knowledge of the pact shocked him, and he warned Desai not to go ahead without the approval of the Congress Working Committee. 'Jinnah says one thing and Liaqat repeats it', he wrote to Desai on 24 January. 'I am letting you know what I see from this distance. I fear what I see.'[220]

Wavell believed that Gandhi knew of the proposals, for he held that Desai was 'an important and experienced politician' who would not go ahead without being sure of his ground. He considered the proposals to be 'undoubtedly important' and moderate, and wanted the war cabinet to accept them.[221] Mudie thought that the proposals

[216] Ibid. [217] Diaries, *BDC*, file no. 7. [218] Ibid.
[219] V.P. Menon to Jenkins, 27 January 1945, *TOP*, vol. 5, p. 476.
[220] Gandhi to Desai, 13 February 1945, *BDC*.
[221] Wavell to Amery, (T), 14 January 1945, *TOP*, vol. 5, pp. 400–2.

'were exactly what we have been working for. The move has come from the Congress and the League. So there can be no question of H.E.'s receiving a rebuff'. The initiative had been taken by the leaders of the Congress and the League in the Legislative Assembly. 'It is definitely right wing and gives an opportunity, which may never occur again, of splitting the Congress.'[222]

Churchill, however, demanded an explanation for 'this new, sudden departure'.[223] Could Desai deliver the goods, and would the interim government support the war effort? Would the Quit India movement be withdrawn? The cabinet suggested that Jenkins, rather than Wavell, should meeet Desai. 'In other words, they felt that the bridge should be further tested by a sagacious but lighter weight quadruped before my lord the elephant himself puts even a portion of his weight on an uncertain structure.'[224]

But Wavell had already arranged to meet Desai on 20 January, and was satisfied by his explanations. The Viceroy would have the final say in deciding the portfolios: the only change would be that he would consult party leaders before making any appointment. Desai told him that the new councillors would not take orders from Jinnah or Gandhi and said that 'he never contemplated outside control of the Centre. He was against any immediate attempt by the provisional government to promote a long-term solution, until the atmosphere seemed more favourable'.[225] There was no further reaction from the war cabinet.

Despite his denials, British officials in India were certain that Jinnah knew about the Desai–Liaqat pact. Wavell instructed Colville, the Governor of Bombay, to ascertain whether Jinnah thought Desai's proposals were worth pursuing and whether he would be willing to discuss them with the Viceroy and Desai.[226] Jinnah was emphatic that there had been no 'authorized discussion' between Liaqat and Desai. Then he said that Colville's communicating the points in Wavell's letter 'was the first approach to him in the matter'. He said '"this conversation is the starting point"'. He agreed to meet Wavell in Delhi and to call a meeting of his Working Committee immediately.[227]

[222] Mudie to Jenkins, 15 January 1945, Ibid., p. 403.
[223] Minute by Churchill, 16 January 1945, Ibid., p. 404.
[224] Amery to Wavell, 18 January 1945, Ibid., p. 419.
[225] Wavell to Amery, (T), 20 January 1945, Ibid., pp. 423–5.
[226] Wavell to Amery, 22 February 1945, Ibid., p. 596.
[227] Colville to Wavell, 24 February 1945, Ibid., pp. 607–8.

Jinnah tried to commit Jenkins 'to negotiations with him and through him to the League Committee as though the proposals came from me and not from Desai, and Desai were not directly concerned.'[228] After meeting him on 26 March, Wavell's impression was that Jinnah's disclaimer of all knowledge of the pact was 'an obvious falsehood I am sure . . . He is playing his usual slippery game in fact.'[229] Jinnah's tactics were probably inspired by Desai's offer of parity with the Congress at the centre. But his mistrust of the Congress was echoed in his desire that the *British* present the proposals, for he probably believed that once they put them down on paper, they would stand by what would then be a British offer. Having made the overtures in the first place, the Congress would accept an identical British one, and the concept of parity would at once be formalized and institutionalized. But the stalling tactics of the war cabinet deprived Jinnah of any British reed to lean on; this, coupled with his inability to trust Congress *bona fides*, was the main reason why the Desai–Liaqat pact come to nothing, despite the reported interest of many Leaguers in taking office under its terms.[230] The point is important and discounts the oft-made contention that the Congress was never prepared to compromise.

Jinnah's interest in the Desai–Liaqat pact was perhaps also stirred by the difficulties most League ministries were finding themselves in by February 1945. The release of Congress MLAs in the NWFP led to the defeat of the League ministry and the return of the Congress to office. In Sind, as we have seen, Hidayatullah had defied Jinnah and coalesced with Maula Baksh's Azad Muslim party. In Assam, Saadullah had been obliged to turn to the Congress for support to preserve his position. The Congress had acted on Gandhi's advice to act as they thought best in the light of the local circumstances. Nazimuddin's ministry was defeated in the Bengal legislature by a snap vote on 28 March, and the assembly had been prorogued by the Speaker. Intrigues within the ministry and the provincial League meant that the Governor did not know on whom to rely to form a new government, so he had imposed Section 93. In the Punjab, the Unionists had won a by-election against the

[228] Jenkins to Symington, 25 February 1945, Ibid., p. 616.
[229] Wavell, *Journal*, entry for 26 February 1945, p. 114.
[230] *Statesman*, 23 January 1945; Hallett to Colville, 27 March 1945, *TOP*, vol. 5, pp. 749–51.

League.[231] With the League more or less off the political map of India, participation in a government at the centre would have given it a much-needed, tangible gain at the all-India level.

The enhancement of the League's prestige between 1942 and 1945 owed much to the British and the Congress. For tactical reasons, the British recognized the League's claim to speak for Muslims at the all-India level. The Cripps offer went far to concede the right of cession to the Muslim majority provinces, and so gave some substance to the possibility of Pakistan. In Sind and in Bengal, the League came into power as a result of official reactions to the ministries which were governing in those provinces until October 1942 and March 1943 respectively. However, as their support for the Unionists against Jinnah showed, the British did not necessarily want the League to govern all the Muslim majority provinces: what mattered most to them was the success of the war effort.

Like the British, Congress leaders gave recognition to the principle of Pakistan in 1942 and in 1944, regardless of Jinnah's position in the Muslim majority provinces. They thus undoubtedly gave substance to the demand for Pakistan, and indirectly built up the stature of the League at the all-India level.

There is some evidence that the League's call for Pakistan strengthened its appeal to Muslim popular sentiment, but it did not necessarily strengthen its hold over provincial Leaguers or Muslim groups, who were often not committed to the sovereign Pakistan of Jinnah's definition, but were interested in provincial power. The provincial Leagues relied on Jinnah to some extent to look after their interests with the Viceroy against the Congress at the all-India level, but retained autonomy in the provinces; and Jinnah found it difficult to assert control over them. With Pakistan as a slogan the all-India League was a party which depended for support at the provincial level on bargains with Muslim leaders who either rejected this aim or whose overriding interests lay chiefly in intercommunal parties or coalitions. The solidification of Muslim opinion against the Congress during the war had not, then, necessarily resulted in the solidification of the Muslim political community in favour of a sovereign Pakistan by April 1945.

[231] Memorandum by Amery, 5 April 1945; Wavell to Amery, 20 March 1945, *TOP*, vol. 5, pp. 830–2, 712 respectively; NWFP Governor's report, 23 March 1945, *CC*, vol. 16; FRs for Sind for February and March 1945, HP file nos. 18/2 and 18/3/45.

CHAPTER 4

The Success of the Muslim League: June 1945 to March 1946

The Simla Conference June–July 1945

Since October 1944, Wavell had urged Whitehall to allow him to include representatives of leading Indian parties in his Executive Council. An official administration, he argued, could not cope efficiently with post-war economic and political problems; nor would it enjoy the popular support necessary to mobilize India's resources for a successful offensive against Japan. But it was not before May 1945 that Whitehall reluctantly agreed that Wavell call a conference of Indian leaders at Simla the following month.[1]

On 15 June 1945, Wavell announced that he would invite Indian leaders to discuss the formation of a new Executive Council which would be 'more representative' of organized political opinion. The reconstituted Council would continue the war against Japan; tackle problems of post-war development until a new and permanent constitution could be agreed upon.[2]

Knowledge of an impending British initiative aroused widespread interest in India. The Congress Right welcomed Wavell's announcement of the Simla Conference as 'the fulfilment of our joint prayers and efforts'.[3] Their unstinted support to the war effort raised hopes among the Unionists that at least one of their number would be represented in the Executive Council among the Muslim members. Glancy encouraged their expectations, for they had 'from the very beginning' of the war consistently and unconditionally supported the war effort, while the Muslim League has at the best remained neutral'.[4] Wavell assured Glancy that he had no intention of hand-

[1] For Wavell's account of his discussions with the Cabinet, see his *Journal*, pp. 118–135.

[2] *Statesman*, 15 June 1945.

[3] Rajagopalachari to Sapru, 15 June 1945, *TBSC*, vol. 20.

[4] Glancy to Colville, 4 May 1945, L/P&J/5/248, p. 84. Colville sent Glancy's letter

ing over the interim government to any one party. An interim government of the kind proposed might prove a useful step towards inducing Muslims to abandon the objective of Pakistan.

Though Gandhi protested against the provision for parity between 'Caste Hindus' and Muslims in the proposed new Council, the Congress Working Committee, whose release from prison was announced by Wavell in his broadcast on 15 June, authorized Azad to accept the Viceroy's invitation to come to Simla.[5] Congressmen were instructed[6] that they were attending the conference on the understanding that the suggested arrangements were on 'an interim and temporary basis only, and especially in regard to communal parity'. The principle of such parity was 'an evil when and if accepted in the Centre and cannot be extended to the Provinces'. While communal parity in the limited and temporary sense could be agreed to, Congress would not accept the right of the League to nominate all the Muslim members of the new government, and would nominate individuals belonging to all communities. The continued ban on the AICC was described as 'an obstacle in our way and must be regarded as coercion'. The congress would also seek clarification from the Viceroy on the withdrawal of Indian troops from South-East Asia after the end of the war with Japan.

These points were raised by Azad and Gandhi when the Conference opened on 25 June. Wavell agreed that the Congress could nominate Muslims and Scheduled Castes, 'but said the principle of parity must be maintained'.[7]

Jinnah displayed a persecution complex, fearing that the Muslims would always be in a minority in the new Council because the other minorities, for example, the Sikhs and the Scheduled Castes, would always vote with the Hindus, and that the Viceroy would be reluctant to use his veto. Wavell tried to reassure him. 'I said I doubted his assumption' and pointed out that the Viceroy and Commander-

to Amery and asked him to draw Wavell's attention to it. Wavell was at that time having discussions with the British cabinet in London. A note in the margin said that Wavell had seen Glancy's letter. Colville to Amery, 7 May 1945, L/P&J/5/248, p. 83.

[5] Azad to Viceroy, (T), 21 June 1945, AICC file, G-26, 1945–6, p. 45.

[6] Confidential Note containing Instructions to Congressmen attending the Simla Conference, 25 June 1945, AICC file, p. 52, G-58. An undated, probably earlier, note, simply titled 'Memorandum' is almost identical to the Instructions of 25 June, and can be found in AICC file no. 41, 1945.

[7] Wavell to Amery, (T), 25 June 1945, *TOP*, vol. 5, pp. 1151–4.

in-Chief would ensure fair play for Muslims. Jinnah proposed that if a majority of Muslims were opposed to any decision, it should not go by vote and claimed that the League had the right to nominate all Muslim members to the Council. Wavell would not accept this and further told him that he also had it in mind to nominate a Unionist Muslim. Jinnah reacted sharply to the proposal of Unionists representing Muslims.

The wrangle over credentials continued when Wavell stated that there was nothing in the proposals to brand the Congress as a communal organization. Jinnah interjected here that the Congress represented only Hindus, a statement to which Dr Khan Sahib took vehement objection. Wavell concluded that Congress represented its members and both Congress and Jinnah accepted this.[8]

The main problem at Simla was, of course, the method of selecting new members of the Executive Council.[9] In the light of Jinnah's claims, Wavell circulated a statement of matters to be decided by the Conference.[10] The statement was divided into two parts. Part A was for settlement between the parties and the Viceroy representing the British government. It committed the parties to the tasks set out in the Viceroy's broadcast on 15 June, the selection of men of ability to the Council, with all portfolios, except that of the Commander-in-Chief, going to Indians. The new government would work under the existing constitution. All parties agreed to these points. On point (iv) of the statement, which provided for communal parity, Azad reiterated the Congress view that members of the Council should be appointed not on a communal but on a political basis. Part B of the statement was for agreement between the parties themselves. If all parties agreed to Part A, they would decide on the strength and composition of the Executive Council by parties and for communities and the method by which panels of names would be submitted to the Viceroy to enable him to make his recommendations to the British Government. Delegates wanted to have private discussions on this part of the statement, and the Conference adjourned till the next day.[11]

When the Conference met the next morning, Jinnah maintained a

[8] Wavell to Amery, (T), 25 June 1945, *TOP*, vol. 5, pp. 1155–6.
[9] Wavell to Amery, 25 June 1945, Ibid., p. 1157.
[10] Wavell to Amery, (T), 26 June 1945, Ibid., pp. 1162–4. Also Wavell to Amery, (T), 26 June 1945, Ibid., pp. 1164–5.
[11] Wavell to Amery, (T), 26 June 1945, Ibid., p. 1165.

rigid attitude and refused to see Azad. The Congress reiterated that they would not accept the League's demand for the exclusion of Congress Muslims. Khizar, meanwhile, was apprehensive that the Congress and the League would strike a bargain which would include the substitution of a Congress–League ministry for the Unionist ministry in the Punjab. The proposals would be 'disastrous' for the Punjab if a Punjabi Muslim independent of the League were not included in the Council. Khizar's fear reflected the likelihood that a League–Congress settlement at the Centre would change the balance of power in the provinces.

The critical point of the Conference had now been reached, and, for Wavell, the main stumbling-block was the attitude of Jinnah, that is, his claim to nominate all Muslim members.[12] The attitude of the Congress 'so far has been conciliatory and reasonable'. Wavell did not expect trouble from the Sikhs and Depressed Classes.[13] When the Conference met on 29 June, it was clear that the parties had failed to agree. So Wavell decided to take the initiative himself, and asked the parties to submit lists of their nominees for the Executive Council. The Congress agreed to submit a list which would include members of all communities. The Viceroy agreed to a suggestion by Khizar that the lists should be submitted secretly to him. Jinnah said he would consult his Working Committee, and Wavell feared that he 'may decline to submit a list at all'.[14]

Reports from the provinces suggested that Jinnah was under pressure from Muslim Leaguers not to break up the Conference. Saadullah and Nazimuddin were dependent on Congress support; Liaqat was anxious to take office.[15] In the NWFP, 50 per cent of educated Muslims did not think Jinnah had the right to nominate all Muslims. Aurangzeb was discredited and with him the local Muslim League. In the Punjab, some Muslim Leaguers were keen on a Congress–League settlement and the Unionists had recently defeated the League in a by-election in the constituency of Dera Ghazi Khan.[16] By winning the by-election from Shikarpur, where he had lost to the League's candidate only a year earlier, Maula Baksh had turned the tables on the League in Sind. Dow described the

[12] Wavell to Amery, (T), 27 June 1945, Ibid., pp. 1165–6.
[13] Ibid., p. 1167.
[14] Wavell to Amery, (T), 29 June 1945, Ibid., pp. 1171–3.
[15] Wavell to Amery, 1 July 1945, Ibid., p. 1182.
[16] *Statesman*, 3 July 1945.

League's hold over Sind Muslims as 'tenuous', and thought that Hidayatullah would require little persuasion to break away from the League.[17] Jinnah's position within the party was weakened by the fact that the League did not have a majority in any province, and all provincial Leagues were riven by dissensions. "Pakistan", had, until now, failed to unite provincial Muslim leaders. Jinnah, therefore, was under great pressure from other Leaguers. He told Wavell more than once, ' "I am at the end of my tether; I ask you not to wreck the League." '

Jinnah finally refused to submit a list, on the ground that Wavell had not accepted his right to nominate all Muslim members to the Executive Council.[18] But Wavell did not want the Conference to break down 'before every possible effort has been made'. He proposed to send Amery his own list of nominees for approval. He would then show the list to Jinnah and other party leaders. If either the League or the Congress or both rejected the list he would close the Conference and disclose the names put forward by him in a broadcast.[19]

In the Cabinet, Amery supported the course of action suggested by Wavell. But other members raised objections. Simon said that Wavell's proposal was not in accordance with the original plan, according to which the parties were supposed to submit lists. Now one of the principal parties had refused to put forward any names but the Viceroy proposed to go ahead with a list of his own. Grigg thought that leaving out the League would mean that the British 'risked losing our friends without getting any security that the resultant arrangements would in fact be workable.' The Cabinet knew that the Congress had submitted a list of names, but wanted to 'avoid a situation in which the Muslim League could be held up as the one obstacle to progress.'[20] The Cabinet wanted Wavell to persuade Jinnah once again. If the latter did not agree the Cabinet wanted Wavell to report back.[21] The Cabinet were 'afraid of the whole onus of failure being thrown on Muslims'.[22] In fact, Simon,

[17] Dow to Wavell, (T), 2 July 1945, *TOP*, vol. 5, p. 1191; and *Statesman*, 3 July 1945.

[18] Jinnah to Wavell, 9 July 1945, *TOP*, vol. 5, p. 1213; note by Wavell, 8 July 1945, Ibid p. 1208.

[19] Wavell to Amery, 9 July 1945, *TOP*, vol. 5, p. 1214.

[20] Cabinet C.M. (45) 13th Conclusions, minute 9, Ibid., p. 1222.

[21] Amery to Wavell, (T), 10 July 1945, Ibid., pp. 1223–4.

[22] Amery to Wavell, 10 July 1945, (T), Ibid., p. 1224.

Grigg and Butler all wanted the proposals to break down: Grigg felt that Amery was only concerned in selling four hundred million Indians 'to a handful of greedy Hindu industrialists.'[23] This provoked Wavell to point out that given British undertakings to India 'I do not see how we can now take a high moral line and say that we will hand over only to people of whose motives we approve.' The League and the Congress were the most important parties, and 'I do not see how we can disregard either or both of them any more than you could disregard the Conservative and Labour Parties at home'.[24]

Jinnah emerged victorious at Simla. On 11 July, Wavell showed him his list. It was rejected by Jinnah although Wavell had gone as far as he could to meet Jinnah 'even at the risk of alienating Congress by excluding Nationalist Muslims who are particularly disliked by the League'.[25] Wavell included the names of 4 Muslim Leaguers and a Unionist Muslim. But Jinnah refused even to discuss the names unless he could be given the absolute right to select all Muslims and some guarantee that any decision which the Muslims opposed in the Council could only be passed by a two-thirds majority—in fact a kind of communal veto. Wavell told him these conditions were entirely unacceptable.[26]

Wavell decided to close the conference. The Cabinet did not want his provisional list to leak out,[27] so he could not show his list to other leaders as he had wanted to. He would simply tell them its communal and party composition and say that the League felt unable to accept them. At the last meeting of the conference on 14 July, Jinnah claimed parity inside the Council '*with all other parties combined*. If he really meant this', commented Wavell, 'it shows that he had never at any time an intention of accepting the offer, and it is difficult to see why he came to Simla at all.'[28]

Congress leaders were understandably bitter at Wavell's decision to close the conference. Within a week of their release from prison and able to cope with strenuous work only with difficulty, they had

[23] Amery to Wavell, (T), 11 July 1945, Ibid., pp. 1228–9.
[24] Wavell to Amery, 22 July 1945, Ibid., pp. 1290–1.
[25] Wavell to Amery, (T), 11 July 1945, Ibid., pp. 1224–6.
[26] Ibid.
[27] Cabinet C.M. (45) 14th conclusions, Minute 5, 12 July 1945, Ibid., p. 1235.
[28] Wavell, *Journal*, entry for 14 July 1945, p. 155. Italics in original. Also Wavell to Amery, (T), 14 July 1945, *TOP*, vol. 5, pp. 1247–8.

accepted Wavell's invitation to Simla. They had submitted their list to Wavell, but he had never shown them his and given them an opportunity to express an opinion on it. In his interview with Azad, Wavell had not raised any objection to any name on the Congress list. Jinnah's refusal to submit a list was for the Viceroy sufficient ground to wind up the conference. 'The Working Committee found themselves helpless in the face of this extraordinary attitude of the Viceroy . . . The Conference as a whole had no say in the matter at any stage'.[29] In Congress eyes, the conference could not have succeeded so long as the British gave 'one party the power to veto all effort'. The Congress Working Committee never learned that the directive not to embarrass Jinnah came from the war cabinet. Gandhi did not deny that Wavell had made an honest attempt to break the political deadlock, but his pithy comment on the Viceroy's ending the conference was that ' "An honest attempt should have ended honestly".'[30]

As in the case of the Desai–Liaqat Pact of January 1945, it is significant that the Congress accepted the principle of parity as a temporary expedient to get into a coalition government, with the Act of 1935 still holding sway. Not even the British accepted the League's claim to a monopoly of the Muslim nominations to the executive council. But the war cabinet destroyed their own initiative partly because they were averse to any political liberalization—Churchill had agreed to it because he was advised of its inevitable failure[31]—partly because their dislike of the Congress was at once too intense and petty to allow that party to wear a halo. To say that Jinnah's demand killed Wavell's attempts to reconstruct the executive council[32] implies that the British had no possibility of salvaging their efforts to ease the political stalemate. The options *were* discussed by them; they considered Jinnah's claims unfounded and wrong, but they chose to let him get away with it.

As for Jinnah, it is doubtful that he ever wanted a settlement.

[29] Draft letter from Azad to Wavell, 14 July 1945, AICC file no. G-58, 1945–6, pp. 30–1. The letter was not sent, but it reveals the frustration and disappointment of Congress leaders.

[30] Quoted by Pyarelal, *Mahatma Gandhi: The Last Phase*, vol. 1, part 1, p. 132. Pyarelal was Gandhi's personal secretary and one of his closest companions.

[31] Cabinet meetings, 31 May and 8 June 1945, CAB 65/33.

[32] R. J. Moore, 'Jinnah and the Pakistan Demand', *Modern Asian Studies*, 17, 4, 1983, p. 550.

Khaliquzzaman and Nazimuddin told Francis Mudie, the Home Member, that Jinnah was anxious to get out of the whole thing. Quite apart from his right to nominate, he was afraid that if the League came into a central government they might have to take action that would prejudice their Pakistan demand.[33] Jinnah's obduracy was received with mixed feelings in different quarters. In the UP and the NWFP, the League thought its action had been welcomed. Many educated Muslims and the Sind and the Punjab Leagues were disappointed at the breakdown.[34]

The Elections of 1945–6

The elections in Britain in July 1945 brought the Labour party into power. Congress circles expected quick action from the new government,[35] but Labour's desire to settle the Indian problem did not necessarily mean that they were in any hurry to end the empire. It did, however, accept the recommendation of a Governors' Conference held in Delhi on 1–2 August that elections to the provincial and central legislatures should be held in the coming winter: the Governors agreed unanimously that an official government could not solve post-war problems.[36] On 21 August Wavell announced that the elections would take place. What gave the elections immense significance was Attlee's statement in Parliament on 11 September; that the 'broad definition of British policy contained in the Declaration of 1942 . . . stands in all its fullness and purpose'. Wavell would undertake discussions with new representatives in the provincial legislatures to ascertain whether it was acceptable or whether some alternative or modified scheme would be preferable. Their election would be followed by positive steps to set up a constituent assembly which would frame a new constitution.[37] Obviously, the imminence of the British departure was clear to all parties and sections of public opinion, though the British government had not fixed a date for it, or even declared it to be an immediate aim of policy.

[33] Enclosure to Mudie to Jenkins, 16–17 July 1945, *TOP*, vol. 5, p. 1269.

[34] Dow to Wavell, 17 July 1945, L/P&J/5/261;FR for Punjab for first half of July, HP file no. 18/7/45.

[35] Government of India, Information and Broadcasting Department to Secretary of State (T), 1 August 1945, *TOP*, vol. 6, p. 1.

[36] Governors' Conference, 1–2 August 1945, Ibid., pp. 3–4 and 23.

[37] Pethick-Lawrence to Wavell, (T), 18 September 1945, Ibid., pp. 270–1.

If the Cripps offer stood as the basis of British policy, it meant that the right of provinces to opt out of an Indian Union stood with it. For Jinnah, it was necessary, if he had any hope of achieving a sovereign Pakistan, to get a majority in the legislatures in the Muslim majority provinces. Wavell knew that Jinnah attached 'more importance to the number of seats the League can win both in the Central Assembly and in the Provincial Assemblies than to the ability of the League to form Ministries in the Muslim majority provinces'.[38] The League must also win the support of the Muslim masses, especially in the Punjab and Bengal, where a plebiscite might eventually be necessary to decide the case for Pakistan. Thus, the 'immediate and paramount issues' before Jinnah were Pakistan and to make good the League's claim to represent the Muslims of India.[39]

Jinnah's task was not easy. The League organization in most places was poor; the leaders were mostly men of some social standing and did not bother themselves with mass contacts and local committees.[40] Mamdot, for example, had not allowed mass contact committees on his estate.[41] In the NWFP, the League was divided and lacked funds. Aurangzeb stood discredited because of the corrupt methods he had used to retain himself in power. In Sind, the provincial League was riven by factions. In Bengal, the tussle between Nazimuddin and Suhrawardy culminated in the former not being given the League ticket for the elections.[42]

Nevertheless, Jinnah appears to have been able to assert his authority over the provincial Leagues. The Central Parliamentary Board of the League had the final say in the selection of candidates for the provincial and central legislatures.[43] In Sind, G.M. Syed's

[38] Wavell to Pethick-Lawrence, 5 November 1945.

[39] *Dawn*, 31 August 1945. Jinnah must have taken Attlee's statement at its face value: he could not have known of the reasons behind it. For the discussions which led to Attlee's statement, see Cabinet India and Burma Committee meetings on 29 August 1945, *TOP*, vol. 6, pp. 173–80; 31 August 1945, Ibid., pp. 188–90; 3 September 1945, Ibid., pp. 202–209; and 6 September 1945, Ibid., pp. 225–30.

[40] Wavell to Amery, 12 August 1945, *TOP*, vol. 6. p. 59.

[41] Khan Rab Nawaz Khan to Jinnah, 25 March 1943, *Jinnah papers*, quoted by I.A. Talbot, 'The 1946 Punjab Elections', *Modern Asian Studies*, 14, 1, 1980, p. 68.

[42] Cunningham to Wavell, 9 October 1945, L/P&J/5/222; Dow to Wavell, 20 September 1945, L/P&J/5/261; Casey to Wavell, 10 September 1945, R/3/2/56.

[43] *Quarterly Survey of the Political and Constitutional Position of the British in India*, nos. 34 and 35, L/WS/1/1559.

group were not given any tickets, which stirred them to put up their own candidates against Jinnah's in every constituency.[44] Jinnah got his way in the Punjab as well. The provincial League was divided; and most provincial Leaguers did not want Firoz Khan Noon, who had resigned from the Viceroy's executive in October to contest the elections in the Punjab, to stand as the League's candidate for Rawalpindi. They regarded him as an outsider and were afraid that he would take the credit for the League's success in the Punjab. That he was nevertheless allowed to contest from Rawalpindi at Jinnah's bidding[45] points to the increasing authority Jinnah had come to exercise over the provincial League since the break with Khizar in June 1944.

That the AIML was able for the first time to have the final say in the selection of candidates suggests that it was expanding its own organization instead of relying entirely on provincial Muslim Leagues or parties; and that it also had its own provincial machinery. In the Punjab, for example, the League's Committee of Action had started propaganda to popularize the party even before Khizar's expulsion from it. Permanent paid workers were employed to carry out propaganda in the rural areas, and a centre was set up in Lahore to train volunteers and to employ members of the Punjab Muslim Students Federation during their vacations. The Committee of Action moved its office to Lahore in May 1944 and Liaqat Ali Khan, then General Secretary of the League, supervised the organization of propaganda, which included preaching in mosques. The stake the AIML had in the province is illustrated by the fact that it donated half the money for the party's activities in the Punjab; the rest was raised by the provincial League.[46] It was when Jinnah had his own machinery in the provinces, that "Pakistan" was popularized. It could be used to brand provincial Muslim politicians who were lukewarm or opposed to it as traitors to Islam, and it could suggest that the League was the only party offering a guarantee of political

[44] *Statesman*, 3, 5 and 9 January 1946 and 1 February 1946. That the majority of Syed's candidates were defeated was a personal triumph for Jinnah.

[45] Firoz Khan Noon, *From Memory* (Lahore, 1966), pp. 184–90.

[46] This account is based on FR for Punjab for first and second half of May 1944, HP file no. 18/5/44, and Glancy to Wavell, 8 May 1944, *TOP*, vol. 4, pp. 953–6. On the organization, powers and functions of the MLWC, Committee of Action and Central Parliamentary Board, see K.B. Sayeed, *Pakistan: The Formative Phase*, pp. 184–196.

security and opportunity at the all-India level; where decisions on the political future of India would be taken.

In the Punjab, the brunt of the League's attack was directed against the Unionists. The party had ruled the province since 1920, and had successfully countered the influence of both the Congress and the Muslim League. It was not easy for the League to fight through the maze of power and influence that the Unionists had built up in the last twenty odd years. Writing in *Dawn* on 2 September, a League sympatizer observed that panchayat officers in most cases were nominees or relatives of Unionist MLAs. The Unionists represented the jagirdars, honorary magistrates and government grantees. Therefore, the bureaucracy and aristocracy were dependent on each other, and their influence over the peasants had been demonstrated in the elections of 1937, The success of the League would not come

> 'by working in the top strata of the Punjab Muslims alone . . . the League should work from the bottom upwards. The villager must be contracted (sic) by mass propaganda . . . the Congress was successful in the U.P. not because it won over the landlords but . . . because it made the peasantry class conscious.'[47]

It was in this tactic that the cry for Pakistan could be made most effective. The Punjab League's election manifesto was believed to have been drawn up by G. Adhikari, a Communist leader, and touched up by Jinnah.[48] In December 1944, Muslim Leaguers in the province were being told to associate with Communists to draw on their supporters.[49] Since 1944, the Communists themselves had decided to infiltrate the Congress, League and the Akalis and were working among the Muslim masses with "Pakistan" as their slogan, which may be taken as an indication of its popular appeal. The Communist contribution to the League's victory in the elections cannot yet be ascertained from the material available. Not that their part in drawing up the League's manifesto implies any significant Communist or radical influence within the League. Landlords were the largest single group within the provincial and all India Leagues, though a struggle between them and more radical elements may

[47] 'Need for All-Out Effort in the Punjab', by 'A Punjab Peasant', *Dawn*, 2 September 1945.

[48] FR for Punjab for second half of November 1944, HP file no. 18/11/44 and *Civil and Military Gazette*, 8 November 1944.

[49] FR for Punjab for first half of December 1944, HP file no. 18/12/44.

have been taking place in the party.[50] But if the manifesto was drawn up by them with Jinnah's knowledge, it shows the lengths to which he was prepared to go to win the majority of Muslim votes in the Punjab and to oust the Unionists.

The Unionists—and their British supporters—were attacked on any pretext which presented itself. The Unionist decision not to contest any seat for the Central Assembly gave rise to the League's argument that if the central elections were beyond their scope of work, their demand for a seat in the Viceroy's executive was also not within their sphere of action. *Dawn* editorialized about

> 'the disreputable caucus known as the Unionist Ministry of the Punjab. That reactionary junta who has long fattened on the ignorance of the Punjab masses and traded on the latter's dread of the bureaucracy . . . Most shamefully servile of all Indian Ministries, the Khizr Cabinet had learned to depend upon the support of permanent officials through whom it bestowed patronage for its own nefarious political and personal ends.'[51]

Wavell's favourable reference to the Unionists even induced Jinnah to proclaim: 'When we fight for Pakistan we are fighting against the British and not against the Hindus.'[52] Muslim Leaguers alleged official interference in favour of the Unionists and the provincial League passed a resolution demanding the dismissal of the ministry and the 'liquidation' of bureaucratic machinery. Glancy declined a demand by the provincial League to issue a communique assuring voters that the provincial election would be entirely free from official interference.[53] This only intensified attacks on the Unionists and the British by the Muslim League.

Evidence of official interference and pressure comes from both League and British sources. Campaigning in Mamdot's constituency, a League worker asked Jinnah for one lakh rupees from the League's central fund as official pressure was 'too much'.[54] The British Deputy Commissioner in Attock wrote to his parents that Khizar was sympathetic to his application for leave.

[50] Sayeed, *Pakistan: The Formative Phase*, p. 207; and W.C. Smith, *The Muslim League*, 1942–1943 (Lahore, 1945), pp 25–6.

[51] *Dawn*, 2 December 1945. [52] *Dawn*, 29 December 1945.

[53] *Civil and Military Gazette*, 11 December 1945.

[54] Amiruddin to Jinnah, 28 January 1946. S. Jafri, (ed.) *Qaid-e-Azam Jinnah's Correspondence with Punjab Muslim Leaders*, pp. 37–8.

> 'Actually, certain interested parties—which I think includes the Premier—want me to get out of Attock as I am not prepared to swing the Elections for the Unionist Party (which is the party in power).'[55]

Again, the Deputy Commissioner of Lyallpur reported that 'nearly 80 per cent' of the subordinate Muslim staff, both revenue and District Board had active League sympathies and a large number of them had been used as instruments by the League for submitting false and forged applications of Muslim League voters. Official interference inspite of Government instructions regarding neutrality in the matter 'is largely on the side of the League rather than the Unionist Party.'[56] As it turned out, the League achieved its greatest victories in constituencies where it had made the strongest allegations about official interference.[57] Earlier, Glancy expressed the view that the Unionists suffered 'at least as much' as any other party from the activities of officials who were not impartial.[58]

The defection of 30 Muslim Unionists to the League since 1944 made the League's task easier, but it did not imply a walkover for the League in the provincial elections. The ex-Unionists included Daultana, Mamdot, and Ghazanfar Ali, all big landlords. At the beginning of October 1945, Major Mumtaz Tiwana, the biggest Tiwana landowner and one of the pillars of the Tiwana tribe, joined the League.[59] He was followed by Firoz Khan Noon, who resigned from the Viceroy's Council to work for the League and to counter the influence of Khizar, who was his cousin.[60] Families were divided—would Muslims vote for Khizar or Mumtaz? And who would win when two candidates of great social and religious influence were pitted against each other—for example, Mustafa Shah Jilani and his Unionist opponent, Makhdum Murid Husain Qureshi? The Qureshis claimed descent from the Muslim saint Bahauddin, the hereditary guardian of the shrines of Bahauddin, who was said to have descended lineally from Hasham, the grandfather of the Prophet. One of his brothers was a *Sajjad Nashin*; Murid Husain himself was President of the *Zamindara* League. The Jilanis came from Jilan in Persia, had enjoyed a grant of

[55] Allan Arthur to his parents, 15 October 1945, *Allan Arthur Papers*.
[56] Glancy to Wavell, 1 December 1945, L/P&J/5/248.
[57] Glancy to Wavell, 28 February 1946, L/P&J/5/249.
[58] Glancy to Wavell, 2 February 1946, Ibid.
[59] *Statesman*, 4 October 1945.
[60] F.K. Noon, *From Memory*, p. 184.

Rs. 12,500 from the Mughals, and were regarded as one of the most influential families in Multan.[61] Mamdot was opposed by Mohammad Ghulam Sarwar, who belonged to an important landowning family of Ferozepur district, and was also a *pir*. The influence of Daultana in Multan was offset by Major Ashiq Husain, regarded by his followers as a hereditary saint. With many men of influence pitted as candidates against each other, social influence could not have been the decisive factor in the League's win in the Punjab in 1946. It may have counted where a candidate of influence was set up against one with less influence or a political unknown. But it must also be remembered that the Punjab was not a province of many big landlords—most of the landed classes in the province comprised of small peasant proprietors. It was to them the League had addressed its appeal since November 1944. But it was not before November 1945 that the provincial League set up branches in *tehsils*.[62] The League's entry into the villages, then, occurred at a very late stage; only three months before the polling for the provincial elections took place in the Punjab.

Even so, the organization of the League was much better than that of the Unionists. The calm in the Unionist headquarters in Lahore was explained by the secretary of the Unionist Party thus:

> 'We are a rural party . . . . We do not believe in public meetings . . . . Our men go to villages and talk to local notables who wield influence over voters. They explain to them the work we have done and the benefits our legislation has conferred on peasants. Villagers, we know, will follow them.'

His remarks accounted for the difference in the propaganda technique of the two parties. The League held forty to fifty meetings a day all over the province. The Unionist Party's average was 'not even one a day'.[63] Almost a statement a day was issued from the League office in Lahore, criticizing the government or explaining their stand on one thing or another. Ghazanfar Ali used to preside over a daily round table conference with a European cartoonist and a number of journalists working for the League.

It was in the countryside that the issue was to be decided, for only 12 of the 85 Muslim seats were allotted to the urban areas. The game

[61] L. Griffin, *Chiefs and Families of Note in the Punjab*, vol. 2 (Lahore, 1940), pp. 374–9 and 396–7.

[62] FR for Punjab for first half of November 1945, HP file no. 18/11/45.

[63] *Statesman*, 24 November 1945.

was tough; at the beginning of February 1946, the League and the Unionists were reportedly running neck and neck in the villages.[64] In some constituencies a voter was alleged to be richer by almost half a year's income if he pledged his vote. It was estimated that over 15 *crores* had changed hands during the elections, which were certainly not a poor man's show. In some constituencies they cost 7 to 10 *lakhs* of rupees. There were cases of whole villages pledging themselves to the highest bidder.[65] Paper, petrol and transport played an exceptionally important part in the Punjab elections, and prices of buses soared. Most of the 100 trucks ordered by the League in December 1945[66] were used in the Punjab to cart their potential voters from distant villages to polling booths. The *Statesman* commented that the success or failure of a candidate could depend on his ability to provide transport. 'This is particularly true of rural areas where promise of a joyride is all the price one need pay for a voter.'[67]

Students, politicians, and *ulema* carried out religious propaganda for the League. Politicians would often preach in mosques after the Friday prayers.[68] Students had earlier campaigned against Unionists who had cooperated with the National Defence Council in 1941.[69] Aligarh Muslim University started a special election training camp for students in August 1945,[70] and more than one thousand students worked for the League in the Punjab and Sind alone. Student leaders were in constant touch with Jinnah.[71] Their youthful idealism may have made them more reliable than some party politicians as propagandists for the League. Ali Ahmad Faziel, a League worker writing in *Dawn*, was especially keen that college students be trained as party workers in different areas. The League would provide at least one trained worker for every 1000 voters; therefore at least 800 chief workers would have to be trained, and every constituency was to have 'at least' 12 such workers. A minimum of six of these workers should belong to the constituency in which they would campaign for the League, and in addition an equal number of outside workers.

[64] *Civil and Military Gazette*, 4 February 1946.
[65] *Civil and Military Gazette*, 8 February 1946.
[66] *Dawn*, 21 December 1945. [67] *Statesman*, 18 December 1945.
[68] *Dawn*, 2 October 1945.
[69] K.B. Sayeed, *Pakistan: The Formative Phase*, p. 290.
[70] *Dawn*, 30 August 1945.
[71] Sayeed, *Pakistan: The Formative Phase*, p. 290.

The headquarters of the constituency would act as the link between the provincial committees and individual field workers. They would be assisted in everyday affairs by the League's National Guard. Muslim League newspapers put students in the 'vanguard' of the League's election campaign in the Punjab. Daultana declared that in many districts in Multan division, student workers had been able to turn the tide in favour of the League.[72]

Now that the League was expanding its organization into the countryside, it was able to exploit the religious appeal of Pakistan effectively, and its propaganda was based on the identification of Pakistan with Islam. For example, Firoz Khan Noon openly preached that a vote cast for the League was a vote in favour of the Prophet.[73] Omar Ali Siddiqi, leader of the Aligarh Election Delegation to the Punjab declared that 'the battle of the Karbala is going to be fought again in this land of the five rivers.'[74] A poster issued in Urdu over the signature of Raja Khair Mehdi Khan, the League candidate in Jhelum district, asked Muslims to choose between 'Din' and 'Dunya'; in the 'battle of righteousness and falsehood.'

Din	*Dunya*
On one side is your belief in the Almighty and your conscience	On the other side you are offered squares and *jagirs*
Righteousness and faithfulness are on one side	The other side has to offer *Lambardaris* and *Zaildaris*
One side is the rightful cause	On the other is *Sufedposhi*
One side has Pakistan for you	The other has *Kufristan* (reign of infidels)
On the one side is the problem of saving Muslims from slavery of Hindus	As opposed to this there is only the consideration of personal prestige of one man
On one side you have to bring together all those who recite the *Kalima* (the basis of Islam)	On the other is Baldev Singh and Khizar Hyat

[72] *Dawn*, 4 January 1946.
[73] Glancy to Wavell, 27 December 1945, L/P&J/5/248.
[74] *Dawn*, 19 December 1945.

On the one side is the consideration of the unity and brotherhood of all Muslims	On the other side is the *Danda* (big stick) of bureaucracy and terror of officialdom
On the one side are the lovers of Muslim League and Pakistan	On the other are the admirers of Congress and Unionists
On the one side is the honour of the Green Banner	On the other is the Government of Khizar Ministry

. . . for the sake of your religion, you have now to decide in the light of your strength of faith, to vote for . . .’[75]

Ulema from the UP, Punjab, Bengal and Sind and local *pirs* threatened Muslims with excommunication; which included a refusal to allow their dead to be buried in Muslim graveyards and a threat to debar them from joining in mass Muslim prayers, if they did not vote for the League. Those who opposed the League were denounced as infidels, and copies of the Holy Quran were carried around ‘as an emblem peculiar to the Muslim league’.[76]

The religious appeal of Pakistan was admitted by Khizar when he declared that the Unionists were for Pakistan; that Muslims would be voting for Pakistan whether they voted for a Muslim League candidate or a Muslim Unionist.[77] The banners flown on the election camps of the Unionists and League were an identical green, bearing the Muslim legend of the Crescent.[78] Khizar was on the defensive and lacked conviction in adding that intercommunal cooperation was necessary in the Punjab. The Unionists argued that the crucial electoral issue for voters was *not* Pakistan, to which the Unionists were already committed; the choice was

> ‘between chaos, disorder and communal bitterness on the one side, which is the only prospect held out by the Muslim League group, and a stable and efficient administration offered by the Unionists in the interests of the masses to which the majority of the Muslims of the province belong.’[79]

[75] Translation enclosed in Glancy to Wavell, 28 February 1946, L/P&J/5/249. I have italicized some non-English terms.

[76] Glancy to Wavell, 27 December 1945, L/P&J/5/248. See also Glancy to Wavell, 16 January and 2 February 1946, L/P&J/5/249.

[77] *Statesman*, 28 October 1945.

[78] *Civil and Military Gazette*, 8 February 1946.

[79] *Statesman*, 28 October 1945.

The election manifesto of the Unionist Party stressed the economic achievements of the ministry including the reduction of the agricultural debt by two *crores* of rupees. Provincial autonomy, complete independence, free and compulsory primary education for the poor, a reduction in military expenditure were the party's aims.[80] But the economic achievements of the Unionists seem to have had little influence on the Punjabi Muslim voter in 1946.

That Khizar's Pakistan, implying intercommunal cooperation, was rejected so decisively by the Muslim voter points to the success of the communal propaganda of the League and to the appeal of a communal Pakistan for Muslims. But though the cry for Pakistan had now become the most successful means of politicizing the Muslim masses, it is by no means clear what they understood by it. Statements by Punjab Leaguers based precisely on Jinnah's definition of Pakistan as a sovereign state[81] are hard to find, as are statements opposed to it or even a discussion on Pakistan as part of a federation. To most Leaguers in 1945–6, Pakistan appears to have stood for some sort of general salvation from Hindu domination and symbolized and Islamic revival in India.

What counted most in the League's victory in the Punjab in 1945–6? The great effort it made; the fact that for the first time the League's organization had reached down to contact the Muslim voter, partly accounted for its win. The appeal was essentially religious and attempted to convince Muslims of the benefits of Pakistan. Propagandists were directed when they visited a village to: 'Find out its social problems and difficulties to tell them [the villagers] that the main cause of their problems was the Unionists [and] give them the solution—Pakistan'.[82] Soldiers were told that the Unionists had not done anything for them after the war.[83] For the students who campaigned for the League, Pakistan held out the promise of the resurgence of Islam—'our aim is essentially to reorientate Islam in the modern world, purge our ranks of the reactionary Muslim Church and to free ourselves from economic and political bondage'.[84] This seemed a far cry from the assurance given by Jin-

[80] *Civil and Military Gazette*, 29 November 1945.

[81] See, for example, Jinnah's reply to Patel in *Statesman*, 19 November 1945.

[82] Translation of pamphlet issued by the election board of the Punjab Muslim Students Federation, quoted by Talbot, 'The 1946 Punjab Elections'. *Modern Asian Studies*, 14, 1, 1980, p. 75.

[83] *Statesman*, 10 November 1945. [84] *Dawn*, 4 December 1945.

nah to the Pir of Manki Sharif in November 1945 that Pakistan would be based on the laws of the Quran in which the shariat would be established,[85] but it showed that Pakistan could mean, as it was intended to mean, all things to all men. S.E. Abbott, then Secretary to Khizar, attributed the League's victory to the Muslim belief in the inevitability of Pakistan.[86] The League had presented the elections as a plebiscite for Pakistan.[87] The claim had not been contradicted by the British, who would actually transfer or confer power. To that extent, their silence on the subject also contributed to the League's victory.

In Bengal, the League's influence in urban areas had been rising since its coalition with Huq in 1937. After provincial Leaguers fell out with Huq in 1941, they had organized demonstrations against him in several towns of the province. The popularity of the League in urban Bengal was evident by 1944, when Huq's Muslim candidates lost every seat in the elections to the Calcutta Corporation to the League. Radical Leaguers like Suhrawardy built up a base among Muslim labour during the League's tenure in power from 1943–5. Involved in ministerial politicking, Huq had gradually lost the rural base which had swept him into power in 1937.[88] In 1946, Bengal League candidates were personally selected by Suhrawardy and approved of by Jinnah. "Pakistan" as Bengal Leaguers presented it to their voters would consist of an autonomous Bengal and Assam, and would lead to prosperity for backward Muslims. At a Bengal League conference, Liaqat Ali Khan promised the abolition of *zamindari* without compensation—a promise which could have only won the League support of the poor Muslim peasantry of Bengal.[89] But were Bengal Leaguers thinking of the sovereign Pakistan of Jinnah's conception? It seems unlikely. Ispahani, one of Jinnah's most loyal lieutenants in Bengal, told the Governor in January 1946 that Muslims needed opportunities for self-advancement, administratively and otherwise, and Casey's 'definite

[85] Sayeed, *Pakistan: The Formative Phase*, p. 208.

[86] Letter to author, 15 February 1981.

[87] Wavell to Pethick-Lawrence, 22 October 1945, *TOP*, vol. 6, p. 377. For Pethick-Lawrence's reasons for not clarifying Whitehall's stand on the League's propaganda, see his letter to Wavell, 9 November 1945, Ibid., pp. 466–7.

[88] This paragraph is based on Sen, *Muslim Politics*, p. 127ff. See also Ispahani to Jinnah, 8 January 1942, 14 January 1942, 16 June 1942, *Jinnah–Ispahani Correspondence*, pp. 234–5, 235–7, 276 respectively.

[89] Sen, *Muslim Politics*, pp. 196–7.

impression' was that adequate safeguards would be acceptable to the Muslims. Ispahani said he realized very well that the day of small states was past, and that if the British imposed an interim government of India, which had adequate safeguards for the Muslims, it would be accepted.[90]

The League's success in Bengal and Sind can be partly accounted for by the fact that it did not face any serious, organized opposition in these provinces. Huq's party was in disarray; in Sind, no Muslim stood on the Congress ticket as this would have been fatal for any chances of victory.[91] The Congress lacked the money and organization required to contest Muslim seats in every province. The release of Congress prisoners less than three months before the elections added to their difficulties and large amounts of money were needed in the Muslim majority provinces, especially in the Punjab and Bengal, which, for the Congress, 'held the key position' in the election. But it was in these two provinces that the provincial Congress groups were riven by factions, and organizational work never really got under way.[92] Congress strategy in Muslim constituencies sometimes confounded its own supporters. For example, in Sind the Congress negotiated with the League for a coalition, even as it was fighting the League in other provinces. Azad's offer to the League of a coalition in Sind 'came as a great surprise' to Congressmen in the Punjab. Anti-League Muslims 'cannot understand these things, nor can the rest of us'.[93] The Congress allied with Nationalist Muslims, Ahrars, Momins—indeed, with any anti-League Muslim party. It carried out propaganda for Nationalist Muslims, and the League and the Congress vied with each other in the virulence of their appeals to religious loyalty. The Congress used Muslim divines in the UP and Bengal. League ministries during the war were condemned as the stronghold of the British.[94] In Bengal, Nationalist Muslims alleged that one of the 'wonders' of the League ministry during the war was the 'man-made famine' of 1943.[95] To this the

[90] Entry in Casey's Diary, 2 January 1946, *TOP*, vol. 6, p. 732.

[91] FR for Sind for second half of December 1945, HP file no.-18/12/45.

[92] Azad to Patel, 21 October 1945, Patel to Prafulla Ghosh, 26 October 1945, *PC*, vol. 2, pp. 24–5 and 122 respectively.

[93] B.S. Gilani to Patel, 10 February 1946, Ibid., pp. 301–2.

[94] See, for example, *Hindustan Standard*, 11 February 1946.

[95] *Amrita Bazar Patrika*, 29 November 1945, and 3 December 1945; *National Herald*, 26 February 1945.

League reported that Hindus, who were in a majority in the Viceroy's executive council, had refused to send food to Bengal and were therefore responsible for the famine.[96] League newspapers published reports of Hindu volunteers donning Turkish caps while campaigning for Nationalist Muslims.[97]

The League, however, had the whip-hand in Muslim religious propaganda against the Congress. The *Morning News* in Calcutta claimed that the *Jamiat-ul-ulema-i-Hind*, which campaigned for the Congress was working for *Hindiat*, while the *Jammat-i-Islami*, which supported the League, stood for the *Islamiat*.[98] The *Jammat-i-Islami* accused the *Jamiat-ul-ulema-i-Hind* of making a distinction between religious and secular matters.

> 'They remembered the prayer, but they forgot the chain of armour donned by the Prophet Muhammad when he went forth to fight the unequal battle with the infidels . . . They misled the Muslims to the unworthy tenets of *ahimsa*.'[99]

Its attempts to outdo the League in religious propaganda, without having a widespread popular base among Muslims, profited Congress little, and only contributed to the atmosphere of communal bitterness.

Only in the NWFP was the Congress successful in both Hindu and Muslim constituencies. Here, in spite of defections from the Congress to the League before the elections, the Congress was the better organized party. Aurangzeb stood discredited because of the undignified methods he had used to remain in power and was not even given a League ticket. Although the Congress and their Red Shirt allies used the religious appeal (the tri-colour was marked with the *Kalima*),[100] it was not this alone that won the election for the Congress. The Congress was successful in representing the League as a catspaw of the British. It appealed to the less well-to-do, over whom the Khans were losing their hold. Moreover, the provincial League was disorganized, and it was only on 10 December that a Committee of Action was set up. The fact that Mamdot was

[96] Congress worker (name illegible) to Sadiq Ali, 5 December 1945, AICC file no. P-24, 1945–1946, p. 28.

[97] *Morning News*, 30 November 1945.

[98] *Morning News*, 25 October 1945.

[99] *Morning News*, 28 October 1945.

[100] *Star of India*, 28 February 1946.

appointed as its convenor[101] suggests that the League found it difficult to get a reliable man from the province to head the committee.

All candidates in the NWFP attached importance to personal contacts with voters and visited individual houses or mohallas. Election officials reported a growing sense of political discipline in canvassing, addressing and organizing mass meetings. Appeals to tribal and sectional loyalties were made, but they may not have made much difference in a province where a Khan only had to declare his loyalty to the League, and his relatives would support the Congress. They would also give their tenants a free running, and it was 'a tenantry which had been primed that they would be allowed to take over the Land belonging to the Khan if the Congress came to power.'[102] The election saw a fight more on ideological than on personal grounds.[103] The League's charge that the Congress was using office to win votes was balanced by the fact that most Muslim officials had League sympathies, and even some British officers and their wives campaigned for the League.[104] Pakistan did not have much appeal for the Pathans, because, according to Cunningham, they did not think they would be dominated by the Hindus or anyone else![105]

Nevertheless, the League did not fare so badly in the province, contesting all 33 Muslim seats and winning 15. It also won the special seats reserved for landholders, none of which was contested by the Congress. The Congress won 19 Muslim seats and lost 8. Anti-League parties secured 58.75 per cent of the total Muslim vote.[106] The extent of the League's success in Muslim constituencies in 1945–6 can be gauged from the fact that it won 76 per cent of the total Muslim vote in India—a very far cry indeed from the 4.8 per cent it had obtained in 1937! Its achievements in the Punjab were remarkable: it defeated, and unseated, 57 Unionists in Muhammadan rural constituencies; the Congress in 9 rural constituencies; and swept the Ahrars from 5 urban seats. The Unionists defeated the League in only 11 rural constituencies. With a total of 62 wins in ru-

[101] *Dawn*, 11 December 1945.

[102] Caroe to Wavell, 8 May 1946, L/P&J/5/223.

[103] *Report on the General Elections to the Central Legislative Assembly and the NWFP Legislative Assembly* (Peshawar, 1946), p. 10.

[104] A. Ghaffar Khan, *My Life and Struggle* (Delhi, 1969), p. 175.

[105] Cunningham to Wavell, 27 February 1946, *TOP*, vol. 6, p. 1086.

[106] Nehru to Wavell, 8 May 1946, Reforms Office file no. 70/46/R, 1946.

ral areas, all 9 urban seats and both the women's seats, the League chalked up 73 seats in the Punjab legislature, and polled 65.10 per cent of the votes polled in Muslim constituencies.

In Bengal, it did even better, obtaining 83.6 per cent of the Muslim votes polled. The Krishak Praja party secured only 5.3 per cent, and the *Jamiat-ul-ulema* and Nationalist Muslims, both supported by the Congress, won 1.2 and 0.2 per cent of the Muslim votes polled.

The NWFP was the only province where the League failed to secure a majority of Muslim votes: anti-League parties obtained more than 58 per cent of the votes polled. Nevertheless, of the extent of the League's victory, and its appeal to Muslims, there was no doubt. The gains of the League clearly represented a turning of many Muslims from essentially provincial concerns to rally behind the only Muslim party which would take care of their interests at the all-India level, in the bargaining for the spoils of the transfer of power. The League's success also represented a solidification and politicization of the Muslim religious community, a rallying to "Pakistan", but whether that meant the victory of Jinnah's conception of a sovereign state can perhaps be questioned.

With the election results out, there arose the question of the formation of governments in the provinces. In Bengal and Sind, the League had enough seats to form ministries, but in the Punjab it needed the support of 10 more members to obtain a majority in the legislature. Here the League offered 3 portfolios to the Sikhs if they would enter a Muslim League coalition.[107] But Pakistan was the stumbling-block. The Sikhs objected to the League's insistence on Pakistan, to which the Muslim League leaders replied that the ministry came under the Act of 1935 and that all India issues did not come into question. The Sikhs retorted that there was no all India issue for them.[108] Negotiations between the League and the Congress failed because the League refused to enter into a coalition with any non-League Muslim group.[109] This was in contrast to the years before 1945, when the AIML had not always been able to prevent provincial Leagues from coalescing with non-League Muslim parties. Jinnah's authority was now apparently sufficient to prevent such coalitions. Every candidate for the elections had been selected

[107] *Statesman*, 26 February 1946.

[108] *Civil and Military Gazette*, 28 February 1946.

[109] *Statesman*, 6 and 9 March 1946.

with his approval; their victory was therefore a personal triumph for him.[110]

On 7 March, the Congress, Akalis and the Unionists formed the Punjab Coalition Party, under the leadership of Khizar. The strength of the Coalition worked out to at least 10 more than that of the League. Glancy accordingly called on Khizar as leader of the coalition to form a ministry, despite the contention of Muslim League leaders that they represented the largest individual party.

Deprived of constitutional power, the League organized demonstrations against the Ministry. Muslim students were directed by provincial League leaders to demonstrate before Khizar's residence in Lahore. Communal feeling had been strengthened by an election fought on the slogan of Pakistan; and Congress leaders advised Hindu students not to start counter-demonstrations,[111] while the League demanded Glancy's dismissal. Local Muslim Leaguers were directed 'to organize the Muslim masses to prepare them for the struggle that lies ahead. Khizar Quisling Ministry . . . is an insult to the determined will of the Mussalmans and a blot on the fair name of this Province'.[112] The Congress was condemned for joining the Unionists whom it had formerly derided as reactionaries.[113] A coalition which included so small a percentage of Muslims was a strange anomaly in the Province, especially when the party which commanded a majority of the Muslim votes found no place in the government. It did not augur well for the future.

[110] See note by 'F.M.', *TOP*, vol. 6, pp. 767–8.
[111] *Statesman*, 10 March 1946.
[112] *Eastern Times*, 13 March 1946.
[113] *Eastern Times*, 13 March 1946. On this paragraph see also Glancy to Wavell, 15 March 1946, L/P&J/5/249.

CHAPTER 5

The Cabinet Mission:

March to July 1946

If, as some scholars have suggested, the emergence of Pakistan as a sovereign state through the partition of 1947 was the inevitable result of the politicization of two intrinsic 'nations', the question of how and when that politicization occurred to make that inevitable arises. In the case of the Muslim community in the majority provinces the first essential for such a development was their unification behind the AIML, capable of focussing their political weight at the central negotiating table. In Chapter 4 a case has been made for thinking that this prerequisite was not achieved until 1945, and then the imminence of the British relinquishment of central authority appears to have contributed much to confirm the League's claim to speak for the Muslim community as a whole. But was the consolidation of the League's claim a superficial product of momentary crisis rather than a fundamental and lasting political unification of Muslim communalism? Carried to its logical extreme, such a view would suggest that Jinnah and the League adopted "Pakistan" as a mere political slogan which would draw Muslim religious sentiment behind the League's candidates and align Muslim provincial leaders and parties into conformity with its central directorate. It is, however, argued in this thesis that Jinnah and the League intended the claim to a sovereign Pakistan to be more than a bargaining lever to extract the greatest possible constitutional concessions for the Muslim community from both the British and Congress in an eventual Indian federation; and that at Simla in 1946 Jinnah played this tactic so that both the other parties had to concede Pakistan before, or when, power was transferred to Indians. It is, therefore, necessary to review the negotiations with the Cabinet mission in some detail in order to test the seriousness of purpose with which Jinnah contended for a sovereign Pakistan.

Pakistan was the issue which dominated all discussion on the political future of India at the Governors conference held in August 1945 to discuss the political fallout from Simla. Most Governors held that Jinnah should be asked to define Pakistan. His intransigence at Simla had raised his popularity among Muslims. Glancy warned that Pakistan, in its crude form, was a potent political slogan and might well carry the day. If Pakistan became an imminent reality, there would be civil war in the Punjab.[1] The election propaganda of the League in the Punjab had taken the line that 'these elections will decide whether there is to be Pakistan or not, and that if the League win in the Pakistan provinces no further vote by the legislature or plebiscite will be needed'.[2] Significantly, at least one Governor, Clow, was of the view that the British themselves had contributed to the growth of the Pakistan idea because they had given recognition to it in the constitutional proposals of 1942 without ever asking Jinnah what he meant by it.[3] Jinnah's demand at Simla that the League must be given parity with all other parties combined made it difficult for the British to make any constitutional advance without first accepting Pakistan. But, as Evan Jenkins, then Private Secretary to the Viceroy, observed, he had never defined it; and the Rajagopalachari formula had failed in its attempt to bring Jinnah out into the open. 'It failed', concluded Jenkins, 'and I do not think that any other attempt is likely to succeed at present'.[4] Wavell's wry comment on Jenkins' note was that it would 'obviously be difficult to bring Jinnah into the open over this, but we may have to try some day'.[5] Now, in October 1945, he favoured a clarification of the British stand on Pakistan. 'We clearly could not agree to permit any Province to stand out of the new constitution, or to secede at a later stage, on the result of elections to the Provincial Assembly or of a purely Muslim plebiscite'.[6] Of course, it would not be easy for the British to make such a declaration: with the present Congress attitude, the British should avoid any action which would turn the League against the Government as well.[7] The British had to balance against the advantage of reassuring the minorities the disadvantage of alienating the Muslim League. Although the denial of the claim for a Muslim plebiscite would annoy Jinnah,

[1] Glancy to Wavell, 16 August 1945, L/P&J/5/248.
[2] Wavell to Pethick-Lawrence, 22 October 1945, *TOP*, vol. 6, pp. 337–8.
[3] Enclosure to Clow to Colville, 23 August 1945, Ibid., p. 149.
[4] Note by Evan Jenkins, 23 July 1945, R/3/1/105, pp. 34–5.
[5] Handwritten note by Wavell on Jenkins' note above.
[6] Wavell to Pethick-Lawrence, 22 October 1945, *TOP*, vol. 6, p. 377.
[7] Menon to Abell, 20 November 1945, R/3/1/105, p. 119.

'it is fairer to Jinnah to deny it now than to let him assume its validity throughout the elections and tell him afterwards that we are quite unable to accept it.'[8]

Faced with the prospect of making a declaration about an issue on which it would be difficult to please either party, Pethick-Lawrence was unable even to justify a renewal of the Cripps proposals. The British, he argued, had never said they accepted Jinnah's assumption. It would be better if the British said nothing in favour of the Cripps plan as one of the parties might then refuse to enter into negotiations. The British could consider alternatives to it—for example, the right of smaller areas of a province to opt out.[9] The British Cabinet decided that the Viceroy could tell Jinnah that if Muslims insisted on self-determination in 'genuinely' Muslim areas this would be conceded. But there would be 'no question' of compelling large non-Muslim populations to remain in Pakistan against their will.[10] Pethick-Lawrence also put aside the right of provinces to opt out of an Indian union if 60 per cent of the population voted to do so in a plebiscite, as the balance of Hindu and Sikh votes would probably turn the verdict against Pakistan.[11] Pethick-Lawrence's apparent attempt at keeping all options open disclosed his desire to avoid taking a stand on any issue; indeed, the Labour government had very little idea of what constitutional settlement they could obtain in India. The British could not give up the idea either of a union government or Pakistan. They could announce that the principle of Pakistan would only be recognized after attempts to form a single constitution-making body had failed. Alternatively, they could say that no progress could be made on the basis of a union government; that if the Muslims insisted on self-determination in 'genuine' Muslim areas this would be conceded, but large non-Muslim areas would not be forced to stay in Pakistan against their will.[12] How Muslims and non-Muslims would give expression to their wishes he did not say.

Much has been made of the Labour party's commitment to Indian independence. However, a closer look at Labour's imperial attitude reveals a woolliness and illusions about decolonization which

[8] Note by Jenkins, 22 October 1945, R/3/1/105, p. 104A.
[9] Pethick-Lawrence to Wavell, 9 November 1945, *TOP*, vol. 6, pp. 466–7.
[10] Cabinet India and Burma Committee meeting, 14 January 1946, Ibid., p. 787.
[11] Note by Pethick-Lawrence, 14 February 1946, Ibid., pp. 978–9.
[12] Ibid., pp. 980–2.

blurred a commitment to empire which was as strong as that of the Conservatives. Redolent of Amery in 1943, Bevin had favoured marriages between British soldiers training in different parts of the Commonwealth and local women.[13] Attlee's desire, in January 1942, to do for India what Lord Durham did for Canada did not manifest an interest in Indian independence, for Durham only wanted to consolidate the empire by concession and reform.[14] As late as 1945, Attlee shared with the Conservatives a horror of self-government for Indians. His talks with Nehru and Krishna Menon in 1938 did not include discussion of the terms of any treaty between an Indian constituent assembly and the British, otherwise their strongly differing attitudes to any treaty provisions would have been revealed at that stage. The British knew that the Congress would never agree to foreign bases on Indian soil, while the Labour party subscribed to a widely held official British idea that a transfer of power should be conditional upon satisfactory arrangements to safeguard British economic and military interests in India. It would, of course, have been unrealistic to expect the British not to conceive the prospects the loss of empire would have on their international position. As Deputy Prime Minister in the war cabinet, Attlee asked the India Office in January 1945 to investigate how British troops could be kept on Indian soil once India received dominion status. Evidently he was contemplating treating India on a different footing from other dominions, for in those countries British troops had marched out as soon as dominion status was given.[15] Independent Labour opinion shared the dominant official desire for defence arrangements with an independent India, while Bevin's speech to the pre-election Labour party conference in May 1945 reconciled socialist revolution with empire:

> 'You will have to form a government which is at the centre of a great Empire and Commonwealth of Nations, which touches all parts of the world, and which will have to deal . . . with every race and with every difficulty, and everyone of them has a different outlook upon

[13] C. Thorne, *Allies of a Kind* (London, 1978), pp. 708–9, V. Rothwell, *Britain and the Cold War 1941–1947* (London, 1982), p. 224: See also N. Mansergh, *The Commonwealth Experience* (London, 1969), p. 402.

[14] Mansergh, *The Commonwealth Experience*, p. 38.

[15] Thorne, *Allies*, p. 640. War Cabinet India Committee paper 1(45)5, 9 January 1945, *TOP*, vol. 5, p. 381.

life . . . . Revolutions do not change geography and revolutions do not change geographical need.[16]

Following the assumption of office by the Labour party in August 1945, the priority accorded to defence emanated from the top: Attlee was Minister of Defence until December 1946. On 14 January 1946, the cabinet decided that the pledge of independence in the Cripps offer was 'not a blank cheque but had been conditional on a scheme being devised on which all parties agreed.'

> 'We had a moral responsibility not to hand over the country to Indians without being satisfied that the succession governments were fully aware of the military and economic problems which a self-governing India would have to face and that they had concerted reasonable plans to meet them . . . It was agreed that the risk . . . was that in effect we set ourselves up as the sole judge of what solution was reasonable both economically and from the defence aspect. If no solution was reached which we could regard as reasonable, logically we should continue governing India even if it involved rebellion which would have to be suppressed by British troops.'[17]

Labour's commitment to the maintenance of British power was understandably greater than its so-called commitment to Indian independence.[18] British interests were paramount; the political decision to transfer power rested on the strategical premise that Indian security required that India remain in the Commonwealth.[19] The logical conclusion of this idea should have been that if Indian security had dictated that she leave the Commonwealth, the British would not have taken any decision to transfer power! Official thinking on India's participation in imperial defence seems to have taken the line that Britain might be weakened by war; India might receive dominion status or even independence; but with India in the Commonwealth, Britain could preserve her global primacy. It has been observed that the awareness that British manpower and economic resources were barely adequate for a world role only reinforced

[16] For example, *New Statesman and Nation*, 22 March 1946, p. 149; Labour Party *Report of the Annual Conference 1945*, p. 115, quoted in P.S. Gupta, *Imperialism and the British Labour Movement 1914–1964* (London, 1975), p. 281.

[17] Cabinet India and Burma Committee meeting, 14 January 1946, *TOP*, vol. 6, pp. 788–9.

[18] As suggested, among others, by V. Brittain, *Pethick-Lawrence* (London, 1963), p. 134; and H. Tinker, *Experiment with Freedom* (Oxford, 1967), pp. 33–4.

[19] Cabinet Far Eastern Planning Committee Paper GEN 77/94, *TOP*, vol. 6, pp. 780–1.

British determination 'to reconstruct solid foundations for permanent Great Power Status'.[20] Labour's offer of independence to India was, then, conditioned by the effort to preserve *Pax Britannica*.

From August 1945 onwards, the British were also concerned over the problem of law and order. The large crowds which enthusiastically greeted political prisoners on their release from jail, the inflammatory speeches of Congress leaders against the bureaucracy, had a demoralizing effect on British officials.[21] Nehru justified his speeches by saying that he did not see how violence could be avoided, if legitimate aims could not otherwise be attained, However, Wavell noted that Nehru's attitude was 'quiet and friendly throughout', even though 'he seems to me to have reached the state of mind of a fanatic'.[22] The fact was that Congress leaders distrusted the British especially after their experience at Simla.[23] Gandhi admitted that Nehru's speeches were 'hot', but only if the British had no intention to part with power.[24]

The question of the loyalty of Indians in the armed forces and Civil Service also concerned the British keenly. Auchinleck felt that if they were honest about leaving India, there could be no justification for reinforcing the British garrison in the country save at the request of an Indian government.[25] Both he and Wavell were against trying the loyalty of Indian troops too highly in an attempt to repress their own countrymen, and advised Whitehall against using Indian troops in Indonesia. Being imbued with nationalist ideas they might not wish to suppress freedom movements elsewhere.[26]

Popular unrest at the trial of three INA officers on the charge of waging war against the King led to demonstrations and riots in Bombay, Calcutta and Delhi from November to February 1946. British officials did not know what the policy of the government

[20] Rothwell, *Britain and the Cold War* p. 3. For a fuller discussion of these points, see Anita Inder Singh, 'Imperial Defence and the Transfer of Power in India, 1946–1947', *International History Review*, November 1982, pp. 568–88.

[21] For example, Colville to Wavell, 2 November 1945; Dow to Wavell, 3 November 1945; Wavell to Pethick-Lawrence, 16 November 1945, *TOP*, vol. 6, pp. 429–30, 437–8, 488 respectively.

[22] Enclosure to Wavell to Pethick-Lawrence, 4 November 1945, Ibid., pp. 440–1.

[23] Casey to Wavell, 2 December 1945, Ibid., p. 589.

[24] Gandhi to Jenkins, 13 November 1945, Ibid., p. 481.

[25] Auchinleck to Viceroy, 22 August 1945; John Connell, *Auchinleck*, p. 792.

[26] Ibid., pp. 823–4; and Wavell to Pethick-Lawrence, 17 October 1945, *TOP*, vol. 6, p. 360.

was, and the authority of the government was being undermined.[27] The three INA men, in Nehru's words, 'became symbols of India fighting for her independence . . . The trial dramatised . . . the old contest: England versus India'.[28] Official intelligence reports noted that the situation in respect of the INA is one which warrants disquiet. There has seldom been a matter which has attracted so much Indian public interest and, it is safe to say, sympathy'. The Congress had led the outcry, but the Sikhs, who had great influence in the rural areas of Central Punjab, were organizing daily meetings where demands on behalf of the INA were voiced.[29] Muslim soldiers belonging to the INA were campaigning for the League in the elections.[30] The League, probably moved by considerations of expediency, had decided to defend Muslim officers of the INA, and the trial of Muslims was expected to make their effect on the Muslim public and the League alike. INA weeks and days were being organized in towns and villages. It was clear that sympathy for the INA 'is not the monopoly of those who are ordinarily against Government. It is equally clear that this particular brand of sympathy cuts across communal barriers . . . In many cases officers of the INA belong to influential families'.[31] There were also indications that 'majority opinion' in the Indian Armed Forces was in favour of leniency. So 'abstract justice must to some extent give way to expediency'.[32] The policy would be revised and only those accused of murder and brutality would be brought to trial, and in future the charge of waging war against the king would be dropped.[33] Auchinleck, with his knowledge of the men he had commanded, wrote that the pleasure and relief which followed the commutation of the sentences on the three officers were born of the conviction that confirmation of the sentences would have resulted in violent internal conflict.

[27] FR for Bengal for second half of January 1946, HP file no. 18/1/46.

[28] Nehru, quoted in Connell, *Auchinleck*, p. 810.

[29] Note prepared by Intelligence Bureau, enclosed in Government of India, Home Department to Secretary, Political Department, India Office, 20 November 1945, *TOP*, vol. 6, pp. 512–13, referred to hereafter as Intelligence Bureau note.

[30] *Star of India*, 28 January 1946.

[31] Intelligence Bureau note, *TOP*, vol. 6, pp. 513–4.

[32] Governor General (War Department) to Secretary of State, Ibid., p. 572.

[33] Auchinleck to Wavell, 22 January 1946, and Wavell to Auchinleck, 23 January 1946, quoted in Connell, *Auchinleck*, pp. 812–13.

> 'This feeling does not . . . spring universally from the idea that the convicted officers were trying to rid India of the British and therefore, to be applauded, whatever crimes they might commit, but from a generally genuine feeling that they were patriots and nationalists and that, even if they were misled they should be treated with clemency, as true sons of India. In this connexion, it should be remembered . . . that *every* Indian worthy of the name is today a "Nationalist", though this does not mean that he is necessarily "anti-British" . . . . It is no use shutting one's eyes to the fact that any Indian officer worth his salt is a "Nationalist".'[34]

With political and economic unrest on the rise, a conciliatory gesture was needed to placate Indian opinion, and the result was the Labour government's decision to send the cabinet mission to India.[35] But even as the cabinet decided to send a ministerial team to discuss the transfer of power, it had not, as we have seen, ruled out repression as a political alternative if that proved necessary to secure British interests. Earlier, the cabinet had considered a suggestion by Auchinleck to increase the size of the British garrison in India. Indian opposition to such a move was anticipated, and was sought to be countered with the deception tactic that the troops were really in India for a short spell of training before they left for Indonesia![36] But in February 1946, two things led the Labour government to change its mind. First, on 4 February, the Chiefs of Staff reported that British troops could not be moved from the Middle or Far East without seriously disrupting the British position in those areas. At home, demobilization was apace, and the shortage of manpower was 'forcing' the Cabinet Defence Committee to make reductions with the result that 'we are now left with an irreducible minimum in all areas where our commitments continue'.[37]

The crumbling imperial military base was signalled further by the mutinies of the Royal Indian Air Force and Royal Indian Navy in January and February 1946. The mutinies came without any warning to the British. Although the Air Force mutiny was quickly suppressed, in the naval mutiny the strikers captured twenty British

[34] Ibid., pp. 945 and 949.

[35] India and Burma Committee meetings on 19 November 1945 and 14 January 1946, CAB 134/341 and 342 respectively; Pethick-Lawrence to Wavell, 21 November 1945 and cabinet paper, 22 November 1945, *TOP*, vol. 6, pp. 516–17 and 522–3 respectively; cabinet meeting, 22 January 1946, CAB 128/5.

[36] Auchinleck to Chiefs of Staff, 22 December 1945 and 18 January 1946. Cabinet Defence Committee meeting, 11 Jan. 1946, *TOP*, vol. 6.

[37] Alanbrooke to Auchinleck, (T), 4 February 1946, L/WS/1/1008, Ibid., p. 120.

ships in Bombay[38] and in Karachi, they retaliated with the ships' guns after British troops opened fire.[39] Congress, League, and occasionally Communist flags flew side by side in Bombay, where industrial labour also joined the strike.[40] Congress and League leaders did not incite the mutineers—they used their influence to bring the strikes to an end.[41] But racial sentiment was now very strong, and with the loyalty of the armed forces in doubt, the British now thought of constitutional expedients to avert violence.

This, then, was the background to the Cabinet Mission, which arrived in India on 14 March 1946. Its aim, as described by Attlee, was to get machinery set up for framing the constitutional structure in which Indians will have 'full control of their own destiny and the formation of a new interim government'.[42]

The Mission noted that their administrative weakness did not make it possible for the British to face the situation 'with the same confidence as in the past owing to doubt whether the forces behind law and order' were reliable. 'They felt this lack of confidence for the first time'. If the negotiations failed and the armed forces had to be called in, they must be certain that they 'will not be handed over to those whom they have had to suppress'. Although it would be difficult to give any set undertaking of support, it would be necessary if their support was to be obtained. 'The general conclusion from this was that negotiations must succeed and we must refuse to permit a breakdown'.[43] Nor could the British impose a solution. For 'the hookum principle . . . ceases to apply if the authority issuing the hookum is forthwith going to step down from the gadi'.[44]

The consequences of a failure of negotiations seized much of the attention of British officials in India and in the India Office. They realized that an attempt by the Congress to paralyse communications and the administration would be successful, even if the police and armed forces remained loyal. In any case, the services would be

[38] *Statesman*, 20 February 1946. [39] *Statesman*, 22 February 1946.

[40] *Times of India*, 23 February 1946.

[41] Mudie to Wavell, 27 February 1946, L/P&J/5/252. See also Colville to Wavell, 27 February 1946, L/P&J/5/167.

[42] Cabinet delegation to Cabinet Office, (T), 25 March 1946, *TOP*, vol. 7, p. 6.

[43] Note of meeting between Cabinet delegation and Viceroy's Executive Council on 26 March 1946, Ibid., p. 7.

[44] Croft to Monteath, 1 April 1946, Ibid., pp. 73–4.

unlikely to remain 100 per cent staunch. Some sections of the Air Force, Navy and Signals units might mutiny. There were chances of a mutiny by the police as well. For their part, British officers were weary and depressed. Indian officers were naturally looking over their shoulders and ahead. Communal antagonism was developing among them and over wide areas they would fail to stand up to a severe test.[45]

The British favoured a transfer of power to a united India, which would keep the army undivided, and be of the greatest advantage to them strategically. In considering the military implications of their future policy with regard to India, they had to bear in mind that in any future war their strategic requirements in India were that they should be in a position to have recourse to her industrial and manpower potential and to use her territory for operational and administrative bases. It was therefore important that India should be secure from external aggression and internal disorder. For defence purposes, 'it is essential' that she should remain a single unit.[46] Neither the League nor the Congress was told about these intentions. Partition would destroy the homogeneity of the Indian army and would be resorted to 'if the only alternative is complete failure and consequent chaos'. If it had to be adopted, 'every effort should be made to obtain agreement for some form of central defence council to be set up which will include not only Pakistan, Hindustan and the Indian States, but also Burma and Ceylon'.[47] The British were, however, anxious that both parties accept a settlement. The Congress might not want to stay in the Commonwealth at all; Pakistan, if formed, could remain in it, but would be economically and militarily unviable.[48] If the Congress alone made a settlement with the British, the British would be bound to support the Congress in dealing with any Muslim disturbances which eventuated.[49] With a British decision on Palestine which favoured the Jews in the offing, the British would have to cope with trouble from Muslims in

[45] Enclosure to Thorne to Abell, 5 April 1946, Ibid., pp. 150–1; Enclosure to Auchinleck to General Mayne, 3 May 1946, Ibid., pp. 407–8.

[46] Defence Committee Paper dated 12 June 1946, Ibid., pp. 889–90.

[47] Attlee to Cabinet delegation, (T), 13 April 1946, Ibid., pp. 260–1.

[48] Note by Abell discussed by Mission and Wavell on 16 May 1946, Ibid., pp. 568–9.

[49] Note by Croft and Turnbull, enclosed with Minutes by Croft, Turnbull and Pethick-Lawrence, 25 April 1946, Ibid., pp. 336–7.

India and in the Middle East, and this would pose 'a very grave threat to the defence system of the Commonwealth'. It would also defeat plans for a Middle East Security system. If there was no agreement between the Congress and League the British would have to produce a settlement. Allowing the Congress alone to join the interim government would mean that the British would get involved in the suppression of Muslims. This situation the British wished to avoid, for the Muslims had supported them during the war and wished to preserve their association with the Commonwealth.[50] The British could range themselves behind Pakistan, leaving Hindustan free to work out her own destiny as she pleased. This course of action would also avoid a situation in which the British would find themselves staying on in Hindustan and suppressing Hindus.[51] The political logicality of a withdrawal into Pakistan did not appeal to British defence chiefs. Pakistan would be in two halves, and the forces needed to defend it would be as great as those needed to defend India. Pakistan had insufficient resources for defence, the cost of which would fall on Britain. An alliance with Pakistan might push the Congress into a defence treaty with the USSR, and the British position in Pakistan and in Europe could be endangered. The British would also have to contend with minorities in Pakistan, who might act as a fifth column.[52] So if repression was difficult, scuttle humiliating, Pakistan economically and militarily unviable, the only alternative left was that the negotiations for a transfer of power to an undivided India must succeed. It was the only basis on which the British could hope to secure their long-term aim of maintaining India within the imperial security system; and therefore made every effort to achieve it.

When the Mission arrived in India, there were reports of rising communal tension from all provinces, and forebodings of civil war from the Punjab, where the Sikhs, especially, feared Muslim domination in any form of Pakistan.[53] In the NWFP, Muslim League volunteers had started carrying spears in their processions.[54]

[50] Note by Croft and Turnbull, Ibid., p. 337.

[51] Meeting between cabinet delegation and Wavell on 15 May 1946, Ibid., pp. 563–4.

[52] Note by Abell discussed by cabinet delegation and Wavell on 16 May 1946, Ibid., p. 569. In writing these two paragraphs, chronology has been sacrificed for coherence—also to avoid subsequent repetition of the points discussed.

[53] Jenkins to Wavell, 15 April 1946, Ibid., p. 272.

[54] FR for NWFP for second half of March 1946, HP file no. 18/3/46.

Even as the League negotiated with the British and the Congress, Liaqat Ali Khan talked of ' "Pakistan or death" ',[55] and Firoz Khan Noon proudly proclaimed: 'If we find that we have to fight Great Britian (sic) for placing us under one Central Government of Hindu Raj, then the havoc which the Muslims will play will put to shame what Jenghiz Khan and Halaku did'.[56] In the Punjab, Sind and NWFP, the Muslim League National Guards were being reinforced and Shaukat Hyat Khan called on Muslim ex-military personnel to enlist in the force.[57] All Commissioners in the UP reported deteriorating communal relations. There were also tendencies for labour disputes to take on the colour of inter-communal strife. The Sind government discerned the sinister role of the RSS 'in every recent violent communal incident',[58] and the RSS declared its creed to be Hindustan only for the Hindus.[59] The effect of RSS propaganda brought to the notice of Muslims can be imagined: 'Trust not a Muslim. A Muslim is a *goonda* incarnate. Muslims are our eternal enemies . . . Strengthen your ranks so that after 5 or 6 years when your strength reaches sufficient proportions you may be able to swoop down upon Muslims and free the country of these "mlechhas." . . . Every Hindu must keep daggers and spears at his home and carry a sharp knife with him'.[60]

From the start of the negotiations, Wavell thought that Cripps and Pethick-Lawrence paid too much deference to Congress leaders and their wishes. He thought that the first interview with Gandhi was 'a deplorable affair', with Pethick-Lawrence displaying 'his usual sloppy benevolence to this malevolent' politician. The interview closed with a little speech by the Secretary of State expressing 'penitence' for 'Britain's misdeeds in the past!' The Viceroy was 'horrified' at the deference shown to Gandhi; 'when he expressed a wish for a glass of water, the Secretary was sent to fetch it himself, instead of sending for a chaprassi; and when it did not come at once Cripps hustled off himself to see about it'. Gandhi, in Wavell's eyes,

[55] *Civil and Military Gazette*, 26 March 1946.
[56] *Eastern Times*, 11 April 1946.
[57] *Eastern Times*, 11, 16 and 29 May 1946; *Star of India*, 25 April 1946.
[58] FR for Sind for first half of May 1946, HP file no. 18/5/46.
[59] Letter to Secretary, AICC, from Tula Singh. AICC file no. G-60, 1945–1946, pp. 37–8.
[60] *Star of India*, 11 May 1946, *Goonda* is a bad character. *Mlechha* means foreigner.

was a 'remarkable old man, certainly, and the most formidable of the three opponents who have detached portions of the British Empire in recent years: Zaghlul and de Valera being the other two. But he is a very tough politician and not a saint'.[61]

Interviews with Jinnah and other Muslim Leaguers revealed their fear that, in spite of their electoral success, the party would be left out in the cold by the British and the Congress; their inability to define Pakistan; their expectation that the British would unfold a settlement,[62] which they would accept or reject. All Muslim Leaguers broke down under Cripps' cross-examination of the practical implications of Pakistan. Jinnah, in Wavell's words, 'talked for one hour on the history of India (largely fanciful) and the cultural differences between Hindu and Muslim (also somewhat fanciful)'.[63] The other Leaguers could adduce no real argument, except perhaps 'vague phrases' such as balance of power, prestige, psychological effect, but 'a good deal of hate' against Hindus.[64] Such were the men for whom Wavell confessed to having sympathy; whom he and Alexander thought should not be let down.[65]

The cabinet delegation's opinion of the definition of Pakistan by Leaguers probably reflected the official British dislike of the Pakistan solution, for Jinnah had made clear to them and to the parliamentary delegation which visited India in January 1946 the essential elements in the League's demand for Pakistan. Jinnah had emphasized parity, which underlined Muslim nationhood; the League would never enter a coalition government, the possibility of which had existed only during the war. 'All that is finished', he told the editor of the *Statesman* on 31 January 1946.[66] The League would never agree to a coalition government being set up even as an interim measure as it would relegate the demand for Pakistan to the background.[67] He dismissed as 'complete humbug' the Congress offer to serve under his leadership in an interim government. The

[61] Wavell, *Journal*, p. 236.

[62] Note by Cripps, 30 March 1946, *TOP*, vol. 7, pp. 59–60. Entries for 4 and 17 April 1946, Alexander diaries, Churchill College, Cambridge.

[63] Wavell, *Journal*, p. 237.

[64] Ibid., p. 240; Alexander diaries, entry for 2 April 1946.

[65] Wavell, *Journal*, p. 368; Alexander diaries, entry for 20 June 1946.

[66] Attlee to India Committee, 3 February 1946; note by Rankin on Woodrow Wyatt's talk with Jinnah on 8 January 1946, *TOP*, vol. 6, pp. 876–7, 798–9 respectively.

[67] *Hindustan Standard*, 30 January 1946.

Congress, he said, had always insisted that such a government should be responsible to a legislature which meant that it would be 'quickly overthrown'. It would not work at all. 'We should be fighting like Kilkenny cats all the time'. The League would never enter a constituent assembly for a united India; any attempt to impose one would be resisted, if necessary, by force. Jinnah's promise of good neighbourliness to India only underlined his determination to achieve a sovereign Pakistan. Relations with India would be purely diplomatic, without any common currency, armed forces, transport. For him, division of the armed forces was the crux of the matter. After the British transferred power, Pakistan would remain within the Commonwealth with a British Governor-General and would encourage British investment.[68] Jinnah's reliance on the British both before and after the transfer of power was an essential element in the demand for a sovereign Pakistan. He was, after all, aware that the Congress would not agree to British supervision of the constituent assembly, dominion status for India and alliances between India and any power bloc.[69] At one level, then, the future Pakistan's dependence on the British would win their support for it against the Congress, which sought the termination of the Raj. Assuming that the Congress got its way on Indian non-alignment, the British, with Pakistan in the Commonwealth, would be able to keep a foothold on the subcontinent, which would simultaneously be a military guarantee for Pakistan against Indian or other aggression. Between a Pakistan dependent on British help for its defence and a non-aligned India there could hardly be a common military policy; hence the question of having a common army, whether or not under British command, would not arise. The League demanded a full Pakistan; its "inability" to define the boundaries of which was rationalized by the realization that any definition would circumscribe that demand, whereas if they did not "define" it they might even get the maximum they wanted. If the British gave an award they would enforce it; and it would be accepted by the Con-

[68] Attlee to India Committee, 3 February 1946; note on Wyatt's interview with Jinnah, 8 January 1946; Wavell to Pethick-Lawrence, 29 January 1946, *TOP*, vol. 6, pp. 875–8, 798–9, 862 respectively; also Wyatt's memorandum, 29 March 1946, note by Cripps, 30 March 1946, *TOP*, vol. 7, pp. 54, 59–60 respectively.

[69] Among the many statements by Nehru on these points, see the reports in *National Herald*, 5 March 1946; confidential note for AICC by Nehru, 15 March 1946, Nehru papers; *Hindustan Times*, 6 April 1946.

gress. For the League and Jinnah, the British held the balance between them and the Congress.

Congress leaders stressed immediate rather than long-term demands. Gandhi demanded abolition of the salt tax, the release of political prisoners and the dismissal of Ambedkar from the government.[70] On behalf of the CWC, Azad wrote that the Congress would proceed on the basis of independence, and that the future constitution would have to be dealt with by a constitution making body. Before a constitution making body was set up, there must be an interim government which must be in charge of all subsequent stages, itself setting up the constitution making body as well as conducting the administration of the country. Members of the interim government should be chosen by the provinces—11 out of 15 members could be provincial representatives; four representatives of the minorities could be chosen by the legislature or the provincial governments. The Congress envisaged a federation in which fully autonomous provinces would have residuary powers. In accordance with the Cripps plan of 1942, no areas would be compelled to join the federation. The League must allow a plebiscite of the total population in the Muslim majority provinces, and the states must attend the constitution making body. Owing to the exigencies of the moment, the Congress was prepared to give up its earlier demand for a constitution making body elected on the widest possible franchise. Instead, provincial legislatures could act as a federal college to choose a constitution making body, and the federal college would vote together and not in provincial compartments.[71]

The Congress proposals were inspired by Gandhi's faith that the cabinet mission was sincerely desirous of transferring power 'but wanted a face saving device for Jinnah'. Gandhi said that the reference to self-determination in the Congress formula referred 'only to matters like Municipal Government'. Jayakar pointed out the difficulties against accepting such an interpretation to which Gandhi replied that 'matters would be cleared up at the right time.'[72] Patel held that Nehru had 'incautiously' gone on laying the clause on self-determination, but he was clear that

[70] Note of interview between cabinet delegation and Gandhi, *TOP*, vol. 7, p. 117.

[71] Note of interview between cabinet delegation, Wavell and Azad on 3 April 1946, Ibid., pp. 111–13.

[72] Note by M.R. Jayakar, 6 April, 1946, *MRJC*.

> 'the formula cannot be interpreted in any way more liberally than the interpretation given to it in the Congress Resolution of 1942, i.e., that it only confined full provincial freedom to remain out so as to enjoy full control over internal (?) affairs, under the control of the Governor General. His interpretation in other words was the same as Gandhi's on the previous evening . . . If the Constitution framed as a result of discussion was not favourable to certain Muslim areas & if plebiscite was favourable, they would be permitted to remain out on the footing with Residuary powers enjoyed by them under the Governor General. . . . Talking of Jinnah's threat of bloodshed he laughed it out and said Congress could control the situation by persuasion if not by force, . . .[73]

Having ascertained the views of the Indian parties, the mission accepted Cripps' view that there could be no agreement on the constitution of the Interim Government until a broad agreement had been reached upon 'the fundamental question of whether there shall be one India only in the future, or two or more Indias'.[74] Cripps concluded that there were only two possible solutions which stood any chance of acceptance by the Indians. Scheme A envisaged an Indian Union which would consist of three principal parts—the Hindu majority provinces, the Muslim majority provinces, and the Indian States. The Union Government would control such subjects as Defence, Foreign Affairs and Communications. A wider range of optional powers might, by agreement, either be exercised by provinces cooperating as groups, and thereby constituting a third tier, or be transferred to the centre. Scheme B provided for two Indias, Hindustan and Pakistan, to either of which the States could federate. The boundaries of Pakistan would be determined on the principle that the Muslim majority districts would have a right to form a separate and sovereign state, with a defensive and offensive treaty of alliance between the two Indias. They would, however, have no common executive and therefore no common control of defence or foreign policy.[75]

Attlee agreed with the Mission that Scheme A would be preferable: Pakistan would be weak and would be strengthened only in so far as it could rely upon its treaty with Hindustan. Without defensive agreement with India, no scheme of defence would be of any

[73] Note by Jayakar on interview with Patel, 7 April 1946, Ibid.

[74] Memorandum by Cripps, undated but probably around 8 April 1946, *TOP*, vol. 7, p. 174.

[75] Ibid., pp. 175–6.

value.[76] Scheme B would destroy the homogeneity of the Indian army. Even if all were acting in common for the defence of India, co-operation would be far from easy unless all acknowledged a central directing authority.[77]

The Mission now tried to get the parties to agree to one of the alternatives set out by Cripps. They decided to tell Jinnah that they did not believe that the *full* claim for Pakistan had any chance of acceptance or could be supported by them.[78] On 16 April, Jinnah was told that he could not reasonably hope to receive both the whole of the territory, much of it inhabited by non-Muslims, which he claimed and the full measure of sovereignty which he said was essential. If the full territories were insisted upon then some element of sovereignty must be relinquished if there were to be a reasonable prospect of agreement. If, on the other hand, full sovereignty was desired, then the claims to the non-Muslim territories could not be conceded.[79] Jinnah was then asked whether he would be willing to discuss a possible constitution on the basis of Scheme A.[80]

'I have never seen a man with such a mind twisting and turning to avoid as far as possible direct answers', wrote A.V. Alexander, who was friendly to the League's view point.

> 'I came to the conclusion that he [Jinnah] is playing this game, which is one of life and death for millions of people, very largely from the point of view of scoring a triumph in a legal negotiation by first making large demands and secondly insisting that he should make no offer reducing that demand but should wait for the other side always to say how much they would advance towards granting that demand.'[81]

Characteristically, Jinnah said that the Congress should make a statement first. Confronted with Pethick-Lawrence's admonition that 'if the Delegation gave an award in the Muslim League's favour and then Great Britain withdrew her troops, the Muslims would be exposed to grave dangers', Jinnah's reaction suggests that, inspite of his success at the polls, he was relying on the continuing presence of

[76] Cabinet Meeting on 11 April 1946, Ibid., pp. 229–30.
[77] Attlee to cabinet delegation and Wavell, (T), 13 April 1946, Ibid., p. 260.
[78] Meeting between cabinet delegation and Viceroy on 13 April 1946, Ibid., pp. 251–2.
[79] Note of interview between cabinet delegation and Jinnah on 16 April 1946, Ibid., p. 281.
[80] Ibid., pp. 281–3.
[81] Entry for 16 April 1946, *Alexander Diaries*.

the British in India. He said that 'he was 100% in favour of agreement but what if there were no agreement. The situation was unprecedented. The British Government was asking the Indian people to take self-government and the Indians were unable to do so'. But he could make no alternative suggestion. He said that it was Congress which should say what it wanted. He thought he had little to lose in a setback and left it to the British to produce a settlement.[82]

When it became clear that Jinnah had not accepted either scheme, the Mission thought they would have to propound the basis of settlement themselves.[83] Cripps held that a Pakistan confined to Muslim districts alone was not acceptable to the League and would be impracticable; and there was no justification for including large non-Muslim areas in Pakistan. He concluded that 'there is no practicable scheme whereby the Muslim-majority areas can be brought together to form an independent Sovereign State wholly separated from the rest of India'. Nor would a separate Pakistan state solve the communal difficulties.[84] Nevertheless, Muslims desired some practical form of self-government. There should, therefore, come into being a three-tier constitutional arrangement, the bottom tier of which would comprise the provinces and States which expressed a desire to join Hindustan or Pakistan. At the top would be a Union of India embracing both Pakistan and Hindustan.

The Mission decided to discuss the proposals with Jinnah first; and to warn him that 'it was the last suggestion' which the Delegation had to make in the hope of promoting agreement between the parties and that 'unless Mr. Jinnah had some positive proposition to make the Delegation would have to deal with the Congress and do what they could for the Muslim Community'.[85]

Jinnah agreed to put the proposals before his Working Committee if they were accepted by the Congress. The Mission were now encouraged to put Plan A before the Congress, as Gandhi's main objection to Pakistan was to it having sovereignty and 'now it appeared that Mr. Jinnah was for the first time prepared to consider

[82] Note of interview between cabinet delegation and Jinnah, 16 April 1946, *TOP*, vol. 7, pp. 284–5.
[83] Cabinet delegation to Attlee, (T), 18 April 1946, Ibid., p. 314.
[84] Memorandum by Cripps, 18 April 1946, Ibid., p. 305.
[85] Meeting of cabinet delegation and Wavell, 24 April 1946, Ibid., p. 324.

something less than a sovereign Pakistan'.[86] Azad himself raised the question of the three-tier constitution when he met Cripps on 26 April. He thought he could get the Working Committee to agree to a single federation which could be broken down into two parts legislating separately for optional subjects.[87]

With both Azad and Jinnah willing to negotiate on the basis of the three-tier solution, the Mission now invited them to nominate 4 representatives each to meet the Delegation and the Viceroy.[88] Azad raised objections to Pethick-Lawrence's reference to 'predominantly Hindu and predominantly Muslim provinces'. The Congress had never agreed to such a division. It however recognized that there might be provinces which wished to delegate to the Central Government subjects in the optional list, while others might agree to delegate only compulsory subjects like Foreign Affairs, Defence and Communications. Also, the Cabinet Delegation had left no choice to a province in the matter of joining or not joining a group. There might be provinces which did not wish to join any particular group. The Congress Working Committee agreed to the provinces having full powers for all remaining subjects as well as the residuary powers, but it 'should be open to any Province to exercise its option to have more common subjects with the Federal Union'.[89]

Jinnah blew hot and cold as usual. He accepted the invitation to Simla to discuss proposals which envisaged, in the final analysis, an Indian Union; but he enclosed a copy of a resolution passed by the Subjects Committee of the all India Muslim League Legislators Convention on 9 April. The resolution stated that 'the Muslim Nation will never submit to any constitution for a United India and will never participate in any single constitution-making machinery set up for the purpose'.[90]

To both Azad and Jinnah, Pethick-Lawrence replied that their objections would be discussed at the Conference, for the British had never considered that acceptance by Congress and the Muslim League of their invitation 'would imply as a preliminary condition full approv-

[86] Meeting of cabinet delegation and Wavell, 26 April 1946, Ibid., p. 342.

[87] Meeting between Cripps and Azad, 26 April 1946, Ibid., p. 345.

[88] Pethick-Lawrence to Azad and Jinnah, 27 April 1946, Ibid., p. 352.

[89] Azad to Pethick-Lawrence, 28 April 1946, Ibid., p. 357.

[90] Jinnah to Pethick-Lawrence, 29 April 1946, Ibid., pp. 371–2. Muslim Convention resolution, Ibid., p. 373.

al by them of the terms set out in my letter'. The terms were a 'proposed basis for a settlement'.[91]

Jinnah began the proceedings at Simla by refusing to shake hands with Azad and Ghaffar Khan.[92] His vagueness on many points was probably due to his deliberately unconstructive attitude. He suggested that the foreign policy of the Union should be decided by consultation 'as between members of the Commonwealth'; to which Cripps reminded him that 'there was no common Foreign Policy of the Commonwealth'. Pethick-Lawrence raised the point that even if the Centre had a limited field, there must be someone responsible for the common army and he must have a popular mandate—how could he be responsible to two legislatures that might have different policies? Jinnah answered that 'the executive could settle all these matters and he was definitely against a Union Legislature'. He did not suggest how the executive should proceed. When Nehru agreed with Wavell that a Union Court would be necessary to deal with disputes between the units, and might also deal with fundamental rights as included in the Constitution, Jinnah's reaction was that, on the assumption that there would be no communal trouble once the Union was set up, 'there was no need of a Court'.[93] After some time, he said that if there was to be a Union Legislature its members should be elected in equal numbers by group legislatures.

The Congress was against group legislatures and executives. This would mean 'a sub-federation, if not something more and we have already told you that we do not accept this'. It would result in creating three layers of executive and legislative bodies, an arrangement which would be cumbersome, static and disjointed, leading to continuous friction. 'We are not aware of any such arrangement in any country'.[94] Wavell assured Nehru that the scheme 'was designed to get over a psychological difficulty. It was not claimed to be ideal from the administrative point of view'. The Congress, said Nehru, would exercise no compulsion on units to stay in an all India federa-

[91] Pethick-Lawrence to Azad and Jinnah, 29 April 1946, Ibid., pp. 374 and 375 respectively.

[92] Pethick-Lawrence to Attlee, 5 May 1946, Ibid., p. 431; and Alexander diaries, entry for 5 May 1946.

[93] Simla proceedings on 5 May 1946, *TOP*, vol. 7, pp. 429 and 430.

[94] Azad to Pethick-Lawrence, 6 May 1946, *TOP*, vol. 7, p. 434.

tion. But it was against splitting up India; the Union of India, 'even if the list was short, must be strong and organic'. He appealed to the League to come into the constitution-making body on the assurance that there would be no compulsion.[95]

Jinnah declined the invitation but he said that if groups could have their own legislature and executive, the League would accept the Union subject to argument about its machinery. Nehru pointed out that Jinnah had accepted no feature of the Union. The Union without a legislature would be 'futile and entirely unacceptable'.[96]

In the afternoon, Jinnah expressed himself against one constitution making body, and said that the constitution should not be for more than five years in the first instance. Alexander told him that this was 'too short'. 15 years would be more appropriate. The Congress was justifiably suspicious about Jinnah's intentions. Patel seized upon Jinnah's statement: 'there we have it now; what he has been after all the time'[97]—implying that in the long run, Jinnah would never be interested in a Union.

The Delegation now decided to present points which were intended as a compromise to the Congress and the Muslim League. There would be a Union government and legislature dealing with Foreign Affairs, Defence, Communications, fundamental rights and having the powers to raise finances for these subjects. All remaining powers would be vested in the provinces. Groups of provinces would be formed and such groups would determine the provincial subjects which they desired to take in common. The groups could set up their own executive and legislatures. The Union legislature would be composed of equal proportions from the Muslim and Hindu majority provinces, 'whether or not these or any of them' formed themselves into groups, together with representatives of the States. The Union and Group constitutions would contain a provision whereby any province could by a majority vote of its legislative assembly review the terms of the constitution every 10 years. The constitution making body would include representatives from each Provincial assembly in proportion to the strengths of the various parties in the assembly on the basis of one-tenth of their numbers. The Constituent Assembly would be divided into three sections

[95] Simla proceedings, 6 May 1946, Ibid., pp. 436–7; and Alexander diaries, entry for 6 May 1946.

[96] Ibid., p. 437.

[97] Wavell, *Journal*, p. 259; Alexander diaries, entry for 6 May 1946.

representing Hindu and Muslim majority provinces and the States. The Hindu and Muslim groups would meet separately to decide the provincial constitutions for their group, and if they so wished, the group constitution. When these had been settled, it would be open to any province to opt out of the group. Thereafter the three bodies would meet together to settle the Union constitution.

These points were communicated to Jinnah and Azad for comment.[98] Jinnah saw Congress inspiration behind the new formula, especially on grouping. He protested that the meeting had adjourned for the Mission to consider further the matters arising out of the Congress rejection of a Union government vested with powers to deal with only three subjects and grouping. New proposals had now been made, and 'By whom they are suggested, it is not made clear.' The League would never agree to one constitution making body or to the proposed method of forming the Constituent Assembly. Jinnah wanted not one Constituent Assembly but three, which would meet together only for the purpose of deciding the Constitution of the Union Government.[99]

The Congress delegates wanted a declaration from the Mission that acceptance of the terms for negotiation would not make them binding on either party; and that the Constituent Assembly would be free to throw out any items and to add or to amend the suggestions before it. The difficulty about parity between six Hindu majority provinces and five Muslim majority provinces was 'insurmountable.' the Muslim majority provinces represented nine crores of the population as against over nineteen crores of the Hindu majority provinces. Azad pointed out that the proposals limited the discretion of the Constituent Assembly. Two or three constitutions might emerge for separate groups, joined together by 'a flimsy common super structure left to the mercy of the three disjointed groups'. There was also compulsion in the early stages for a province to join a particular group—'why should the Frontier Province which is clearly a Congress Province, be compelled to join any group hostile to the Congress?'[100]

When the conference met again on 9 May, Nehru suggested that the Congress and League could sit together with an umpire accepted by both parties, whose decision would be final. Jinnah agreed to sit

[98] Turnbull to Azad and Jinnah, 8 May 1946, Ibid., pp. 462–3.
[99] Interview between Wyatt and Jinnah on 9 May 1946, Ibid., pp. 475–6.
[100] Azad to Pethick-Lawrence, 9 May 1946, Ibid., pp. 476–7.

with Nehru and 'consider whether this proposal could be accepted and, if so, who the umpire would be'.[101] But on 11 May, Jinnah said he had not agreed to anything or to an umpire. If there was to be arbitration the first question which would arise would be the partition of India. The matter had been settled at the elections and it was 'inconceivable' that it should ever be the subject of arbitration'.[102]

With the Congress and League unable to reach any agreement, inspite of some concessions to both sides, the Mission now decided that the time had come for them to make their own statement, which had been in preparation for some time. The League and the Congress were shown copies of the statement before it was published on 16 May. An account of the conversations between the British, Congress and League is important, for they contained the seeds of future bickering between all three parties. Cripps and Pethick-Lawrence told the representatives of the League, which included Liaqat Ali Khan, Ismail Khan and Abdur Rab Nishtar, that 'sections of the constitution-making body would meet to decide the character of the provincial constitutions within the Group, and the Group constitution. The decision would be taken by representa tives of the Provinces within the section'. If a province, such as the NWFP, refused to come into the meetings of the sections of which it was a part, 'the sections would . . . proceed without those representatives'. Cripps told Rab Nishtar that each section of the constitution-making body would be entitled to frame the constitution for the provinces within it whether they attended or not, and also to determine whether there should be a group and what the group subjects would be, 'subject only to the right of a Province to opt out after the constitution had been framed'. The option, said Cripps, would be exercisable 'after the whole picture including the Union Constitution had been completed'.[103] This, of course, meant that grouping in practice would not be voluntary at all. Cripps said that the statement was not negotiable and that it was intended to go ahead with convening the Constituent Assembly on the basis of it. The only alterations which could be considered would be those agreed upon by the two main parties. The League representatives

[101] Simla proceedings, 9 May 1946, Ibid., p. 490; Alexander diaries, entry for 9 May 1946.

[102] Simla proceedings, 11 May 1946, *TOP*, vol. 7, p. 508.

[103] Meeting between Pethick-Lawrence, Cripps and members of the League on 16 May 1946, Ibid., p. 577.

wanted a copy of the note of the explanations which they had been given. It was agreed that Rab Nishtar might see the note of the meeting and take notes from it 'but these would not have the status of an official record.'[104] Pethick-Lawrence told Liaqat that 'it would require a majority of each of the major communities' in the Constituent Assembly to depart from the basic provisions set out in the Statement. Cripps said that the League could 'cease to participate' in the Assembly if it failed to comply with the basic provisions. Sovereignty 'would not be given until the constitution had been framed'. An Act of Parliament to set up the new constitution 'would not be appropriate'. He thought that 'all that would be necessary' was an act of cession by the Crown to the constitution-making body or to the new Government.[105]

As the notes taken by Rab Nishtar would not constitute an official record, the passage on the sovereignty of the Constituent Assembly was excluded from the official record of the meeting. Rab Nishtar 'did not fail to notice this omission when he saw the notes and commented on it to me . . . there is no doubt that this question of sovereignty is an important one to the Muslims and they will have taken careful note of what was said'.[106]

Somewhat different assurances were given by Wavell to Nehru and Azad when they discussed the Statement on 16 May. The Viceroy told them that the Constituent Assembly 'might be regarded as a sovereign body, for the purpose of constitution-making, and that when agreement was reached it would remain for Parliament to repeal the Government of India Act, 1935, and for formal steps of recognition to be taken'.[107] Wavell also told them that the Interim Government 'must be under the existing constitution'.[108]

This was the background to the Statement of 16 May. Gandhi asked Cripps and Pethick-Lawrence whether the procedure laid down for the Constituent Assembly was subject to alteration by a majority of votes, and also by a majority of both of the major communities voting. Cripps said that 'there was in fact on a strict interpretation nothing in paragraph 19(vii) making it clear that the majority of each of the two major communities was required for

[104] Ibid., p. 579. [105] Ibid., pp. 579–80.

[106] Addendum, Turnbull to Abell, 22 May 1946, Ibid., p. 580.

[107] Meeting between Wavell and Azad and Nehru on 16 May 1946, Ibid., pp. 581–2.

[108] Ibid., p. 581.

such a decision unless it were held to be a decision which raised a major communal issue'.[109] Indeed, the said paragraph read:

> 'In the Union Constituent Assembly resolutions varying the provisions of paragraph 15 above or raising any major communal issue shall require a majority of the representatives present and voting of each of the two major communities.'[110]

The Congress understood that the Constituent Assembly would be a sovereign body for the purpose of drafting the constitution as well as for entering into any treaty with the British government. It would be open to the Assembly 'to vary in any way it likes the recommendations and the procedure suggested by the Cabinet Delegation.'[111] The statement had not said anything about either of these points; Wavell had assured Nehru and Azad that the assembly would be a sovereign body for the purposes of constitution-making.

Azad raised valid questions about grouping. Paragraph 15 (5) of the Statement read that 'Provinces should be free to form Groups with executives and legislatures, and each Group could determine the Provincial subjects to be taken in common'.[112] But clause (3) of the same paragraph stated that 'All subjects other than the Union subjects and all residuary powers should vest in the Provinces'.[113] However, paragraph 19 said that provincial representatives would divide up into the three sections, and these sections would proceed 'to settle the Provincial Constitutions for the Provinces included in each section, and shall also decide whether any Group Constitution shall be set up for those Provinces and, if so, with what provincial subjects the Group should deal'.[114] The Congress discerned a basic discrepancy in these provisions. The basic provision gave full autonomy to a province to do what it liked and subsequently there appeared to be a certain compulsion in the matter which infringed that autonomy. It was true that a province could opt out later if it wanted to. But it was not clear how a province or its representatives could be compelled to do something which they did not want to do. A provincial assembly could give its mandate to its representatives not to enter any group or a particular group or section. Also, the Punjab would dominate Section B and Bengal Section C. It was

[109] Meeting between cabinet delegation and Wavell on 18 May 1946, Ibid., p. 616.
[110] 16 May statement, Ibid., pp. 589–90.
[111] Azad to Pethick-Lawrence, 19 May 1946, Ibid., p. 639.
[112] 16 May statement, Ibid., p. 587.
[113] Ibid., p. 587. [114] Ibid., p. 589.

conceivable that this dominating province might frame a constitution against the wishes of Sind or the NWFP; it might even lay down rules nullifying the provision for a province to opt out of the group.[115] Azad was told that once the Constituent Assembly had been formed, 'there is naturally no intention to interfere with its discretion or to question its decisions.' When the Constituent Assembly had completed its labours the British government would recommend to Parliament such action as would be necessary for the cession of sovereignty to the Indian people, 'subject only to two provisos . . . namely, adequate provision for the protection of minorities and willingness to conclude a treaty to cover matters arising out of the transfer of power'. For these reasons independence could not precede the new constitution.[116]

The status of the Interim Government cropped up again in correspondence between Congress leaders and the Mission. 'Has the cry "Independence in fact" no foundation?' asked Gandhi.[117] Wavell subsequently wrote to Azad that the spirit in which the Government was worked would be of much greater importance than any formal document and guarantees: 'if you are prepared to trust me, we shall be able to co-operate in a manner which will give India a sense of freedom from external control' as soon as possible. The British government would treat the Interim government 'with the same close consultation and consideration as a Dominion Government'. It was his intention 'faithfully to carry out' the undertaking in the Statement that the interim government would be given the greatest possible freedom in the day-to-day administration of the country.[118] This letter was important, for it was on the basis of the assurances given by Wavell that the Congress subsequently agreed to enter the interim government.

Jinnah protested at the Statement's preference for a united India; the provision for one constitution-making body and for union finances; and the absence of parity between Hindu and Muslim majority provinces in the Union executive and legislature.[119] On the question of parity, Wavell pointed to the alternative safeguards

[115] Azad to Pethick-Lawrence, 20 May 1946, Ibid., p. 640.

[116] Pethick-Lawrence to Azad, 22 May 1946, Ibid., pp. 659–60.

[117] Gandhi to Pethick-Lawrence, 22 May 1946. Also Azad to Wavell, 25 May 1946, Nehru to Wavell, 25 May 1946, Ibid., pp. 660, 690–2, 693–4 respectively.

[118] Wavell to Azad, 30 May 1946, Ibid., p. 738.

[119] Statement by Jinnah on 22 May 1946, Ibid., pp. 663–9.

provided and had urged that the Muslim League could hardly expect to receive parity in an Indian Union. Jinnah asked Wavell what would happen if Congress rejected the proposals and the League accepted them. Wavell said 'he could not give any guarantee but speaking personally he thought that if the Muslim League accepted them they would not lose by it and that His Majesty's Government would go on with constitution-making on the lines they had proposed as far as possible in the circumstances.' Jinnah asked whether the Muslim League would in such circumstances be invited to join the Interim Government and be given their due proportion of the portfolios. The Viceroy had said that 'he thought that he could guarantee that the Muslim League would have a share in it'. Jinnah wanted a written assurance on these points as it would help him with his Working Committee.[120] Jinnah was shown the text of two verbal assurances which were to be given to him. No written assurance could be given, but Wavell could give him 'on behalf of the Delegation, my personal assurance that we do not propose to make any discrimination in the treatment of either party; and that we shall go ahead with the plan laid down in our statement so far as circumstances permit, if either party accepts . . .'[121] This, and a similar assurance by Cripps, were shown to Jinnah and, according to Wavell, 'he seemed satisfied'.[122]

Some sources suggest that initially, many Leaguers were shocked at the absence of parity between the Congress and the League at the centre, and wanted Jinnah to reject the Plan.[123] Others noted that the League was not in a position to launch civil disobedience, and they advocated that the prudent strategy would be to work up the Plan up to the group stage, while refusing to submit to a centre that did not accord them parity. If the Congress did not accomodate them at the centre, the League could withdraw from the constituent assembly and resist the imposition of an unwanted centre.[124] The evidence of both Khaliquzzaman and Chaudhuri Muhammad Ali is that Wavell's assurances of 3 and 4 June that the British would form a government without the Congress if that party rejected the Mission Plan 'played a decisive role in determining the final attitude

[120] Meeting between cabinet delegation and Wavell on 3 June 1946, Ibid., p. 784.
[121] Verbal assurance given by Wavell to Jinnah on 3 June 1946, Ibid., p. 785.
[122] Assurance by Cripps to Jinnah, Ibid., p. 786. See also Wavell to Abell, 3 June 1946, p. 785.
[123] Note by Wyatt, 25 May 1946, Ibid., pp. 684–5.
[124] Moore, *Escape from Empire*, pp. 121–4.

of the Muslim League leaders'. Many Leaguers, including Jinnah, feared that the Congress would use its majority in the constituent assembly to break the Plan.[125] Jinnah's own inclination seems to have been to accept the Plan. He reportedly told the Muslim League council that the Plan conceded the substance of Pakistan and provided a machinery for achieving a fully sovereign state in ten years. Rejection would mean that the League had given up constitutional methods and had become a revolutionary body: why shed blood when they could achieve their goal by peaceful methods? Groups would have power on all subjects except defence, communications and foreign affairs. Defence would remain in British hands until the new constitution was enforced.[126] Jinnah evidently envisaged a long drawn out process of constitution making, a British presence until it was complete, and British enforcement of their interpretation of the Mission Plan. He was, after all, aware of disagreement with the Congress both on grouping and on parity; it is hard to see how he and the Congress would have ever agreed on the British having the last word on the constitution.

According to M.A.H. Ispahani, Jinnah was requested by his working committee to take a decision on the Mission Plan. The general consensus in the committee was that if the League turned down the proposals, they would be drawing on themselves the onus of failure. They accepted in the hope 'that it would ultimately result in the establishment of a complete, sovereign Pakistan'. But Jinnah was unsure that he had taken the right decision and on consideration 'he would rather have rejected the proposal'.

> 'But it was too late . . . All that he could do was to hope that the Congress would either reject the proposal or ask for such amendments or put such interpretation on it as would vitiate their acceptance of it.'[127]

The issue of parity provided him with his first occasion to find fault with the Congress and the British. Jinnah said he would only enter the Interim Government on the basis of parity with the Congress, and asserted that Wavell had assured him on 3 June, before he

[125] Khaliquzzaman, *Pathway to Pakistan* p. 362 and C.M. Ali, *The Emergence of Pakistan* pp. 59, 60, 69.

[126] *Star of India*, 7 June 1946.

[127] M.A.H. Ispahani, *Qaid-e-Azam Jinnah As I Knew Him* (2nd edition, Karachi, 1966, pp. 168–9); League resolution, *TOP*, vol. 7, p. 839.

met the League Working Committee that portfolios would be distributed on the 5:5:2 ratio. This was 'one of the most important considerations' which weighed with the Working Committee.[128] According to Woodrow Wyatt, 'Jinnah *did* promise the Muslim League Council and Working Committee that he would not go into an Interim Government without parity'.[129] Wavell thought that the British must adhere to the 5:5:2 ratio as the most helpful basis of settlement. But he had given Jinnah no assurance that he would get it. However, the Congress reiterated its opposition to parity. 'What was proposed now was not Hindu/Muslim parity, but Muslim League and Congress parity. This cut out all the non-League Muslims'.[130]

The Mission tried to discuss alternatives to parity: Pethick-Lawrence even suggested that 'we were not committed to parity and he was not able to see why we should necessarily have it.'[131] The next day, Cripps said he had met Jinnah who seemed willing to discuss portfolios and had agreed not to discuss parity. So Wavell wrote to Nehru and Jinnah asking them to discuss personnel for the new Interim Government.[132] Jinnah replied tha the League had accepted the May 16 statement on the basis of parity. Also, there would be no point in discussing portfolios until the Congress had given their decision on the Statement.[133] Pethick-Lawrence secured Attlee's agreement to a proposal made by the Delegation on 3 June that if the Congress refused to come in, while the League agreed, the latter would be invited to go on with their won constitution making. The centre would have Muslim League representatives and representatives of minorities with seats reserved for the Congress but held temporarily by officials or non-Congress Hindus.[134] But Pethick-Lawrence said 'he would not like to be committed to asking Jinnah to form the Government'.[135]

[128] Jinnah to Wavell, 8 June 1946, Ibid., p. 839.

[129] Interview between Wyatt and Jinnah, 11 June 1980, Ibid., p. 867. Italics in original.

[130] Meeting between cabinet delegation and Azad and Nehru on 10 June 1946, Ibid., p. 855. See also note of Wyatt's interview with Gandhi on 10 June 1946, Ibid., pp. 857–8.

[131] Meeting between cabinet delegation and Wavell, 11 June 1946, Ibid., p. 862.

[132] Wavell to Nehru and Jinnah, 12 June 1946, Ibid., p. 877.

[133] Jinnah to Wavell, 12 June 1946, Ibid., p. 885.

[134] Cabinet delegation and Wavell to Attlee, 3 June 1946, para. 4 (b), Ibid., p. 789.

[135] Meeting between cabinet delegation and Wavell on 14 June 1946, Ibid., p. 918.

Nehru gave Wavell a list of his nominees for the interim government on 13 June. The list included 5 Congress, 4 Muslim League, 1 Congress Scheduled Caste, 1 Congress woman, 1 independent Muslim and 3 other minority representatives. Wavell said the League would never agree to the list and suggested that he would meet Jinnah. Both Nehru and Jinnah appeared willing to consider a 5:5:3 basis, with the Scheduled Caste outside Congress.[136] If no agreement could be reached, the Mission would make a statement, setting out its own proposals for the formation of an interim government.[137]

The Statement of 16 June contemplated an interim government composed of 6 Congress representatives, all of them Hindus and including one Scheduled Caste, 5 Muslim Leaguers, 1 Sikh, a Parsi and a Christian. This composition was not meant to be taken as a precedent for the solution of the communal question, but was intended as 'an expedient' to solve the present difficulty.[138] Paragraph 8 of the statement, however, promised if both parties or either of them proved unwilling to join in the setting up of a coalition Government 'on the above lines, it is the intention of the Viceroy to proceed with the formation of an interim Government which will be as representative as possible of those willing to accept the Statement of May 16'[139] Differing interpretations of this provision by the British and the Muslim League were to culminate in the League's call for "Direct Action" on 29 June.

Jinnah claimed that though the Viceroy had not promised him parity with the Congress in the interim government, 'he had conducted the discussion on the basis of parity' and that it was on this basis that he had agreed to come in. Pethick-Lawrence said he 'quite understood his position' and it was true that the Viceroy was endeavouring to construct an Interim Government on the basis of parity, but he had not found it possible to do so. 'Accordingly, if Mr. Jinnah had given a promise on this basis to take part in the Government he was released from this promise when the basis was changed'.[140] Jinnah said nothing more on this point.

[136] Meeting between cabinet delegation and Wavell on 13 June 1946, Ibid., pp. 913–14.

[137] 16 June statement, Ibid., pp. 954–5.

[138] Ibid., p. 954. [139] Ibid., p. 955.

[140] Meeting between Jinnah, Alexander and Pethick-Lawrence on 17 June 1946, Ibid., p. 960.

Wavell now assured Jinnah, against the wishes of Pethick-Lawrence, that the names of those invited to join the interim government in the Statement of 16 June 'cannot be regarded as final', but that 'no change in principle will be made in the statement without the consent of two major parties.' He also promised that the 'proportion of members by communities will not be changed without the agreement of the two major parties'.[141] This assurance by the Viceroy was to further complicate the chances of agreement, for the Congress had decided that they would nominate a Muslim out of their own quota. They had in mind Zakir Husain, who, as the British recognized, 'is not known to have any definite political affiliations, but had been associated with Mahatma Gandhi as an expert on education'.[142]

Jinnah now published his correspondence with Wavell in the press, and provoked the Congress to refuse to enter the interim government because of the assurances given by the Viceroy to him. Within the Mission, even Alexander agreed that the British could not accept the principle that the League could have a monopoly of appointing Muslims. The Delegation failed to persuade the Congress leaders not to include a Muslim in their own quota.[143] The Congress Working Committee decided not to enter the Interim Government, but added, while reiterating their objections to the Statement of 16 May, 'we accept your proposals and are prepared to work them with a view to achieve our objective'.[144] In effect, Congress would accept the long-term plan, with reservations.

Wavell thought that the Congress had outmanoeuvred the British because of their ability to 'twist words', in formally accepting the 16 May statement.[145] The British had hoped that their threat to form an interim government of one party if the other party rejected their long-term plan would compel both to accept it and join the interim government, but this tactic had resulted in both parties accepting

[141] Wavell to Jinnah, 20 June 1946, paras. 5 (i) and (iv), Ibid., p. 989. This was sent in reply to Jinnah's letter of 19 June 1946, Ibid., pp. 974–7.

[142] Draft Cabinet paper, on instructions to be given to Viceroy regarding resumption of negotiations for Interim Government, para. 8, by Pethick-Lawrence, July 1946, L/P&J/10/73.

[143] Meeting between cabinet delegation and Congress members on 23 June 1946, Ibid., pp. 1012–15.

[144] Azad to Wavell, 25 June 1946, Ibid., p. 1036.

[145] Note by Wavell, 25 June 1946, Ibid., pp. 1038–9.

the plan with conflicting reservations. Since Congress had not accepted the interim proposals, the Mission decided to tell Jinnah that new negotiations for an Interim Government would be stated after a while; and that Jinnah would be told that 'we could not support his objection' to the Congress including a Muslim in their own quota.[146]

Accordingly, Jinnah was informed that Azad's letter of 25 June constituted acceptance of the long-term plan, though Wavell pointed out that 'the Delegation had said in their Statement of May 25th that they did not accept the Congress interpretation'. In reply to Jinnah's charge that the reservations made by the Congress 'were most vital and broke the whole thing', Pethick-Lawrence said that 'the Muslim League reservations were quite as fundamental'.[147] When Jinnah charged the Delegation with departing from the 16 June statement, Pethick-Lawrence told him that 'the Delegation were not asking for Mr. Jinnah's opinion of their conduct'. Alexander tried to console Jinnah by telling him that he appreciated his sacrifices, but requested him to use his influence with the League Working Committee and to come into the interim government on the basis of their acceptance of the 16 May statement. On 29 June, the Cabinet Delegation returned to Britain.

British officials now debated the basis on which the League and the Congress should be called in to form the interim government. Penderel Moon suggested that the 6:5:1 basis could be adhered to.

> 'If, for any reason, including the non-co-operation of either of the major parties, it is impossible to form a Coalition Government . . . then the Congress as the largest single party should be called upon to form a Government; *but the intention of doing this should not be disclosed*, except possibly at the last moment to Jinnah. . . . If we had the courage to recognize the Congress' right to include a nationalist Muslim in their quota of representatives, the League would *not* have refused to co-operate. The League could not possibly go into the wilderness on the ground that an extra Muslim was being included in the Government in place of a Caste Hindu. The League is relatively weak and quite unused to fighting. If it decides to fight it will fight on strong ground and not on an absurdity.'[148]

'Of course what prevented us from doing that which Moon refers to in last para', commented Pethick-Lawrence, 'was the pledges

[146] Meeting between cabinet delegation and Wavell on 25 June 1946, Ibid., p. 1044.
[147] Ibid., p. 1045.
[148] Note by Penderel Moon, 29 June 1946, L/P&J/10/73, p. 341.

we gave Jinnah in the ill-advised letter of Viceroy to Jinnah on 20 June para 5(1) and (4) . . . to which I was at that time strongly opposed'.[149] Turnbull was also in general agreement with Moon. Pethick-Lawrence, drawing up instructions for the Viceroy in consultation with the cabinet, firmly believed that 'it is unreasonable of Jinnah to demand that all the Muslim members should be nominees of the Muslim League in view of the fact that the Muslim League achieved only 76% of the Muslim votes'. If the principle was repudiated, the Congress 'may be prepared not to press for the actual inclusion of a Congress Muslim'. The Viceroy should make it plain to Jinnah that 'we cannot support his claim' that all the Muslims should be nominated by the Muslim League, but that the British agreed with him that a majority of both communities would be required for raising a major communal issue. He should, at the same time, urge upon Nehru the 'essential importance' of Congress not pressing their claim to the inclusion of a Congress Muslim. If the League refused to come in, the Congress would be asked to form the Government, though the Viceroy would oppose it.[150] Wavell favoured the 6:5:3 ratio for the formation of the interim government, to which the cabinet agreed.[151]

Jinnah felt let down by the British. He had assumed that the Congress would not be allowed to join the interim government because of its conditional acceptance of the 16 May statement and its rejection of the statement of 16 June. On 6 July, he wrote to Attlee that the delegation's handling of the negotiations had

> 'impaired the honour of the British Government and have shaken the confidence of Muslim India and shattered their hopes for an honourable and peaceful settlement. They allowed themselves to play in the hands of the Congress. . . . I . . . trust that the British Government will still avoid compelling the Muslims to shed their blood, for, your surrender to the Congress at the sacrifice of the Muslims can only result in that direction.'[152]

A series of statements by Congress leaders against grouping and their assertion that they were not bound by anything except their decision to join the Constituent Assembly, combined with the si-

[149] Handwritten note by Pethick-Lawrence, undated but probably around beginning July, Ibid., p. 339.

[150] Note by Pethick-Lawrence, July 1946, Ibid., pp. 320–3.

[151] Cabinet Meeting on 18 July 1946, Ibid., p. 220.

[152] Jinnah to Attlee, 6 July 1946, Ibid., pp. 200–2.

lence of the British, heightened the apprehensions of the League.[153] *Dawn* commented that if Attlee and his colleagues indicated in Parliament that their silence hitherto,

> in face of Congress leaders' bragging to treat their Statement of 16 May as a scrap of paper, has been due to extreme patience and not cowardice, and if they restate that there shall be no departure from the fundamental basis of that Statement, Muslims would still be willing to play their part honourably and peacefully, provided that such a restatement by the British Government is logically followed up by such action in respect of the setting up of an Interim Government also.'[154]

Pethick-Lawrence's reply to Lord Simon in the House of Lords raised the League up in arms. Simon enquired whether the British government regarded it as 'being quite open' to the Constituent Assembly to frame a constitution 'which squares with Government's framework, or have they a wider ambit than that, so that they can propose something of a different kind? The Secretary of State replied:

> 'I think it would be quite impossible for me to give direct, specific, definite answers as to the precise position of that body . . . The object of setting up the Constituent Assembly is to give Indians the power to make their own Constitution. The only reason we intervened at all was that it was necessary to get both major Parties into the body so that there should be certain understanding between them as to the basis of a new government.'[155]

In the Commons, Cripps stated that the Indian parties were 'at perfect liberty to advance their own views on what should or should not be the basis of a future Constitution'.[156]

Accusing the British of appeasing the Congress, the League rejected on 29 July the 16 May statement, 'due to the intransigence of the Congress on one hand, and the breach of faith with the Muslims by the British Government on the other'. The Congress was bent upon setting up 'Caste Hindu Raj in India with the connivance of the British'. The Council of the League called on Muslims to resort to 'Direct Action to achieve Pakistan . . . to get rid of the present British slavery and the contemplated future Caste-Hindu domina-

[153] Statements by Azad, Patel and Nehru between 6–10 July 1946, *TOP*, vol. 8, p. 517.

[154] *Dawn*, 17 July 1946.

[155] *TOP*, vol. 8, p. 516. [156] Ibid., pp. 516–7.

tion'. As a protest against 'their deep resentment of the attitude of the British', the League called upon Muslims to renounce the titles 'conferred upon them by the alien Government.'[157]

Nehru has often received most of the blame for the passing of the Direct Action resolution by the League. Azad wrote that the League would have come into the Constituent Assembly had it not been for Nehru's press statement of 10 July, which he describes as 'one of those unfortunate events which changed the course of history'.[158] But Nehru, along with other Congress leaders, had expressed himself against grouping throughout the negotiations with the cabinet mission. Azad himself upheld the Congress view that 'there should be no compulsion in the matter of grouping' on 6 July.[159]

Nehru also thought that once the parties entered the constituent assembly, discussion of the political, social and economic problems facing the whole of India would relegate grouping to the background.[160] In any case, Nehru envisaged that grouping would fail on its merits because Section A would oppose it; the NWFP would not join Group B; provincial jealousies would work against grouping, as the NWFP and Sind would not like Punjabi domination.[161] This assumption was not unreasonable: Khizar had expressed similar views to the cabinet delegation in April.[162] But if Nehru expected grouping to collapse *sui generis*, it could hardly have been the *leitmotif* of his statement, or the idea seizing his mind. In fact, the sovereignty of the constituent assembly was at the core of many of Nehru's statements around the beginning of July,[163] and it is difficult to understand why his press interview of 10 July has been singled out by his contemporaries and historians as the *casus belli* of the League's call for direct action. On 10 July, he merely reaffirmed what he had said earlier: that the constituent assembly must be a sovereign body. Nehru's remarks were clearly aimed at the British:

[157] League resolution of 29 July, Ibid., pp. 138–9.

[158] Azad, *India Wins Freedom*, p. 181.

[159] Statement by Azad, 6 July 1946, *TOP*, vol. 8, p. 517.

[160] See, for example, Nehru's note of 10 July 1946, *SW*, vol. 15, pp. 248–9.

[161] Press interview, 10 July 1946, Ibid., pp. 242–3.

[162] Meeting between cabinet delegation and Khizar on 5 April 1946, *TOP*, vol. 7, p. 148.

[163] Nehru's editorial in *National Herald*, 3 July 1946; speech at Jhansi, 4 July 1946; 7 July 1946, *SW*, vol. 15, pp. 233, 234–5, 236–8 respectively.

> 'When the Congress stated that the constituent assembly was to be a sovereign body, the Cabinet Mission's reply was more or less "yes", subject to two considerations: first, a proper arrangement for the minorities, and secondly, a treaty between India and England. I wish the Mission had stated that both these matters were not controversial. It is obvious that the minorities question has to be settled satisfactorily. It is also obvious that if there is any kind of peaceful changeover in India, it is bound to result in some kind of a treaty with Britain.
>
> What exactly the treaty will be I cannot say. But if the British Government presume to tell us that they are going to hold anything in India, because they do not agree either in regard to the minorities or in regard to the treaty, we shall not accept that position . . . if there is the slightest attempt at imposition, we shall have no treaty.
>
> In regard to the minorities . . . we . . . accept no outsiders' interference in it—certainly not the British Government's—and, therefore, these two limiting factors to the sovereignty of the constituent assembly are not acceptable to us.
>
> The only limitation on the party's action would be its anxiety to carry the work of the constituent assembly to successful conclusion. It does not make the slightest difference what the Cabinet Mission thinks or does in the matter.'[164]

The point was reiterated by him on several occasions after 10 July.[165]

Jinnah took exception to the absence of any assurance from Cripps and Pethick-Lawrence that the British would insist on the working of the constituent assembly as laid down in the 16 May statement. He and other Leaguers made this very clear to the British after the passing of the direct action resolution on 29 July 1946.[166] Even moderate Leaguers like Nazimuddin lamented that the 'British have let us down'.[167] All this only underlined the essential political division between the League and Congress: what for the Congress implied British dictation to the constituent assembly was, for the League, a British guarantee against Congress domination. British assurances to the League on grouping would have no value if they were not backed up by a guarantee of British responsibility for the procedure of the constituent assembly. But not only were the

164 Press interview, 10 July 1946, Ibid., pp. 242–3.

165 Nehru's editorial in *National Herald*, 16 July 1946; speech on 20 July 1946; press interview, 29 July 1946; speech, 1 August 1946, Ibid., pp. 255–6, 260–1, 273–4, 276–7 respectively.

166 Wavell to Pethick-Lawrence, (T), 27 August 1946; note by Wavell, 16 September 1946; undated note by Mudie, *TOP*, pp. 311, 525, 212–13 respectively.

167 *Morning News*, 5 August 1946. See also *Morning News* editorial, 31 July 1946.

British unwilling to proceed without the Congress; they seemed to be reneging their assurances on the status and procedure of the constituent assembly, while their rejection of parity at the centre implied that they had not acquiesced in the logic of the two nation theory. Differences with the Congress had prevailed on all these points throughout the negotiations with the cabinet mission; it was the realization that they might, in the end, get nothing from the British which proved the catalyst for the League's call for direct action.

CHAPTER 6

Negotiations for The Interim Government and Direct Action

Discussing the 'novel and serious situation' created by the League's call for Direct Action, the British cabinet advised Wavell that they must not lose the initiative and that it was 'impossible' to allow Jinnah's non-cooperation to hold up progress in the formation of an interim government. The Viceroy was instructed to see Jinnah as soon as possible and to press him to allow Muslim Leaguers to join the interim government. The British could not allow themselves to get into a situation in which both Congress and the League were in opposition and the government had to be carried on by officials indefinitely.[1] The decision to proceed without the League was 'undoubtedly a grave one' but there was 'no practicable alternative'. That Whitehall was prepared to go a considerable distance away from the assurances it had given the League on 16 May is illustrated by Pethick-Lawrence's suggestion that if the Constituent Assembly met without the League 'there appears to be nothing short of the May 16 Statement which would make it necessary for the Provincial representatives to meet in sections.' Paragraph 19 of the statement which laid down this procedure could be varied if a majority of both communities were in agreement. 'As a majority of the Muslim representatives would, in the absence of the Muslim League, be pro-Congress Muslims, such a decision is not impossible. The result would be that the Provincial constitutions of the Muslim Provinces would be framed by a predominantly Hindu body and the possibility of Groups being formed would be very faint indeed.' But the British must not disguise the fact that if the Muslims (Muslim League) were to resort to violence 'we should inevitably be involved in supporting a predominantly Congress Government in putting down the disturbances.'[2] Political considerations can make for the strangest bedfellows.

[1] Secretary of State to Viceroy, (T. 14078), 31 July 1946, L/P&J/10/73, p. 136.

[2] Cabinet Paper C.P. (46) 315, Memorandum by Secretary of State, 31 July 1946, Ibid., pp. 121–6.

Wavell was thinking of extricating the British from a situation in which they were being castigated by Jinnah for letting him down, and, to that extent, indirectly bore the responsibility for the League's refusal to join the interim government. The onus of getting Jinnah in could be thrown on the Congress. The British had 'some chance of using the present situation to good effect if we can put responsibility for satisfying League on Congress'.[3] Wavell also did not take seriously Jinnah's call for Direct Action. He did not expect Jinnah to ask Muslim League ministries to resign. Jinnah, in his opinion, had few lieutenants who would be willing or able to run a mass movement. Also, Jinnah had given no indication that he would start a mass movement.[4]

The cabinet agreed with Wavell that the best tactics would be to call Nehru to make proposals for the formation of the interim government and to secure the agreement of the Congress Working Committee before any details were discussed. If the Working Committee agreed the Viceroy would stress the need for a coalition with the League.[5] So, on 6 August, Wavell invited Nehru, as Congress President, to submit proposals for an interim government on the basis of his letter of 30 May. Nehru was asked to discuss the proposals with Jinnah as a coalition would be the most effective form of government. The Congress Working Committee gave its approval for the Congress to enter the interim government. The Congress would approach the League for cooperation, though they did not expect it in view of their recent resolutions and statements. If cooperation was denied, then 'we shall be prepared to go ahead without it'.[6]

There was in fact little indication that the League would enter the government. Replying to Wavell's invitation of 22 July, Jinnah now argued that in making the proportions 6:5:3 the basis of the new government, the British were reneging on their earlier promises to form a government on the 5:5:3 and 5:5:4 basis in order to appease the Congress.[7] Wavell reminded him that the 6:5:3 basis was

[3] Viceroy to Secretary of State, (T 1587-S), 1 August 1946, Ibid., p. 118.

[4] Viceroy to Secretary of State, (T 1587-S), 1 August 1946, p. 118.

[5] Viceroy to Secretary of State, (T 1609-S), 4 August 1946, and Secretary of State to Viceroy, (T 14197), 2 August 1946, Ibid., pp. 102 and 103 respectively.

[6] CWC Resolution, 10 August 1946, Ibid., p. 217 and Nehru to Wavell, 10 August 1946, Ibid., p. 218.

[7] Jinnah to Wavell, 31 July 1946, Ibid., p. 156.

accepted by the Working Committee of the League in its resolution of 25 June.[8] The League's attitude was echoed in an editorial in *Dawn* on 14 August, which threatened that the moment 'a Hindu Government is set up without the consent and collaboration of Moslems the first shot of aggression will have been fired against them and that will be the signal for Muslims to do or die.'[9]

What the League intended by Direct Action is unclear. Jinnah himself refused to comment—'I am not going to discuss ethics'.[10] Liaqat Ali khan described it as 'action against the law'.[11] Most provincial Leagues called for peaceful demonstrations, and on 16 August itself, Jinnah enjoined upon Muslims 'to carry out the instructions and abide by them strictly and conduct themselves peacefully and in a disciplined manner'. An advertisement in Muslim League papers on 16 August read:

> 'Today is Direct Action Day
> Today Muslims of India dedicate anew their lives and all they possess to the cause of freedom
> Today let every Muslim swear in the name of Allah to resist aggression
> Direct Action is now their only course
> Because they offered peace but peace was spurned
> They honoured their word but were betrayed
> They claimed Liberty but are offered Thraldom
> Now Might alone can secure their Right'.[12]

Direct Action turned violent only in Calcutta. There were many portents of its nature in Calcutta. The *Morning News*, published from Calcutta and whose editor, Akram Khan, was a member of the Calcutta and Bengal Muslim Leagues, asserted in an editorial on 5 August that Muslims 'do not believe in the cant of non-violence.'[13] The conservative landlord Nazimuddin, often at odds with Suhrawardy and his labour supporters, threatened: 'There are a hundred and one ways in which we can create difficulties, specially when we are not restricted to non-violence. The Muslim population of Bengal know very well what "Direct Action" would mean so we need not bother to give them any lead'.[14] Muslims, according to *Dawn's*

[8] Wavell to Jinnah, 8 August 1946, Ibid., p. 203.
[9] *Dawn*, 14 August 1946.
[10] *Morning News*, 2 August 1946. [11] *Morning News*, 2 August 1946.
[12] *Dawn, Eastern Times, Morning News*, 16 August 1946.
[13] *Morning News*, 5 August 1946. [14] *Morning News*, 11 August 1946.

Calcutta correspondent, had 'no faith in non-violence and they are neither hypocrites that they would preach non-violence in words and practice violence in action'.[15] From 10 August Muslim goondas from outside Calcutta armed with sticks, spears and daggers began to appear in the slum areas of the city.[16] A pamphlet written by S.M. Usman, the League mayor of Calcutta proclaimed:

> 'In the month of Ramzan the first open war between Islam and *Kafirs* started and the Mussulmans got the permission to wage Jehad . . . and Islam secured a splendid victory . . . . According to wishes of God, the All-India Muslim League has chosen this sacred month for launching this Jehad for achieving Pakistan . . . . We Muslims have had the crown and have ruled. Do not lose heart, be ready and take swords . . . . Oh *Kafir*! your doom is not far and the general massacre will come.'[17]

On 16 August, the *Star of India* and the *Morning News* advised their readers that the pamphlet was available from the local Muslim League office. Suhrawardy himself did not rule out communal violence. That the Bengal government expected it is illustrated by the fact that troops were confined to barracks on the morning of 16 August.[18]

Europeans were the only groups which emerged unscathed on Direct Action Day in Calcutta.[19] There was in fact considerable evidence that Direct Action would be aimed at Hindus. Earlier in the month, Khurho had told Mudie that it would be 'directed not so much at the British as at the Hindus'.[20] Gazdar, a Muslim League leader from Sind, declared that the Congress was out to crush the League by turning British guns and police bayonets on Muslims. 'I warn them that they will have to pay for Muslim lives thus lost in Hindu blood with compound interest'.[21] An editorial in the *Morning News* advised Muslims that 'any molestation or attempted molestation of British men or women, be they civilian or military, is

[15] *Dawn*, 12 August 1946.

[16] *Report of the Commissioners of Police on the Disturbances of 16–20 August* (Calcutta, 1946), quoted in Richard Lambert, 'Hindu-Muslim Riots', unpublished Ph.D. dissertation presented to University of Pennsylvania, 1951, p. 170.

[17] Extract from Muslim League pamphlet, *Let Pakistan Speak for Herself* (Calcutta, 1946), quoted in Sen, *Muslim Politics*, p. 213. See also Lambert, 'Hindu-Muslim Riots', p. 237.

[18] Burrows to Wavell, 22 August 1946, *TOP*, vol. 8, p. 295.

[19] Ibid., p. 302. [20] Undated note by Mudie, Ibid., p. 213.

[21] *Morning News*, 12 August 1946.

not only against the Bombay resolutions, but also against the spirit and letter of Islam'.[22] The editorial did not express any similar sentiment in favour of Hindus. The Spens Enquiry Commission enquired of Brigadier Thomas Binny, on the general staff of the Eastern Command: '"Had anybody, European or otherwise, any doubt in his mind that this was going to be an attempt against the Hindus?"' Binny answered, '"No."'[23] Official reports from Bengal had warned of the 'potential danger of communal clashes' on 16 August. They also took note of the Hindu feeling that Direct Action would be directed against them in particular. Non-Muslims, except Christians and Europeans, expected and were ready to face violence. Hindu leaders in Calcutta contributed to the atmosphere of hate and violence by calling on Hindu workers to abstain from the hartal organized by the League; to resist it by force if necessary.[24] A prominent Sikh leader in Calcutta declared that 'if rioting did start, the Sikhs would back the Congress and between them they would give the Muslims a good thrashing'.[25] That Hindus were well prepared for violence is indicated by their ready retaliation of attacks by Muslim League processionists as they passed Hindu localities on the morning of 16 August,[26] and the fact that there were eventually more Muslim than Hindu casualties in Calcutta.

Suhrawardy, as Chief Minister and Home Minister, declared 16 August a public holiday with the approval of the Governor. Burrows mentioned the point to Wavell on 8 August. The idea was to minimize the risk of communal conflict on the 16th.[27] Reports of scuffles began to reach police headquarters even before 6 a.m. on the 16th. Some of the early incidents occurred when Hindu shopkeepers refused to comply with demands by Muslim League processionists to close down their shops.[28] Stabbing, arson and looting started early in the day. There were cases of the police participating in the looting; for the rest, they did nothing.[29] The situation became so serious by the afternoon that at 2.40 p.m. the Chief Secretary rang up Burrows' secretary to say that he supported the request of

[22] *Morning News*, 16 August 1946.

[23] Thomas Binny, Staff HQ Eastern Command in Spens Commission Report, quoted by Lambert, 'Hindu-Muslims Riots', p. 172.

[24] Tuker, *While Memory Serves* (London, 1950), pp. 156–7.

[25] Ibid., p. 156.

[26] Burrows to Wavell, 22 August 1946, *TOP*, vol. 8, p. 296.

[27] Ibid., p. 294.

[28] Ibid., p. 296.

[29] Lambert, 'Hindu-Muslim Riots', p. 178.

the Commissioner of Police that the army should be called in at once. Burrows agreed 'on my own responsibility' to their being called in without delay. For the moment, however, troops were not used, because the Governor, on a tour of the city, formed the impression, which he did not detail, 'that the situation was not as bad as I had expected to find it.'[30]

At 4 p.m. Suhrawardy and other League leaders addressed a meeting of Muslims—numbering between 30,000 to 100,000—at the Ochterlony Monument. The Special Branch of Police, by what Burrows described as 'a culpable omission', sent only one Urdu shorthand reporter to the meeting, so that 'no transcript of the Chief Minister's speech is available'. But the Central Intelligence Officer and a reliable reporter deputed by the military authorities agreed on 'one most mischievous statement (not reported at all by the Calcutta Police whose report reached us first). The version in the former's report is:– "He had seen to police and military arrangements who would not interfere". The version in the latter's is:– "He had been able to restrain the military and police". The audience interpreted this as an invitation to disorder; and many of the listeners started attacking Hindus and looting Hindu shops as soon as they left the meeting.[31]

There is no doubt of the complicity of Suhrawardy and the provincial League in the incidents in Calcutta. Days before the rioting, coupons bearing the Chief Minister's signature were issued for the use of Muslim League lorries. Elaborate preparations were made for first aid stations and mobile units by the League for the 16th. The *Statesman* commented:

> 'Some of those disrupting the city's peace were privileged. The bands of ruffians rushing about in lorries, stopping to assault and attack and generally spreading fear and confusion found the conveyances they wanted. On a day when no one else could get transport for their lawful occasions, these men had all they wanted; it is not a ridiculous assumption that they had been provided for in advance.'[32]

S.G. Taylor, then Inspector General of police in Bengal, recollects:

> 'The Chief Minister's own attitude during the rioting was reprehensible to a degree. During the height of the disturbances he drove round Calcutta with the local Army Commander to asses (sic) the situation.

[30] Burrows to Wavell, 22 August 1946, *TOP*, vol. 8, p. 296.
[31] Ibid., pp. 296–7. [32] *Statesman*, 18 August 1946.

As they drove the Army Commander said: "This is all extraordinary; in the Army Hindus and Mohamedans live and work very happily together." To this the Chief Minister replied: "We shall soon put an end to all that."'

Suhrawardy also ordered Taylor to tell the police superintendent in the 24 Parganas district to release all Muslims who had been arrested in connection with the rioting. Taylor retorted that he had no authority to give such an order, and that such orders were illegal. '"Very well then" said the Chief Minister, "you will tell the Superintendent of the Police that if he has occasion to arrest any Mohamedans in the future he will arrest at least as many Hindus!"'[33]

One of the great controversies about the Calcutta riots centres around the role of Sir Frederick Burrows, the Governor of Bengal. Section 52(1) of the Act of 1935 gave the Governor the special responsibility to prevent 'any grave menace to the peace of the province or any part thereof'. But law and order was not a discretionary matter under the constitution, and the Governor was to 'exercise his individual judgement' as to the action to be taken in the carrying out of his special responsibilities.[34]

Burrows himself wrote that in handling the situation, particularly at the outset, 'I had always to consider the susceptibilities of my Ministry. The dual personality of Suhrawardy, as Chief Minister (in charge of the Home portfolio) and as the most influential member of the Muslim League in Bengal, was a constant embarrassment'.[35] As 'slippery as a basket of eels', Suhrawardy combined a reputation as a labour leader backed by the *goondas* of Calcutta with one of being a ladies' man, who, wearing a white sharkskin suit, frequented the club, "The 300", in the city, and had 'all the Western vices'.[36]

Nevertheless, it is not difficult to see why Burrows was charged by the Congress and Hindus for conniving with the League ministry on 16 August. Suhrawardy spent a great deal of time in the Control Room, often attended by some of his supporters. This made it

[33] S.G. Taylor, 'Bengal 1942 to the takeover in 1947,' *S.G. Taylor papers*. Taylor was then Inspector General of Police in Bengal.

[34] *Government of India Act, 1935*, pp. 35–7.

[35] Burrows to Wavell, 22 August 1946, *TOP*, vol. 8, p. 303.

[36] I owe this personal account of Suhrawardy to Mr. W.H. Saumarez Smith, then Deputy Secretary to the Governor of Bengal. Interview with author on 31 October 1980.

difficult for the Police Commissioner, who was handling the situation, to give clear decisions. It was not the function of the minister to direct detailed operations, but the position was delicate as the Police Commissioner 'could not insist' on the extrusion from the Control Room of the Minister responsible for law and order. Short of a direct order from Burrows, there was no way of preventing the Chief Minister from visiting the Control Room whenever he liked; and the Governor was not prepared to give such an order, 'as it would clearly have indicated complete lack of faith in him'. A curfew was imposed on Calcutta only at 9 p.m. It was to last till 4 a.m. Stabbing, looting and arson continued, so the army patrolled some streets. Burrows' tour of the city on the 17th, which was undertaken at about 11 a.m. 'convinced me' that earlier reports had erred on the side of under-estimation. 'I observed very great damage to property and streets littered with corpses. I can honestly say that parts of the city on Saturday morning were as bad as anything I saw when I was with the Guards on the Somme'. It was then that Burrows decided, after consulting with the acting Area Commander, the Chief Secretary and the Police Commissioner, that a military operation would be staged in the area worst affected. The operation began at 3.30 p.m., and it was not until 6.30 p.m. that order was restored in the Bow Bazar area. Reinforcements were called in, and by 20 August, the situation showed a marked improvement.[37]

Why were troops used so late, especially as the police strength in Calcutta—250 with another 250 in reserve—was, to quote S.G. Taylor's understatement, 'quite inadequate to deal with a disaster of this magnitude', and their complicity in the disturbances, either by way of participating in them or being reluctant to open fire, was in no doubt at a very early stage?[38] Brigadier Binny held that troops, if deployed or employed in proper time 'Not only would have been but were sufficient' to prevent or quell the riot.[39] This corroborates Taylor's view. In disturbances which saw the loss of 10,000 lives, when corpses were piling up on the streets even as Burrows toured the city and were beginning to block Calcutta's drainage system, his tardiness in using the army did him no credit, and laid him open to the charge of partiality towards his ministry; and of complacency because there was not 'a single case of any attack on a European or

[37] Burrows to Wavell, 22 August 1946, *TOP*, vol. 8, pp. 217–18, 302.
[38] S.G. Taylor, 'Bengal 1942–1947', *S.G. Taylor papers*.
[39] Spens Commission Report, quoted by Lambert, 'Hindu-Muslims Riots'. p. 179.

even an Anglo-Indian as such'.[40] General Roy Bucher, the Army Commander, recorded that the Bengal government remained inactive even after the army had taken charge. 'Neither then, nor afterwards, did one member of that Government give me any real assistance in bringing order out of disorder'.[41] The ministry was not dismissed, inspite of an assurance by Cripps to Nehru that it would be in any contingency such as this.[42]

Burrows' admission that he did not go into Section 93 because he would not have been able to cope with any agitation by the League, which might then ensue, raises the question of the capacity of the administration to deal with large-scale disorders. Direct Action day in Calcutta resulted in 10,000 deaths, yet only one prosecution was carried out. The only thing which prevented a complete collapse of the administration, according to Burrows, was the three battalions of British troops.[43] Once called in, troops were able to restore order easily—it is this which leads to criticism of Burrows for not calling them in earlier.

Direct Action day passed off peacefully in other provinces, including Sind, which was also governed by a League ministry which had declared 16 August a public holiday. Mudie had also chided his ministers for incitement to violence.[44] In Jorhat in Assam, the communal complexion of an imposing League procession was 'somewhat marred by the fact that it was accompanied by a band comprised mainly of Hindus led by a Chinaman and giving an indifferent rendering of "The British Grenadiers" '.[45]

Jinnah condemned the violence in Calcutta, and declared that the Bengal Provincial League would take action—whatever that might mean—against those who had broken instructions and participated in violence.[46] But as the Congress joined the interim government, he and his lieutenants continued to incite violence. Declaring a *jihad* against the British and the Congress, Ghulam Ali Khan, minister for Law and Order in Sind, proclaimed that anyone opposing Muslims

[40] Burrows to Wavell, 22 August 1946, *TOP*, vol. 8, p. 302.

[41] General Sir Roy Bucher to Nehru, 13 November 1954, *NC*, quoted by Gopal, *Nehru*, vol. 1, p. 330.

[42] Patel to Cripps, 19 October 1946, *Patel Correspondence*, vol. 3, pp. 131–2.

[43] Burrows to Wavell, *TOP*, vol. 8, p. 303.

[44] Minutes of Conference with Governors of Bengal, UP, Punjab, Sind and NWFP, Ibid., pp. 206–7.

[45] Bourne to Wavell, 23 August 1946, Ibid., p. 305.

[46] *Dawn*, 19 August 1946.

in the pursuit of Pakistan 'shall be destroyed and exterminated.'[47] Mamdot announced the League's intention to use 'all methods worthy of an aroused nation . . . Now we have burst our bonds. Now we are determined to stake our all in the Jehad to achieve freedom for Islam in India'.[48] Even as direct action was brought under control in Calcutta, Jinnah's rhetoric—that the inauguration of the interim government would result in 'unprecedented and disastrous consequences'—was dangerous precisely because it did not define the limits or nature of Direct Action.

Direct Action by the League was a new factor for the British to contend with. The British had earlier worked on the assumption that the Congress would be hostile and the League friendly. 'That is certainly not the present position', observed Pethick-Lawrence. 'Jinnah is not only angry with us but is threatening open rebellion. Even if we agree that he was provoked and was perhaps not handled in the best way (which I admit), we cannot ignore his present attitude. He does not even suggest to us a policy which would provide a settlement except the barren slogan of Pakistan. Congress is, at any rate for the moment, friendly'. Whitehall did not know what to do. The situation changed from day to day, and any "ultimate policy" decided on this week would almost certainly by force of events prove to be all wrong next week or the week after.[49]

Wavell remained anxious to get the League into the interim government, for he held that communal violence could not be otherwise halted.[50] But Gandhi and Nehru would not accept grouping in the face of the League's intransigence and the instigated violence in Calcutta. Nor would Congress give up its right to include a non-League Muslim in its own quota.[51] Wavell took their reaction as justification for Jinnah's doubts about Congress; as 'convincing evidence' that Congress always meant to use their position in the Interim Government to destroy the grouping scheme which was the one effective safeguard for the Muslims.[52] There was little condemnation of the political methods which had resulted in the loss of

[47] *Sind Observer*, 3 August 1946, enclosed in letter from Choitram P. Gidwani, President, Sind PCC, 10 August 1946, AICC-file no. G-36, 1946, p. 51.

[48] *Dawn*, 22 August 1946.

[49] Pethick-Lawrence to Wavell, 19 August 1946, *TOP*, vol. 8, p. 263.

[50] Viceroy to Secretary of State, 27 August 1946, (T 1791–S), L/P&J/10/75, p. 401

[51] Gandhi to Wavell, 28 August 1946, and Nehru to Wavell, 19 August 1946, Ibid., pp. 322 and 259 respectively.

[52] Viceroy to Secretary of State (T 1804-S), 28 August 1946, Ibid., p. 398.

hundreds of lives; only a warning that the League would continue to employ such methods if the British did not confirm their promises to the League on grouping.[53] Wavell did not want the British to go ahead with the Constituent Assembly if the Congress failed to accept grouping.[54]

The cabinet disagreed with Wavell's interpretation of the attitudes of Gandhi and Nehru. Pethick-Lawrence also pointed out that the formation of the constituent assembly had been publicly announced: not calling it would be represented as a breach of faith.[55]

Wavell himself was not very consistent on the question of procedure. In his broadcast on 24 August, he accepted the Congress view that any dispute over paragraph 15 of the 16 May Statement could be referred to the Federal Court.[56] But in a letter to Nehru on 28 August, he suggested that the Congress accept grouping as laid down in the Statement as distinguished from the legal interpretation which could be put on it by the Federal Court.[57] '*This approach is new*', pointed out Nehru. The Calcutta occurrences had taken place 'before your broadcast in which you have referred to the Federal Court deciding questions of interpretation'.[58]

The inconsistencies in British attitudes stemmed from the 16 May statement itself, and their acceptance of resolutions which stated contradictory aims of the Congress and the League. The British accepted Azad's letter of 25 June as an acceptance by the Congress of the Statement. The Congress had 'throughout openly held' that they accepted the statement subject to paragraph 15(5)— '"Provinces should be free to form groups and each group could determine the provincial subjects to be taken in common"'. This overrode the subsequent provision that representatives of provinces would meet in sections '"which shall proceed to settle certain constitutions of the Provinces included in each section, and shall also decide whether any group constitution shall be set up for those Provinces, and if so with what provincial subjects the group shall

[53] Ibid., and Wavell to Pethick-Lawrence, 28 August 1946, *TOP*, vol. 8, p. 314.

[54] Viceroy to Secretary of State (T 1791-S), 27 August 1946, *TOP*, vol. 8, p. 311.

[55] Secretary of State to Viceroy, (T 15817), 28 August 1946, L/P&J/10/75, p. 390; and Secretary of State to Viceroy (T 15940), Ibid., p. 368.

[56] Text of Wavell's broadcast on 24 August 1946, *TOP*, vol. 8, pp. 306–7.

[57] Wavell to Nehru, 28 August 1946, R/3/1/117, p. 147.

[58] Nehru to Wavell, 28 August 1946, *TOP*, vol. 8, p. 327. Emphasis mine.

deal" '. The Congress had never moved from this position: the Congress resolution of 10 August reiterated it. Azad's letter of 25 June accepted the British proposals '*with a view to achieve our objective* (which, incidentally, is the avoidance of groups).' The League, on the other hand, did accept the scheme although the basic paragraph 15 contained as its first feature the establishment of a Union.[59] Here Monteath erred. The League accepted the 16 May statement

> 'inasmuch as the basis and the foundation of Pakistan are inherent in the Mission's plan by virtue of the compulsory grouping of the six Muslim Provinces in Sections B and C, [the League] is willing to cooperate with the constitution-making machinery proposed in the scheme outlined by the Mission *in the hope that it would ultimately result in the establishment of a complete sovereign Pakistan, and in the consummation of the goal of independence for the major nations, Muslims and Hindus*'.[60]

The British persisted stubbornly in the wishful thinking that the League was not serious about Pakistan perhaps because it was at odds with the official conception of their future role in India.

The inauguration of the interim government on 2 September was greeted with threats of direct action by the League. Jinnah saw a division of India as the only alternative to it,[61] and there were reports of the organization of direct action from many Muslim majority provinces. The Punjab Provincial League called on all able-bodied Muslims to enlist in the National Guard.[62] Abdulla Haroon was appointed dictator to organize direct action in Sind, and Muslims in the Punjab and NWFP were instructed not to buy anything from Hindu shopkeepers.[63] Jinnah declared that India was on the brink of civil war. Suhrawardy warned that 'the prospects before us are not merely gloomy but just cannot bear contemplation'.[64] Ghazanfar Ali thought Muslims should prepare for direct action rather than indulge in speculation about the outcome of the Jinnah-Wavell parleys,[65] and to wait for the 'final signal for a tremendous struggle for the establishment of Free Pakistan'.[66] The League's Committee of Action defined Direct action as a *jihad* against the enemies of Islam in India.[67]

[59] Notes by Turnbull and Monteath, 30 and 31 August 1946 respectively, L/P&J/5/10/75, pp. 362–4. Emphasis in original.

[60] *TOP*, vol. 7, pp. 837–8.

[61] *Dawn*, 28 August 1946.

[62] *Dawn*, 5 September 1946.

[63] *Dawn*, 5 and 8 September 1946.

[64] *Dawn*, 13 September 1946.

[65] *Eastern Times*, 20 September 1946.

[66] *Eastern Times*, 22 September 1946.

[67] *Eastern Times*, 26 September 1946.

The Congress now tried to go some way in satisfying Jinnah. In a broadcast on 7 September, Nehru stated that the Congress would enter sections, which would then consider the formation of groups.[68] Describing this as a step in 'the right direction', Wavell now wanted to put to the Congress a formula which would make clear that the League would get 'what the Mission wanted by their Statement of 16th May to give them'. Wavell preferred to lose the cooperation of the Congress at the centre and in the provinces 'than go ahead with constitution making on a one-party basis and in a way which the Mission never intended'.[69] He believed that Jinnah now wanted a settlement. This had been indicated by Suhrawardy, and Jinnah had stated that he would accept an invitation by the British government to start a new series of conferences on an equal footing with other negotiators.[70] Of course, the Congress would have to be told of the assurances on grouping which were given to the League on 16 May.[71]

Even as Jinnah stalled on entering the interim government, in spite of the willingness of the Congress to implement the basic principle of the 16 May statement, Wavell continued to urge on the Labour government the need for a breakdown plan. The unprecedented savagery and extent of the communal violence led Wavell to contend on 7 September, and again on 23 and 30 October, that on administrative grounds, the British could not govern India for more than eighteen months. They should therefore be ready to withdraw by March 1948, though Wavell visualized a breakdown as early as January 1947. For Wavell, the "administrative grounds" could be found only partly in the uncertain allegiance of Indians in the civil and armed services to the Raj, for the question was whether loyalist services alone could decisively suppress widespread unrest. Indeed it was in the administrative inability to crush such unrest that the crux of the administrative weakness of the British lay. The increasing Indianization of the services during the war had promp-

[68] *National Herald*, 8 September 1946.

[69] Wavell to Pethick-Lawrence (T 1889-S), 9 September 1946, *TOP*, vol. 8, pp. 470–1.

[70] Wavell to Pethick-Lawrence (T 1895-S), 9 September 1946, Ibid., p. 474; and Wavell to Pethick-Lawrence (T 1897-S), 10 September 1946, Ibid., p. 476.

[71] Viceroy to Secretary of State (T1910-S), 11 September 1946, Ibid., p. 489. See also Secretary of State to Viceroy (T 16574), 11 September 1946, and Turnbull to Monteath and Pethick-Lawrence, 11 September 1946, Ibid., pp. 490–1 and 490 respectively.

ted Wavell to advise the war cabinet to widen political liberalization between 1943–5, but he had not counselled winding up the Raj. It was the deepening political and communal rift, combined with labour unrest, which added a new dimension to the crumbling administrative and military foundations of the Raj after August 1946, especially as it held out the spectre of a sweeping anti-British wave. While Wavell worried about holding responsibility without power,[72] the cabinet pinned their hopes on successful negotiations. The cabinet's reasons for doing so were apparent in the *manner* in which ministers discussed the withdrawal proposals: in each case they pointed to their probable consequences before considering the accuracy of Wavell's estimate of the situation. There is no evidence in cabinet minutes to suggest a willing and long thoughtout British departure from India. The effect of withdrawal on Britain's international prestige weighed most with the Labour government in rejecting Wavell's suggestion to fix a terminal date for the Raj. To leave India before a constitution had been framed would be regarded by the world as an act of weakness and it would seriously undermine Britain's international position. The Chiefs of Staff had advised the essentiality of keeping India in the Commonwealth defence system; and India's cooperation was 'especially necessary' for the maintenance of Britain's strategic position in the Middle and Far East. Only an amicable transfer of power would make this possible. Above all, the British must avoid a situation in which they had to withdraw under 'circumstances of ignominy after there had been widespread riots and attacks on Europeans. It must be clear that we were going freely and not under compulsion'.[73]

To what extent did the Labour government agree with Wavell's appraisal of the administrative machine? On 5 June the cabinet delegation confessed that it was 'extremely weak'. On 23 September, Pethick-Lawrence agreed that it was deteriorating, but that there was no danger of a breakdown. The Viceroy's proposals, if carried out, would lead to a breakdown. The cabinet's anxiety to avoid a breakdown was reflected by their endorsement of A.V. Alexander's

[72] Enclosure by Wavell to Pethick-Lawrence, 8 September 1946, *TOP*, vol. 8, pp. 455–9.

[73] Record of meeting at 10 Downing Street on 23 September 1946, Ibid., pp. 570; cabinet meeting, 5 June 1946, *TOP*, vol. 7, pp. 812–19; Pethick-Lawrence to Wavell, 25 November 1946, *TOP*, vol. 9, pp. 170–1. Chronology has been sacrificed for coherence in this paragraph.

suggestion to strengthen the administration by recruiting additional Europeans on the basis that they would be guaranteed at least fifteen years' service in India or in the Colonial or Foreign Services if they were not required in India for the whole of that period.[74] The proposal was eventually shelved because Wavell warned that it would intensify Indian suspicions of British intentions. It would also have little practical value as the British would face a crisis in India in 1947 or 1948, while the recruits would not have completed training before 1950.[75] In November, Attlee ruled out the re-establishment of British rule for another fifteen years as neither the administrative nor military machine was capable of sustaining it.[76] So the cabinet concurred with Wavell that the administration was shaky, and that the British would not be able to crush a mass revolt. But because they wished to avoid scuttle, ministers did not share his pessimism that it was inevitable. At any rate, they wanted to pursue negotiations until failure became a certainty. In other words, they were reluctant to tell parliament that they expected a breakdown and could do nothing about it.

Wavell was apprehensive of what the British would do if the League embarked on direct action. 'If we allow the Muslims to enter on direct action without making it clear that we have *not* made an alliance with the Congress against the League and do not propose to hold the British forces available for internal security duties for more than a very short time, we shall be accepting a very heavy responsibility'.[77] The British government must decide its policy.

Whitehall did not want to take responsibility for the implementation of the Mission plan. The British could not make a statement that sections could decide their own procedure. Jinnah would then ask for a statement on others 'and we shall be led a considerable distance on the road of laying down in detail' the procedure of the Constituent Assembly.[78]

The tussle between the Congress and the League on the issue of a Nationalist Muslim continued, until Wavell told Jinnah that he

[74] Ibid.

[75] Wavell to Pethick-Lawrence, 23 October 1946, *TOP*, vol. 8, p. 794.

[76] Undated note by Attlee, *TOP*, vol. 9, p. 68. Also Pethick-Lawrence to Wavell, 25 November 1946, Ibid., pp. 170–1.

[77] Wavell to Pethick-Lawrence, 24 September 1946, L/P&J/10/75, p. 160. Emphasis in original.

[78] Secretary of State to Viceroy (T 17341), 25 September 1946, L/P&J/10/75, p. 197.

could not press the Congress further on the issue. Jinnah said nothing about this but said that he must be able to show his Working Committee other gains, for example, the safeguard against being outvoted on major communal issues, the Vice Presidency of the Executive Council, and minorities. Wavell's impression was that the matter of the Vice President was 'obviously one to which Jinnah attached most importance, from the psychological point of view'. On minorities Wavell assured him that no representative would be appointed without the concurrence of the Congress and the League.[79] On the question of a convention on major communal issues that no decision should be taken if either Hindus or Muslims were opposed, Wavell agreed with the Congress that 'it would be fatal to allow major communal issues to be decided by vote in the cabinet'. The efficiency and prestige of the Interim Government would depend on ensuring that differences were resolved in advance of cabinet meetings by friendly discussions. 'A Coalition Government either works by a process of mutual adjustments or does not work at all'. Wavell asked the league to reconsider the resolution of 29 June and to accept the long-term plan of the Mission's formula, that is, to enter the Constituent Assembly.[80] Probably to counter the inclusion of a Nationalist Muslim in the Congress quota, the League nominated a Scheduled Caste representative in its own quota.[81] To this the Congress raised no objection.[82] On 13 October, Jinnah communicated to Wavell the League's decision to enter the interim government.[83]

Why the League entered the Interim Government is not easy to ascertain. Wavell and Pethick-Lawrence had been satisfied that the Congress had 'put their best men' into the government;[84] Wavell expressed his disappointment with the names Jinnah put forward.[85] Nehru considered the inclusion of men of low calibre and standing such as Rab Nishtar and Ghazanfar Ali as indicative of the League's insincerity in making the government a success.[86] Ghazanfar Ali

[79] Viceroy to Secretary of State (T 2025-S), 26 September 1946, L/P&J/10/75, pp. 186–7, and Viceroy to Secretary of State (T 2085-S), 2 October 1946, Ibid., p. 151.

[80] Wavell to Jinnah, 4 October 1946, *TOP*, vol. 8, pp. 654–5.

[81] Viceroy to Secretary of State (T 2160-S), 14 October 1946, L/P&J/10/75, p. 122.

[82] Viceroy to Secretary of State (T 2170-S), 15 October 1946, Ibid., p. 115.

[83] Jinnah to Wavell, 13 October 1946, *TOP*, vol. 8, pp. 709–10.

[84] Pethick-Lawrence to Wavell, 28 August 1946, Ibid., p. 333.

[85] Note by Wavell, 16 October 1946, Ibid., pp. 739–40.

[86] Nehru to Wavell, 15 October 1946, Ibid., p. 735.

seemingly justified the Calcutta riots by saying that they showed Muslims would not submit to any government that did not include their representatives. The Interim Government 'is one of the fronts of the direct action campaign and we shall most scrupulously carry out the orders of Mr. Jinnah on any front that he orders us'.[87] There was not let down in its attacks on the Congress; in the organization of the League's National Guards in many provinces, or any inclination to defuse the atmosphere of communal tension.[88] Liaqat admitted to Abell that the League could only retain its popularity by a policy of 'opposition' and communal propaganda.[89]

The League's entry into the Interim Government did not bring about the expected lull in communal violence. Even as the League joined the government, there occurred in the districts of Noahkhali and Tippera in East Bengal one of the worst communal riots ever seen in india, all the more brutal, because, like the communal killings in Bihar, and in the Punjab in March 1947, they were organized.

Of this there was no doubt in Noahkhali and Tippera. There was evidence of organization behind all aspects of the trouble, which included murder, rape, conversions and forced marriages. The method of attack was consistent. First, a Muslim group approached a Hindu house and told the family that if their wealth was given to this group, they would be protected from other Muslims. Upon the departure of this group, another Muslim group would arrive and tell the Hindus that the only way to escape with their lives was to accept conversion to Islam. Local Maulvis travelled with the second group to perform the conversions. Hindus who resisted were murdered, as were those with influence in the district. A third group would complete the looting and set fire to the Hindu houses. The Hindus who had been forcibly converted were given white caps with "*Pakistan zindabad*" written on them, so that they would be protected from further attacks.[90] Officials found local Muslims sympathetic to the forced conversions,[91] and some were shown the caps which the con-

[87] *Eastern Times*, 9 October 1946.

[88] See, for example, Wylie to Wavell, 14 November 1946, *TOP*, vol. 9, pp. 70–1, FR for UP for first half of November 1946, HP file no. 18/11/46.

[89] Abell to Scott, 16 November 1946, *TOP*, vol. 9, p. 84.

[90] Tuker, *While Memory Serves*, p. 174. Pyarelal, *Mahatma Gandhi: The Last Phase*, vol. 1, part 1, pp. 280–1.

[91] Governor of Bengal to Viceroy (T 2656-S), 22 October 1946, HP file no. 5/55/46.

verted Hindus were made to wear after the conversions had taken place.[92]

Hindu women were raped, their conch shells were broken and their caste marks were erased from their foreheads.

> '"Outside goondas do not loot things of everyday use such as clothes, foodstuffs etc." [observed Kripalani, General Secretary of the Congress]. "They don't drive away cattle . . . Outside goondas are . . . not interested in forcible conversions and marriages. They don't take pirs and maulvis with them to perform conversion ceremonies." '[93]

The performance of the Bengal government was reprehensible. Burrows was on holiday in Darjeeling when the trouble started on 10 October, and his first report to Wavell was dated 16 October from Darjeeling. This was sent in response to a request from Wavell, who had been asked by Congress leaders for a report on the communal incidents.[94] The trouble was organized by a local landlord, Ghulam Sarwar, an ex-Congressman, who had recently joined the League.[95] Suhrawardy stated that the League had nothing to do with the disturbances, and local Leaguers did help to restore order.[96] But the League ministry put pressure on the police to withdraw all criminal cases connected with the rioting. These included murder, rioting, arson, dacoity and in a few cases, rape.[97]

The Bengal ministry's attitude to refugees also left its intentions in doubt. It left district officers in the dark as to the broad policy and details of refugee relief. It relied on "Volunteers", who one British official described as 'young men of the excitable student type' to shepherd and advise the refugees, and appointed junior Muslim officers to important supervisory jobs in Calcutta, but left district officers to arrange food and accommodation for the refugees. No information was given as to how long the refugees should be accommodated or if an attempt should be made to get them away from Muslim areas. 'The only interpretation that seemed

[92] Pyarelal, *Mahatma Gandhi: The Last Phase*, vol. 1, part 1, p. 299. See also Lambert, 'Hindu-Muslim Riots', p. 244.

[93] Statement by J.B. Kripalani, 29 October 1946, quoted in Lambert, 'Hindu-Muslim Riots', p. 184.

[94] Wavell to Burrows, (T), 15 October 1946, *TOP*, vol. 8, p. 729; and Patel to Burrows, 19 October 1946, Ibid., p. 750. See also *Statesman*, 18 October 1946.

[95] *Morning News*, 26 September 1946.

[96] Governor of Bengal to Viceroy (T 291), HP file no. 5/55/46, pp. 32–3.

[97] M.O. Carter, 'Trouble in 1946' *M.O. Carter papers*, pp. 10ff.

possible was that the Bengal . . . ministry was privately sponsoring a kind of transfer of the population in an effort to create "cells" of Muslim resistance, over the heads of its own officers'.[98]

The League's central leadership did not issue any statement condemning the events in Bengal. A plea by Burrows to members of the Interim Government who visited the province to issue such a statement met with a negative response from the League leaders. Liaqat Ali Khan said 'it would probably be better to have such a statement issued by prominent Muslim religious leaders. I said that I appreciated that, but . . . a statement by political leaders would also be of immense advantage. Patel agreed with me. Nishtar said nothing'.[99] Wavell drew attention to speeches made by Liaqat and Ghazanfar Ali which clearly incited to violence. Jinnah only referred to 'what was happening in other parts of India'.[100]

The reorganization of the Muslim League National Guards in October 1946 raises questions about the intentions of the central leadership of the League. Ex-military Muslim personnel had been invited to join the Guards since the end of the war, and many reports show that they were involved in the organization of the riots in Noahkhali,[101] and later in the Punjab. On 1 October 1946, the Guards were reorganized so that the control of Presidents of provincial Leagues over them was withdrawn. The whole organization was given a 'wholly military' character, as opposed to its earlier political cum military character, and was put 'so to speak on a war footing'. The *Salar-i-Ala* was to be appointed by the Committee of Action of the League, and he would appoint provincial *salars* in consultation with the Committee.[102] They pledged to strive for the achievement of Pakistan. Whether the National Guards acted on their own in East Bengal, or whether they were carrying out the orders of the Committee of Action, remains unanswered.

As news of Noahkhali spilled over into Bihar and the UP, these two Hindu-majority provinces witnessed the worst communal vio-

[98] J.M.G. Bell, 'Note on recent experiences in Bengal', *J.M.G. Bell papers*, file 3, item 4.

[99] Burrows to Wavell, 4 November 1946, *TOP*, vol. 9, pp. 5–6.

[100] Note by Wavell on discussion with Jinnah, 22 October 1946, *TOP*, vol. 8, p. 762.

[101] FR for Bengal for first and second half of October 1946, HP file no. 18/10/46.

[102] Note by E.J. Beveridge, 8 November 1946, on the Muslim League National Guards—HP file no. 28/4/46. See also *Star of India*, 14 October 1946.

lence since the beginning of British rule in India. Hindu refugees carried tales of conversions, rapes, the burning of Hindu houses. Propaganda by the Hindu Mahasabha in Bihar added fuel to the desire for revenge. *Searchlight* and the *Indian Nation*, edited by a Hindu landlord, the Maharaja of Darbhanga, put out particularly scurrilous writing after the Noahkhali massacres. *Searchlight* carried reports of *goonda raj* in East Bengal even as the League joined the interim government. The League was attempting to establish Islam by the sword. 'Gone are the days when Hindus . . . proved helpless before successive hordes of invaders.'[103]

The trouble began in Patna with a hartal by Hindus to observe 25 October as Noahkhali Day, which led to an outbreak of rioting. On 26 October, Hindus from villages north of Chapra invaded Muslim *tolas* and killed 20 Muslims. The situation was brought under control by the evening, but the next day rioting spread through eastern and southeastern parts of Jehanabad subdivision in Gaya district and into the western part of Monghyr district. There was evidence of organization of massacres of Muslims in Bihar. Marwari businessmen of Calcutta were believed to have organized them in retaliation for Direct Action day in Calcutta. But it is not possible to detect the hand of a single party in the organization of the violence.[104] Some evidence against the RSS in the UP riots comes from Congress workers.[105]

The Congress ministry in Bihar and Congress leaders in the interim government reacted swiftly to the events in the province. Police opened fire in the Patna and Saran districts on 23 occasions by 31 October. Dow testified that the ministry 'were . . . insistent during the early days of the rioting that the military should shoot to kill larger numbers of the mobs, which generally dispersed, however great their number, as soon as firing was resorted to'.[106] Nehru's threatened bombing of the affected areas—leading to an outcry by the Mahasabha and some resentment among Hindus about the

[103] *Searchlight*, editorial, 21 October 1946.

[104] Dow's reports and the fortnightly reports do not mention any party. This is corroborated by Tuker. Nehru believed it was organized by Marwari businessmen and Hindu landlords. Nehru to Gandhi, 3 October 1946, *NC*.

[105] Statement by Mridula Sarabhai, General Secretary AICC, 13 November 1946, and statement by Shah Nawaz Khan, 13 November 1946, AICC file no. 20, pp. 1–6 and 9–11 respectively.

[106] Dow to Wavell, 22/23 November 1946, *TOP*, vol. 9, p. 149.

alleged ruthlessness with which Hindu mobs were suppressed while Muslim mobs in Bengal were apparently given a free hand.[107]

The attitude of Congress leaders provides a contrast to that of the League, over the riots in both Bengal and Bihar. Kripalani expressed shame that his co-religionists had been betrayed into reprisals.[108] Gandhi's judgement—justified—was that Bihar had disgraced India even as Bengal had done.[109] Wavell, no great admirer of Nehru, praised the work done by him in Patna and Calcutta as having done good, which did 'considerable credit to his courage and energy'.[110] There was evidence of the Congress leaders' concern for Muslims harmed in the violence.[111]

Jinnah's reaction lent credence to the view that he was not interested in a united, independent India. If the League and the Congress did not agree on division, 'What happens is what you see . . . '[112] From 10–14 November, *Dawn* carried provocative epitaphs in black-bordered 'boxes' on the Muslims killed in the riots. The first of these read:

> "Think only of the martyrs of Bihar that they died for Islam. Clustering around the throne of God they must be saying: our Lord! they killed us because we worshipped you. Because we followed your Prophet. Think also this that their souls are watching. Let the blood of those that are dead cleanse the hearts of those that are living. Let it wash their weakness away: make them strong, united, invincible."[113]

The League's attitude to relief work was obstructive. It discouraged Muslim refugees from returning to their villages and encouraged them to leave the province. Muslim League 'helpers' in relief camps concentrated on circulating political manifestoes. Hearing of Dow's tour of the relief camps on 1 November, they arranged demonstrations and processions, and were 'ghoulish enough to dig up the bones and skulls of buried victims and strew them in my path in order to demonstrate the callous neglect of my ministry'. This was carried on under the authority of Firoz Khan Noon.[114] That orders for arranging mass transfers of the population came from Jinnah is

[107] FRs for UP and Bengal for first half of November 1946, HP file no. 18/11/46.
[108] *Searchlight*, 7 November 1946. [109] *Searchlight*, 8 November 1946.
[110] Wavell to Pethick-Lawrence, 13 November 1946, *TOP*, vol. 9, p. 56.
[111] See, for example, Gandhi to Syed Mahmud, 22 January 1946, (in Hindi), *Syed Mahmud papers*.
[112] *Searchlight*, 16 November 1946.
[113] *Dawn*, 10 November 1946. (Original in Capitals.)
[114] Dow to Colville, 10/11 December 1946, L/P&J/5/181.

suggested by Dow's report that both Noon and Nazimuddin realized that it was impracticable to arrange mass transfers of the population, 'but their efforts cannot have much effect so long as Jinnah remains intransigent and openly advocates the movement'.[115] Jinnah's attitude could also account for the fact that Hindus were not encouraged to return to their homes in Eastern Bengal after the Noahkhali violence.[116]

Whatever the ministry may have done by way of firm and effective action in Bihar, the province produced, until June 1947, the largest 'butcher's bill'. Some 20,000 Muslims are estimated to have lost their lives. This raises the question of the ability of the administration in both Bengal and Bihar. In Bengal, Burrows held that there was adequate warning for the authorities to have taken action, but that they failed to do so.[117] On a visit to Calcutta and Noahkhali, Wavell was unconvinced by attempts by the Deputy Inspector General of Police to defend his men against accusations of communal violence and lack of energy. In Chandpur they gave a 'not very convincing' account of why arrests had not been made earlier. 'I cannot believe', concluded Wavell, 'that the district officials had not a considerable amount of warning which ought to have put them on their guard; and when trouble did break out the measures taken seem to have been quite ineffective. The failure to send information more quickly to superior authorities seems to have been inexplicabe'.[118] Tuker gives only one instance of a provincial official in Bihar having known about the Bihar riots in advance.[119] That officials could not be relied upon was illustrated again in the UP, where police did not check people carrying spears, or mounted horsemen who were really destructive gangs, even when Congress workers drew attention to them.[120] The communal sympathies of the District Magistrate of Chittagong had been noted by British officials as early as Direct Action day.[121]

[115] Ibid.

[116] J.M.G. Bell, 'Note on recent experiences in Bengal', *J.M.G. Bell papers*, file 3, item 4.

[117] Burrows to Secretary of State, 18 November 1946, L/P&J/5/153.

[118] Wavell to Pethick-Lawrence, 5 November 1946, *TOP*, vol. 9, pp. 17–18.

[119] Tuker, *While Memory Serves*, p. 181.

[120] Statements by M. Sarabhai and Shah Nawaz Khan on 13 November 1946, AICC file no. 20, pp. 1–6 and 9–11 respectively.

[121] See also J.M.G. Bell, 'Note on recent experiences in Bengal', Bell papers, file 3, item 4.

Another aspect of the administrative problems involved in bringing the riots under control and in carrying out relief work is illustrated by the problem of bad communications and inadequate staff in Bihar, which had a population of 40 million but the same budget as Sind, which had a population of 4.5 million. With a population nearly ten times that of Sind it had only 50 per cent more police than in Sind where they were 'admittedly insufficient.'[122] In January 1946, Bihar had a permanent strength of 13,500 unarmed police, 5,000 armed police and 1,500 military police. This was then considered adequate for the '*normal* needs' of the province. At the same time 3 battalions of internal defence troops were located at Calcutta for use in Bengal, Bihar, Assam and Orissa with a population of over 100 million. The Bihar government had warned the Home Department of the Government of India that these troops were inadequate in a country 'which, even assuming there is a peaceful political settlement seems likely to be torn by communal strife, agrarian uprisings and labour trouble. . . .'[123]

Administrative inadequacy was illustrated when Dow visited the Mishouri district where 60 deaths had occurred. He found no motorable road to it and the only way to get there was by train up to a point and then walk. The road to another village was barely accessible by jeep, and it took an hour to get there. The village itself was off the road and had to be reached by walking through paddy fields. From the 1st November, when 200 Muslims had been massacred there, until the 27th, when Dow visited it himself, nobody had visited it on behalf of the government. 'There was simply no staff, high or low, who could be expected to do it except by neglecting some other duty equally or more important'. Dow did not specify what these might have been. It would be weeks before any police investigation could begin. If the police concentrated on prosecution, they would be diverted from ordinary administration of law and order.[124]

With an administration that was both inadequate and to some extent unreliable, and unable to suppress communal violence except with military help; with an increasing awareness that the adminis-

[122] Dow to Colville, 10/11 December 1946, *TOP*, vol. 9, pp. 328–9.

[123] Secret letter from J. Bowstead, Chief Secretary, Bihar Political Department to Secretary, Government of India, 22 January 1946, Home Police file no. 174/32/45. Emphasis in original.

[124] Dow to Colville, 10/11 December 1946, *TOP*, vol. 9, pp. 329–30.

tration was weak, if not broken down already, with communal passions rising even as news spread of atrocities committed on both communities, partition appeared inevitable by the end of 1946. Developments on the constitutional front confirmed this assumption, despite hopes by both Congress and the British that it could still be avoided.

CHAPTER 7

Prelude to Partition:
November 1946 to February 1947

Between November 1946 and February 1947, the League's attitude to the Interim Government, its attempt to overthrow by force the Unionist ministry in Punjab, its refusal to enter the Constituent Assembly and to accept the Cabinet Mission plan of 16 May 1946—all signified its intent to achieve Pakistan. During these months it also became clear that it would attain its objective as the British were bending over backwards to attract it into the Constituent Assembly, by making concessions to it and ignoring its incitements to violence. The hope of attaining independence for India as soon as possible made the Congress yield to the League and the British, and by remaining the Interim Government, it was caught in a maze of negotiations in which only Jinnah seemed to know where he was going; and the British, as arbiters between the League and Congress, were equally consistent in quickly putting aside old promises, but all the same making new ones in the fond hope that partition could be avoided. If not they still hoped their interests could be safeguarded.

The League never intended the interim government to work as its success would have weakened the case for Pakistan. Liaqat Ali Khan considered it a coalition only in the sense that it contained representatives to two parties; it was 'not a combination in the full sense'.[1] Jinnah also did not regard it as a coalition but only as containing two groups.[2] Indeed, the Interim Government was probably unique in that each party met separately before a cabinet meeting and there functioned in opposition to each other. In this they were not discouraged by Wavell, who saw members belonging to both parties separately, and regarded Congress complaints against the behaviour of the League as inspired by their pique that the League did not recognize Nehru as *de facto* Prime Minister.[3] As the League, un-

[1] Indian Conference in London, 4 December 1946, *TOP*, vol. 9, p. 264.
[2] *Dawn*, 15 November 1946.
[3] Indian Conference in London, 4 December 1946, *TOP*, vol. 9, p. 253.

like the Congress, wanted the Viceroy to retain his special powers, both Wavell and Whitehall were not displeased by differences between the two parties on this issue.[4]

The British believed that 'interference' by the interim government in provincial matters, especially in Muslim majority provinces, would further alienate the League and lessen the chances of its entering the government and the Constituent Assembly. So Wavell did not allow the cabinet to discuss the riots in Bengal and Bihar on the ground that they were a provincial matter.[5] In Sind, a League government which had lost its majority in the legislature was allowed to continue in office until fresh elections were held in November 1946. The constitutional course of calling on the Congress leader in the assembly, who could have commanded a majority, was not resorted to, because Jinnah would not have stood for a Congress government in a Muslim majority province.[6] Mudie allegedly tried to persuade Europeans to support the League and advised the League to offer more portfolios so as to attract waverers and their supporters.[7] Privately, Wavell did not have much faith in Mudie's judgment. But he defended his conduct. 'If what I consider a racket and a public scandal has your approval', rejoined an indignant Nehru, 'then it is obvious that our standards and sense of values differ considerably'.[8]

In the NWFP, the League organized demonstrations when Nehru, whose portfolio included tribal relations, visited the tribal areas. The Mullah of Manki was allowed to carry out religious propaganda among the tribes, and Nehru was lucky not to have been killed on his tour. The governor, Sir Olaf Caroe, made no effort to restrain the Mullah and the League. 'I think that in the circumstances, and given the fact that Nehru's tour was obviously intended to push the Congress cause, it would have been wrong to put active restraint against the League's propagandists going into tribal territory, and an attempt to do so would certainly have led to disturbances.'[9]

[4] Pethick-Lawrence to Attlee, 1 June 1946, PREM 8/247/1946.

[5] Wavell to Pethick-Lawrence, (T), 26 October 1946, *TOP*, vol. 8, p. 825.

[6] Wavell to Pethick-Lawrence, (T), 6 September 1946; Note by Turnbull and Monteath, 7 September 1946; Pethick-Lawrence to Wavell, (T), 8 September 1946, Ibid., pp. 429, 445 and 466 respectively.

[7] Nehru to Wavell, 5 September 1946, Ibid., p. 421.

[8] Nehru to Wavell, 23 September 1946, Ibid., p. 569.

[9] Caroe to Wavell, 23 October 1946, Ibid., p. 787.

To have to work with the League in the Interim Government was, then, no easy task for the Congress; and with the constitutional restrictions, imposed readily by Wavell, on the Interim Government 'interfering' in provincial matters, and with communal violence spreading in Bengal, the Congress was unhappy and frustrated with its position:

> 'Indeed I have come seriously to think whether it serves any useful purpose for me to be in the Interim Government if an important part of India sinks to barbarism or something much worse . . . . What is the good of our forming the Interim Government of India if all that we can do is to watch helplessly and do nothing else when thousands of people are being butchered and subjected to infinitely worse treatment?'[10]

In yet another attempt to cajole the League into the Constituent Assembly, the Labour government, in December 1946, invited representatives of the Congress, the League and the Sikhs to London for fresh discussions. At the same time, the Statement of 16 May was referred to Lord Jowitt, the Lord Chancellor, for a decision on the correct interpretation of paragraphs 15 and 19 of the statement.[11] Jowitt upheld the Mission's interpretation that provincial representatives would form sections, and that the sections—not the individual provinces—would settle provincial constitutions. The sections would also decide whether and to what extent a group constitution should be set up for any province.[12] In a new statement on 6 December, the Labour government announced that its intention had always been that the grouping decision should be taken by simple majority vote in sections. On other questions in the statement which might come up for interpretation, the Federal Court would be asked to decide matters of interpretation and the British government 'will accept such decision so that the procedure both in the Union Constituent Assembly and in the Sections may accord with the Cabinet Mission's Plan'. The Congress was requested to accept the statement so that the League might reconsider its attitude and enter the Constituent Assembly.[13]

Jinnah saw Pakistan being presented to him. Taking aside Baldev

[10] Nehru to Wavell, 15 October 1946, Ibid., pp. 732–3.

[11] Pethick-Lawrence to Lord Jowitt, 29 November 1946, L/P&J/10/111, pp. 100–4.

[12] Jowitt to Pethick-Lawrence, 2 December 1946, Ibid., pp. 47–8.

[13] Statement of 6 December 1946, *TOP*, vol. 9, pp. 295–6.

Singh, the Sikh representative at the London Conference, he offered him any guarantees the Sikhs might require. 'Baldev Singh, you see this matchbox. Even if Pakistan of this size is offered to me I will gladly accept it, but it is here that I need your collaboration. If you persuade the Sikhs to join hands with the Muslim League we will have a glorious Pakistan, the gates of which will be near about Delhi if not in Delhi itself.'[14] As Pethick-Lawrence had earlier perceived, what Jinnah wanted was not an assurance of the intentions of the Cabinet Mission but a guarantee that they would be enforced by the British. He replied to the Statement of 6 December that unless H.M.G. could guarantee that there would be a constitution on the lines recommended by the Cabinet Mission, details about the procedure of the Constituent Assembly were of no interest to him.[15] He would also not accept any decision of the Federal Court which went against him. He promised to call a meeting of his Council to consider that 6 December statement, but gave no assurance that he would ask them to reaccept the Statement of 16 May. The Congress protested that the British should have made their real intentions clear long ago. The Cabinet Mission had accepted the Congress interpretation of the 16 May statement and had told them that there would be no further amendment or change. The 6 December statement created a new situation for the Congress.[16]

On 9 December the Constituent Assembly opened without the League and without any communal incident. Gandhi opposed its meeting without the League, for such a Constituent Assembly was being held without agreement among Indians themselves, and under cover of British arms.[17] Nehru and Patel had reasons to disagree with Gandhi. In December the Assembly passed a resolution that India would be a sovereign, secular republic. The two leaders persuaded an indignant AICC to accept the Statement of 6 December

[14] Baldev Singh to Nehru, 18 September 1955, *NC*, quoted by Gopal, *Nehru*, vol. 1, p. 338.

[15] Secretary of State to Viceroy (T20252), 18 November 1946, L/P&J/10/76, pp. 293–4. See also Indian Conference in London, 4 December 1946, *TOP*, vol. 9, pp. 252–3.

[16] Indian Conference in London, 5 & 6 December 1946, L/P&J/10/111, pp. 60–1, 46–8. See also note of conversation between Jinnah and Wyatt on 9 December 1946; CAB 127/136. On Congress reaction, see also note of interview between Colville and Patel on 10 December 1946, L/P&J/10/76, pp. 59–61.

[17] Confidential notes by Gandhi dated 4 and 17 December 1946, AICC file no. 71, 1946–7, pp. 60 and 61 respectively.

to keep the Constituent Assembly alive. For the significant point about the Constituent Assembly was that it could not be dissolved by the British except by force. It was a weapon with which independence could be achieved. If the Congress rejected it, the British might withdraw the Mission Plan and give the League Pakistan.[18] The Assembly could not, in any case, function without the League or impose a constitution on unwilling provinces. Acceptance of the 6 December statement was 'definitely a climb-down on the part of the Congress but for the good of the people of India principles have sometimes to be swalloed for the sake of expediency'.[19] It appears that Congress leaders thought that Jinnah and the League would enter the Constituent Assembly if they accepted the 6 December statement, which would create some sort of Pakistan within a federation. An unsigned note, probably by J.B. Kripalani, then Congress president, suggests that the Congress favoured accepting the Mission plan with the joint interpretation of it between themselves and Jinnah. Assam, NWFP and Baluchistan would probably secede from Groups B and C, which would frame what group constitutions they could 'inspite of the seceders'. If the British set up or recognized another Constituent Assembly, they would 'damn themselves for ever'. They were duty bound to leave India 'when' a constitution was framed in accordance with the Mission Plan. This was not playing into Jinnah's hands.

The Assembly would frame a constitution for the whole of India and the constitution would contain a specific clause showing in what way boycotters could avail of the constitution.[20] The note is important, because it shows that the Congress had strong hopes that their acceptance of the 6 December statement would bring the League into the Constituent Assembly, and a constitution for a united India would emerge. The confidence of the Congress is suggested by the phrase that the British were 'bound *when* a constitution is framed'; 'if' would have reflected uncertainty.

Even as the Congress debated the 6 December statement, the Labour government had realized the full import of Jinnah's refusal to enter the Constituent Assembly, and the real reason for it—their reluctance to guarantee the procedure of the Constituent Assembly.

[18] *Statesman*, 7 January 1947. *National Herald*, 7 January 1947.

[19] Confidential AICC note, 29 December 1946, probably by Kripalani, AICC file no. G-66, 1946–1947, pp. 149–50.

[20] Ibid.

As the Constituent Assembly met on 9 December, the 'pressure of events' was leading to Pakistan.[21] A withdrawal announcement might still echo of scuttle, but the minutes of the India and Burma Committee meeting on 31 December 1946 are worth quoting, for they show how Labour ministers transformed the political alternative they had hitherto construed as defeat into a moral and political triumph.

> 'The general feeling of the Cabinet was that withdrawal from India need not appear to be forced upon us by our weakness nor to be the first step in the dissolution of the Empire. On the contrary this action *must be shown to be* the logical conclusion, which we welcomed, of a policy followed by successive Governments for many years.... There was, therefore, no occasion to excuse our withdrawal: *we should rather claim credit* for terminating British rule in India and transferring our responsibilities to the representatives of the Indian people.'[22]

But Attlee's heart was not in the announcement, and even as the cabinet decided that the withdrawal statement would be made soon after the British parliament met on 21 January 1947,[23] he was looking for a way out of it. The Congress resolution of 6 January 1947 accepting the 6 December statement obviously renewed his hopes that the League might enter the Constituent Assembly, and a political breakdown avoided. On 8 January, the cabinet decided against making any announcement with a view to overcoming the League's refusal to enter the Constituent Assembly.[24]

But there was no sign of the League entering the assembly. Liaqat Ali Khan said that the Congress resolution of 6 January did not constitute 'true acceptance' of the Mission Plan,[25] and Muslim Leaguers continued their diatribe against the interim government and the Congress. The activities of the League's National Guards increased communal tension in many provinces,[26] and in Sind, Mudie had to tell his League ministers that there was no point in a

[21] India and Burma Committee meetings on 11 and 17 December 1946, CAB 134/342.

[22] Confidential annex to Cabinet C.M. (46) 108th conclusions, 31 December 1946, CAB 128/8.

[23] India and Burma Committee meeting on 20 December 1946 CAB 134/343.

[24] India and Burma Committee meeting on 8 January 1947, CAB 134/342.

[25] Wavell's note on interview with Liaqat Ali Khan, 7 January 1947, *TOP*, vol. 9, p. 481.

[26] See, for example, *Eastern Times*, 2 January 1947, *Dawn*, 5, 10 and 15 January 1947.

Muslim League private army fighting the police of a League administration.[27] On 31 January 1947, the Working Committee of the Muslim League decided that it would remain outside the assembly; that the proceedings of the present assembly were illegal and that it should be dissolved. The Council of the League would therefore not meet to reconsider the Direct Action resolution.

That Jinnah was largely responsible for the resolution was suggested by Mudie's comment that provincial Leaguers in Sind would go by what Jinnah said on an all-India matter;[28] and Wavell himself perceived that other Leaguers would not go against Jinnah.[29] The refusal to withdraw the direct action resolution meant that the League was in opposition to the Cabinet Mission Plan, including the Interim Government formed under that plan and of which it was a member.

The intentions of the League were now made clear in the Punjab. The communal situation had been worsening in the Punjab since October 1946, so that by 29 November, Jenkins had to use his discretionary powers under section 89 of the Act of 1935 to promulgate the Punjab Public Safety Ordinance.[30] Khizar himself was shocked by the deterioration in communal relations coming in the wake of communal riots in Bengal, Bihar and the UP, and on 24 January 1947, he passed with the approval of Jenkins, an ordinance banning the RSS and the Muslim League National Guards under the Criminal Law Amendment Act.[31] Such declarations were always followed by routine searches of party offices. The searches passed off without incident except in Lahore where Muslim Leaguers who had obstructed the police had to be arrested under Section 353 of the Indian Penal Code. They refused to apply for bail. The arrests were followed by disturbances in Lahore on 25 and 26 January. On 25 January, 15 MLAs defied the ban on processions and meetings in two separate batches and also had to be arrested.[32] The League alleged that the ban on the National Guards was an attack on the Muslim League. Ghazanfar Ali, still a member of the Interim Gov-

[27] Mudie to Wavell, 22 January 1947, L/P&J/5/263.

[28] Mudie to Wavell, 8 January 1947, Ibid., p. 489.

[29] Wavell to Pethick-Lawrence, 14 January 1947, Ibid., p. 502.

[30] Jenkins to Wavell, 30 November 1946, Ibid., p. 229.

[31] Jenkins to Pethick-Lawrence, 26 January 1947, Ibid., pp 556–7; *Eastern Times*, 25 January 1947.

[32] Jenkins to Pethick-Lawrence, (T), 26 January 1947, *TOP*, vol. 9, p. 556.

ernment, warned that the Punjab Ministry's action could endanger the peace of the province 'to an extent which cannot be foreseen'.[33] Jinnah expressed 'shock' at the ban on the National Guards and the arrests of provincial League leaders. If there was 'one more mad and inimical action against the Muslim League' by the Punjab government, the reaction all over India would be 'terrific'. He appealed to the Viceroy to intervene and 'save the situation which may otherwise take a very serious turn for which the entire responsibility will rest with the Viceroy and His Majesty's Government'.[34]

Jenkins pointed out that the National Guards had a written constitution of their own and a commander with military titles. They were a party army on the same lines as Hitler's Brown Shirts. All National Guards were presumably members of the League but the converse was not true.[35] There was no need for a similar ban on Congress volunteers as they were not an organized body in the Punjab. The *Akali Jathas* had existed for many years. They were formed *ad hoc* and were not active. The INA was not worth banning from a communal point of view.[36]

Khizar withdrew the ban on 27 January to show that he was not biased against the League as a party. But the demonstrations did not stop. Hartals, meetings and processions were organized in many cities and were most successful in Multan, Lahore, Gujrat and Jullundur.[37] Processionists would shout slogans such as '*Khizar Wizarat murdabad*'.[38] Those taking part in the demonstrations were usually politicians and their wives, and Muslims in rural areas belonging to the poorer classes. The agitation had the sympathy of most Muslims, official and non-official. The processionists made it clear that their aim was to establish Pakistan.[39] Jenkins believed—and Nazimuddin confirmed this—that the aim of the demonstrators was to overthrow Khizar's government by force. The searches on the 24th gave them a starting point. There was evidence that an agitation would have started on 8 February.[40] According to Jenkins,

[33] *Eastern Times*, 26 January 1947.
[34] *Eastern Times*, 29 January 1947.
[35] Jenkins to Pethick-Lawrence, (T), 26 January 1947, *TOP*, vol. 9, p. 557.
[36] Jenkins to Wavell, 28 January 1947, Ibid., p. 570.
[37] See for example, *Eastern Times*, 29 January 1947; *Statesman*, 28 January 1947.
[38] *Civil and Military Gazette*, 28 January 1947.
[39] Jenkins to Wavell, 8 February 1947, *TOP*, vol. 9, p. 654.
[40] Jenkins to Wavell, 15 February and 28 February 1947, L/P&J/5/250.

the main grievance of the League was its failure to form a ministry after winning a majority in the provincial elections of 1946. He thought there might be some truth in the allegation made by Leaguers that they were being victimized by officials, but equally there was evidence of many officials using their influence in favour of the League during the election campaign, and most Muslim officials appeared to sympathize with the League's agitation in the Punjab. It was also likely that Khizar was not conferring on Leaguers rewards such as *jagirs* because of their political hostility. But this was more a question of witholding benefits than of interfering in legitimate rights.[41]

Provincial Leaguers boasted that there had been no communal incidents during the demonstrations, and that this indicated Hindu and Sikh support for them. But this was probably due to the tendency of other communities to abstain from attacks on a government in which they were represented. Restrictions on the press, the exemplary conduct of Sikh leaders who restrained their followers, also prevented the non-Muslim minorities from organizing counter-demonstrations which could have easily degenerated into communal violence. But Hindus and Sikhs were fearful of the Pakistan that the demonstrators clamoured for, especially as the League would give them no assurance about its meaning; and the widespread belief that Muslim Raj was round the corner had a deplorable effect on communal feeling.[42]

Jinnah gave his blessings to the agitation.[43] Liaqat expected the Punjab ministry to fall as a result of the League's show of force. It was an example, he said, of what the League could do all over India although 'I couldn't guarantee that it would always remain non-violent'.[44] The despatch of a batch of National Guards from Bihar under their provincial commander to the Punjab to defy the Public Safety Ordinance[45] could suggest the connivance of the central leadership of the League in the agitation in the Punjab. In any case, the activities of the National Guard must have been known to the leadership, and may well have taken place in accordance with its instructions.

[41] Jenkins to Wavell, 15 February 1947, *TOP*, vol. 9, pp. 721–2.

[42] Jenkins to Wavell, 28 February 1947, L/P&J/5/250.

[43] Jinnah to Mamdot, 23 February 1947, S. Jafri (ed.) *Qaid-e-Azam Jinnah's Correspondence with Punjab Muslim Leaders*, pp. 233–7.

[44] *Eastern Times*, 2 February 1947. [45] HP file no. 33/9/47, p. 94.

Wavell did not reprimand the League for the Punjab demonstrations. The British simply did not know what to do. Compliance with the Mission Plan would mean acquiescing to the Congress demand to remove the League from the interim government. But the British would then be placed in the uncomfortable position of lining up with the Congress against the League. Having earlier acknowledged the validity of a Constituent Assembly, which included only the Congress,[46] the cabinet now contended that an assembly without the League could not be regarded as conforming to the Mission Plan. But it would not be 'practical politics' to disregard it altogether as the Congress might then start civil disobedience,[47] which would plunge the British into the confrontation they had tried to avoid for a year. With the League in active opposition to the Mission Plan as well as the British, political breakdown loomed large. There was only one card to be played, and on 5 February the cabinet decided to issue a withdrawal statement as a 'last attempt' to bring to the Indian parties the 'realities' of the situation. Overturning its earlier objections to Wavell's proposals, the cabinet now justified an announcement on the very grounds on which Wavell had been dismissed.[48] On 11 February, Mountbatten's insistence that Attlee fix a terminal date for the Raj clinched the issue, and two days later, Attlee informed the cabinet that he was 'satisfied' that no announcement would be effective unless the British specified a time limit.[49]

On 20 February 1947, the British announced on the first and penultimate occasion the date for a final transfer of authority to Indians. Urged on a vacillating Labour government as a consequence of the weakness of the British administrative machine by Wavell, and then, after December 1946 by Mountbatten, who made it a condition of the acceptance of his appointment as Viceroy,[50] it

[46] Downing Street meeting, 23 September 1946, L/P&J/10/45.

[47] India and Burma Committee meeting, 5 February 1947, CAB 134/343. For the developments leading to Wavell's dismissal, See Moore, *Escape from Empire*, pp. 202–14.

[48] Confidential annex to cabinet meeting on 13 February 1947, CAB 128/11, and my 'Decolonization in India: The Statement of 20 February 1947', *International History Review*, May 1984, pp. 191–209.

[49] Ibid., and undated note by Mountbatten, (probably around 11 February 1947), *TOP*, vol. 9, p. 674.

[50] Wavell to Pethick-Lawrence, 3 February 1947; Mountbatten to Attlee, 7 January 1947; Attlee to Mountbatten, 16 January 1947; Mountbatten to Cripps, 26 January 1947, Ibid., pp. 595–602, 483, 506, 553 respectively.

was fixed for 30 June 1948. The statement expressed the hope that the Indian parties would work out a constitution by then. If not, the British government would consider 'to whom the powers of the Central Government . . . should be handed over . . . whether as a whole to some form of Central Government . . . or in some areas to the existing Provincial Governments, or in such other way as may seem most reasonable and in the best interests of the Indian people'.[51]

There remained only the need to formulate a strategy to justify the statement in parliament. Mountbatten's insistence may have been the immediate occasion for fixing a terminal date for the Raj, but there was no doubt about the underlying reasons for doing so. The historical and rhetorical part of the statement, confided Attlee to Mountbatten, was needed to keep the opposition in Britain quiet. Accordingly,

> 'While nothing should be said which would suggest that *we are not in a position to prevent Indian parties from seizing power themselves*; it should be pointed out that the problem of transferring power into Indian hands has been exhaustively discussed and progressively effected . . . there must be some date beyond which British administration cannot be continued: that the advice from reasonable authorities in India is that British rule could not be maintained on its existing basis after 1948.'[52]

In the Commons debate on 5 March 1947, Cripps rhetorically posed the question whether, in the absence of agreement between Indians, 'could we have been in any way able to discharge our responsibilities after that later date?' Yet, as Henry Raikes, the Conservative MP from Liverpool, discerned, Cripps had said that one alternative was to fix a terminal date, the other was to carry on for some years. It was impracticable to go on. 'Thus in effect he did not put up any alternative. In effect, he merely said bluntly that there is no possible alternative other than to run out of India, irrespective of to whom we hand over, in the course of the next 16 months.'[53] Henry Raikes's interpretation was confirmed by Wavell's summing up of the advantages to the British of an early withdrawal:

[51] Statement of 20 February 1947, Ibid., pp. 773–5.

[52] Annex to India and Burma Committee meeting on 24 February 1947, L/P&J/10/77. Emphasis mine.

[53] *Hansard*, vol. 434, 1947, cols. 504–9, 541.

'We should . . .thus avoid being responsible for, and probably involved in, any widespread breakdown of law and order which may result from the communal situation or from labour troubles induced by revolutionary teaching or economic conditions. *The worst danger for us* is an anti-European movement which might result in the killing of some of our nationals, and of our having to carry out an ignominous forced withdrawal, instead of leaving in our own time and voluntarily.'[54]

As yet another attempt to get the League into the Constituent Assembly, the statement was a conspicuous failure. Even as the Congress hailed it as 'a courageous document'[55] Jinnah declared that the League would 'not yield an inch' in its demand for Pakistan and that the existing Constituent Assembly was dead.[56] Other Leaguers talked of a transfer of power to two sovereign states.[57] An editorial in *Dawn* welcomed the Statement of 20 February but criticized the British government for

'fighting shy of saying clear things clearly. They might as well have stated categorically that agreements would be entered into with the Congress for the Hindu majority areas and with the Muslim League for the Muslim majority areas. If paragraph 13 has any meaning this is the only manner in which agreements for the transfer of power can be successfully negotiated.'[58]

In the Punjab, the League started a new direct action movement, stopping trains, hauling down Congress flags and the Union Jack from public buildings and using violence in some towns, including Amritsar, Lahore, Multan and Jullundur.[59] Seeking to end the agitation as he believed that the Statement of 20 February had made the Unionist ministry politically irrelevant, Khizar tried to reach an agreement with provincial Leaguers. The terms were approved of or dictated by Jinnah. The ban on carrying arms and wearing uniforms would remain, but private armies could be maintained as a right. Direct action by the opposition was a legitimate weapon against a constitutional government, and special powers would not be used to prevent outbreaks of violence.[60]

[54] Wavell to King George VI, 24 February 1947, *TOP*, vol. 9, p. 809.
[55] Wavell to Pethick-Lawrence, 22 February 1947, Ibid., p. 785.
[56] *Civil and Military Gazette*, 25 February 1947.
[57] Abell to Harris, (T), 25 February 1947, *TOP*, vol. 9, p. 813.
[58] *Dawn*, 21 February 1947.
[59] Jenkins to Pethick-Lawrence, 25 February 1947, *TOP*, vol. 9, p. 814.
[60] Jenkins to Wavell, 28 February 1947, L/P&J/5/250, pp. 78ff.

Dawn described a new movement in the Punjab as 'imminent', for

> 'nothing short of Punjab's sovereign independence. The vast army of Punjabis who will have had training and gained valuable experience in this non-violent struggle may soon be called out to launch a new one. That may well require new techniques, with harsher things than the lathi, the tear gas, and the prison cell awaiting the fighters at the end of their day's work.'[61]

The League also started direct action in the NWFP. Its propaganda suggested that it would achieve Pakistan by shedding blood.[62] The Bengal Muslim League started sending volunteers to Assam.[63] The League's aim was apparently to capture power in the Punjab, NWFP and Assam by force. The Statement of 20 February gave the parties no incentive to come to an agreement, for it promised power either to the centre or to the provinces. If the League could capture power in these provinces it would get Pakistan as of right. Interestingly, Pethick-Lawrence expressed satisfaction at the agreement between Khizar and the League in the Punjab. 'If the Punjab Muslims are, in the last resort, with the League then I think it is really better that fact should be exposed . . . The League have so much to gain by getting into office in the Punjab that I should think the Sikhs could get pretty good terms from them, and if a Muslim League/Sikh coalition does emerge the problems of handing over to more than one authority, if we are driven to that, will be a great deal simplified.'[64]

But the League made no attempt to assuage the fears of the Hindus and Sikhs about the nature of Pakistan, presumably because it intended to use force. The British had always turned a blind eye to its intransigence, partly because they welcomed Congress and League differences on many issues, partly because of their belief that the Congress was out to dominate everybody else, that Jinnah only sought 'justice' for Muslims, that they could not transfer pow-

[61] *Dawn*, 25 February 1947.

[62] Caroe to Wavell, 22 February 1947, L/P&J/5/224. Fortnightly reports for NWFP for first and second half March 1947, HP file no. 18/3/47.

[63] FR for Bengal for first half of March 1947, HP file no. 18/3/47, FR for Assam for first half of March 1947, and Clow to Wavell, 3 April 1947, L/P&J/5/140, FR for NWFP for second half of March 1947, L/P&J/5/224. See also *Eastern Times*, 12 March 1947.

[64] Secretary of State to Viceroy, 27 February 1947, R/3/1/105, p. 108a.

er to only one party; and partly because it was in their own interest to transfer power to an undivided India. The fixing of a terminal date for the *Raj* in the 20 February statement, far from leading to an agreement between the League and Congress, proved the signal for an attempt to carve out Pakistan by direct action by the League.

CHAPTER 8

Divide and Quit

The League celebrated 2 March as 'Victory Day' following the settlement with Khizar. On the same day Khizar announced the resignation of his government because he felt that the Statement of 20 February obliterated the boundaries between the central and provincial spheres of administration and made it incumbent on him to leave the field clear for the League to come to an agreement with other parties. A coalition which included the League was essential for the communal safety of the Punjab, and the League would not negotiate with the minorities as long as the Unionists acted as a buffer between them and the Hindus and Sikhs.[1] Khizar's resignation symbolized the capitulation of one of the greatest bastions of intercommunal provincialism to the political weight of the League at the Centre.

Khizar's resignation shocked his non-Muslim colleagues, who immediately declared that they would not cooperate with a Muslim League government.[2] The Panthic Party passed a resolution opposing the establishment of a Muslim League government, 'so long as its object is Pakistan or Muslim domination of the Punjab, the homeland of the Sikhs'. As he came out of the party meeting, Tara Singh brandished his kirpan and shouted, '*Pakistan murdabad*!'[3] (Death to Pakistan).

The attitude of provincial Congress and Sikh leaders was provocative and hysterical. But it was explicable because the League's attitude during its agitation against the Khizar coalition was one of arrogance towards the minorities and it had never given them any indication of what Pakistan meant or what it might offer them in return for support. The League, as Jenkins pointed out, had also set a foreboding precedent by overthrowing a popular ministry by force, and, after the announcement of 20 February, had made every suggestion that it would capture the Punjab by any means.[4]

[1] Governor of Punjab to Viceroy, (T), 3 March 1947, R/3/1/89, p. 4. See also Jenkins to Wavell, 3 March 1947, Ibid., p. 5.

[2] Jenkins to Wavell, 3 March 1947, Ibid.

[3] *Civil and Military Gazette*, 4 March 1947.

[4] Note by Jenkins dated 16 April 1947, file no. R/3/1/90, pp. 12–13.

On 4 March Hindu and Sikh students took out a procession through the main part of Lahore shouting '*Pakistan Murdabad*', '*Jinnah Murdabad*'[5] and according to *Dawn*, '*Allaho-Akbar murdabad*'.[6] Rioting broke out in Lahore and Multan, and Khizar resigned as caretaker Prime Minister, chiefly because his ministry could not control the situation.[7]

The provincial Muslim League leader, the Nawab of Mamdot, was unable to form a government. Jenkins was suspicious of his claim to have the support of 10 Unionists, including Khizar, and asked him to produce a complete list of his supporters. The claim proved false, so the next day, Jenkins decided to go into Section 93 under the 1935 Act until Mamdot could form a ministry.[8] Mamdot stalled in keeping his appointment with the Governor, and asked him to accept his assertion that the League would command a majority in the legislature. But without evidence that he did in fact have a majority, Jenkins would not let him form a government. The installation of such a ministry would 'be a fraud' on the constitution and the Instrument of Instructions. 'I should simply be inviting one of the Parties to . . . communal conflict to assume charge of it without even satisfying myself of its Parliamentary competence to do so.'[9]

Jenkins' reluctance to allow a League ministry was strengthened by reports of attacks on non-Muslims which were being carried out in the name of the League in several districts of the Punjab, including Rawalpindi, Attock, Multan and Chakwal. Following the provocative speeches made by Hindu and Sikh Leaders on 3 March, he had expected, at the most, rioting in one or two towns. 'What shocked the non-Muslims of the Punjab, and most of the officials, was the savage outbreak of rioting in the Rawalpindi Division and the Multan district.'[10] The rioting was on a scale never seen before in British India, and was characterized by extreme and sadistic vio-

[5] *Statesman*, 6 March 1947, and Note by General Messervy, enclosed in *Auchinleck* to Abell, 22 March 1947, *TOP*, vol. 9, p. 1005.

[6] *Dawn*, 14 March 1947.

[7] FR for Punjab for the first half of March 1947, L/P&J/5/250, and *Civil and Military Gazette*, 6 March 1947.

[8] Mamdot to Jenkins, 5 March 1947, R/3/1/176, p. 19; and Jenkins to Mamdot, 5 March 1947, Ibid.

[9] Governor of Punjab to Viceroy, 5 March 1947, (T 28-G), Ibid., pp. 21–2.

[10] Note by Jenkins of interview with Mamdot and Daultana on 29 March 1947, Ibid., p. 165.

lence. In the rural areas large Muslim mobs banded together from several villages to destroy, loot and kill Sikhs and Hindus. Women and children were hacked or beaten to death and burned alive. There were a number of cases of forcible conversions and forced marriages.[11] In Rawalpindi the attacks were directed against the Sikhs. By 8 March Hindus and Sikhs were being evacuated from Muslim majority districts including Attock, Mianwali, Gujrat.[12]

Officials had no doubt that the attacks on non-Muslims were planned and aimed at exterminating the Hindu and Sikh population. One element of planning was evident from the fact that Muslims would hoist white flags on their houses and then invite Muslim mobs from the neighbouring villages to attack the property not so marked. Hindus and Sikhs were invited to join peace committees and subsequently murdered.[13] Ex-soldiers and pensioners, including VCOs and Honorary Commissioned officers, led the attacks in many areas.[14] That hand grenades, tommy guns and rifles were frequently employed suggested that military deserters and demobilized soldiers played a leading role. The three districts worst affected—Rawalpindi, Mianwali and Attock sent up the greatest number of recruits during the war.[15]

Jenkins discounted the charge that officials had failed to do their duty.[16] There is, however, no reason to accept these denials unquestioningly, simply because the allegations were usually made by Indians. A personal friend of Attlee saw police stand aside in Rawalpindi as Muslims massacred Sikhs.[17] Penderel Moon recollects that not a shot was fired by the police as the two principal bazaars in Amritsar were destroyed and looting went on in almost every part of the city. In Multan many private houses of Hindus were set on fire and 'the inmates had the choice of perishing in the flames or

[11] Note by Messervy, *TOP*, vol. 9, p. 1006.

[12] *Eastern Times*, 18 March 1947.

[13] See Note by Messervy, *TOP*, vol. 9, p. 1006; Jenkins to Wavell, 17 March 1947, R/3/1/89, p. 141; Statement by A.A. Macdonald, Home Secretary, Punjab, in *Civil and Military Gazette*, 11 March 1947.

[14] Jenkins to Wavell, 17 March 1947, R/3/1/89, p. 132; also Auchinleck to Abell, 8 April 1947, R/3/1/176, p. 136.

[15] Letter from Mr. Arthur Williams to author, 22 March 1981, and *Statesman*, 23 March 1947.

[16] Memorandum by Jenkins, enclosed in Jenkins to Mountbatten, 4 August 1947, R/3/1/89, pp. 234–5.

[17] Col. Reginald Schoenberg to Attlee, 11 May 1947, *Attlee Papers*, Box 7.

running the gauntlet of a murderous mob awaiting them below.'[18] The district magistrate of Siria village was informed at 6 p.m. that the village was on fire. Yet it was not until 10 p.m. that he decided to visit the village which lay at a ten minute drive from his headquarters.[19] However, the allegation that districts headed by British officials came out worse in the rioting cannot be substantiated. In Rawalpindi, the Divisional Commissioner, the DIG Police, the Deputy Commissioner and the Superintendent of Police were all British. The Deputy Commissioners of Attock and Jhelum were both Indian when the trouble began, and they had a British and an Indian Superintendent of Police respectively. In Lahore Division, the Commissioner was Indian; the DIG police, the Deputy Commissioner and senior police officers were all British.[20]

The task of the administration was not made easier by the attitude of provincial party leaders. First, there was the complacency of Leaguers. Ghazanfar Ali, still a member of the interim government and perhaps acting under Jinnah's instructions, denied that the League had anything to do with the disturbances in Rawalpindi and suggested to Jenkins that a League ministry be put into power. He also expressed concern that the new Central Powers ordinance, which gave the army more powers to control disturbances, might turn popular feeling against the army.

> 'I was exasperated by Raja Ghazanfar Ali's complacency [wrote Jenkins] and dealt with him rather roughly. I said he did not appear to realize that what had happened in Rawalpindi, Attock and the Chakwal Sub-Division was a general massacre of the most beastly kind . . . . The massacre had been conducted in the name of the Muslim League and senior Military officers thought that it had been carefully planned and organized.'[21]

The League, Jenkins told Firoz Khan Noon, must realize that 'a brutal massacre had been conducted in their name.' The remedy lay in a recognition of the facts and the expression of repentance in some practical form; the League must realize it had never made any attempt to maintain peace or to win over the minorities.[22]

[18] Moon, *Divide and Quit*, pp. 78, 79–81.

[19] Cutting from *Hindustan Times*, undated, HP file no. 33/11/47, p. 97.

[20] Memorandum by Jenkins, enclosed in Jenkins to Mountbatten, 4 August 1947, file no. R/3/1/89, pp. 22, 27–8.

[21] Note by Jenkins of interview with Ghazanfar Ali, 20 March 1947, R/3/1/76.

[22] Note by Jenkins on interview with Noon, 24 March 1947, Ibid.

Meanwhile, Mamdot remained unable to form a ministry. Nor did the League make any attempt to win over the Hindu and Sikh minorities in the Punjab. Some Sikh leaders expressed willingness to discuss an arrangement if the League made an open effort to stop the outrages at Rawalpindi and Multan, and obtained authority from their high command to negotiate freely with other parties in the Punjab.[23] But Mamdot could give no indication of Jinnah's attitude.[24] Jinnah's attitude was clear by his declaration that the League ought to be allowed to form a ministry.[25] Both Wavell and Jenkins thought Mamdot was acting under Jinnah's instructions and Jenkins believed that the League's attitude was intelligible only on the assumption that it believed that if it came to power it could seize and hold the Punjab by force.[26] By May both Jinnah and Liaqat Ali Khan were 'most bitter' that the League had not been allowed to form a ministry in the Punjab.[27]

An inference at the intentions of the central leadership of the League can be drawn by its support for direct action in the NWFP and Assam. On 21 February a large League procession formed in Peshawar city, overpowered the police and broke into the Congress Premier's house. Police had eventually to resort to firing. Communal trouble spread to the rural areas around Peshawar and in Hazara district there were forcible conversions of Sikhs, and burning of gurdwaras.[28] The movement had Jinnah's blessings.[29] Meanwhile, Muslim League National Guards carried out 'direct action' and incited Muslims to violence in Assam.[30]

The part played by the National Guards in the Punjab, the NWFP and Assam, and earlier in the UP and Bengal, raises once again the question of how far their activities were directed by the central leadership of the League itself. Discussing their role in Bengal, J.D. Tyson, then Secretary to the Governor of Bengal, observed

[23] Governor of Punjab to Viceroy, (T), 11 March 1947, R/3/1/89, p. 99.

[24] Governor of Punjab to Viceroy, 13 March 1947 (T 43-G), file no. R/3/1/89, p. 105.

[25] *Civil and Military Gazette*, 14 March 1947 and *Eastern Times*, 14 March 1947.

[26] Note by Abell (?), 8 March 1947, R/3/1/89, p. 51; and Viceroy to Governor of Punjab, (T), 8 March 1947, Ibid., p. 54; Jenkins to Mountbatten, 15 May 1947, Ibid., p. 205.

[27] Viceroy to Governor of Punjab, 5 May 1947, Ibid., p. 195.

[28] Caroe to Wavell, (T), 13 March 1947, *TOP*, vol. 9, pp. 930–1.

[29] FR for NWFP for first half of May 1947, L/P&J/5/224.

[30] Clow to Mountbatten, 3 April 1947, L/P&J/5/140.

that the Guards were organized on an all-India basis and were not subject to the ministry 'or even the party in Bengal' (or indeed of any provincial party).[31] Commenting on the communal massacres in the Punjab, *Dawn* admitted that 'here and there Muslims may have overstepped the limits of self-defence and indulged in disproportionate retaliation.' But people who threatened Muslims and who were now blaming them 'because events have belied their expectations, betray cowardice of a very low order'![32]

Jenkins often implied that the League was responsible for the massacres of the Hindus and Sikhs.[33] Probably quoting official sources, the *Times* reported on 17 March 1947 that the 'chief offenders were said to have been the Muslim League National Guards'.[34] If these beliefs were well-founded, then the question is what the League hoped to accomplish. Initially the disturbances were aimed at ousting Khizar's ministry, and the League must have thought it would then be able to form a government. At another level, Jenkins thought that the massacres were a response to the Congress resolution calling for the partition of the Punjab. Both these explanations imply that the League wanted to take over the whole province before June 1948, under the terms of the 20 February statement, and that it believed that it would hold the Punjab by force.[35] This could also explain why the Sikhs formed the main target of the League's National Guards—some brutish, mindless notion of wiping out the obstacle (Sikhs) to achieve the end (Pakistan) probably prevailed. Jenkins discounted the League's claim to form a ministry and introduced Section 93 as it did not have a legislative majority; and Leaguers from Jinnah and Liaqat Ali Khan downwards alleged that Muslims were being persecuted by officials trying to restore order—an allegation that Jenkins dismissed, as intelligence reports made it clear that the Muslim majority, acting in

[31] Note by J.D. Tyson, 18 April 1947, and Burrows to Mountbatten, 22 April 1947, R/3/2/59A, pp. 48 and 41–2 respectively.

[32] *Dawn*, 20 March 1947.

[33] Governor of Punjab to Viceroy, (T 35-G), 8 March 1947, R/3/1/89, p. 56; Notes by Jenkins of interviews with Noon on 24 March 1947, with Mamdot and Daultana on 29 March 1947, with Mamdot and Shaukat Hyat Khan on 16 May 1947, R/3/1/176, pp. 55, 63–5, 205, 163 respectively; and Jenkins to Mountbatten, 14 May 1947, R/3/1/89, p. 198.

[34] *Times*, 17 March 1947.

[35] Governor of Punjab to Viceroy, 15 May 1947, R/3/1/89, p. 205.

the name of the Muslim League, had been the aggressors.[36] Jenkins was convinced that one of the aims of the organized violence, which continued after 3 June 1947, was simply to discredit his administration. Two days before the transfer of power, he wrote to Mountbatten:

> 'Many of the Leaguers are remarkably smug. They say that as soon as the British leave peace will be restored. It has long been rumoured that Daultana and the like intended to make as much trouble as possible during the last few weeks before the transfer of power so as to discredit the British regime. If this is so, it does not seem to have been appreciated that if all Muslim outrages stop in Lahore on the morning of 15th August, it will for practical purposes be clear that the local butchery was organized by the leaders themselves.'[37]

The communal violence demonstrated the impotence of the Raj in maintaining law and order. The decline in the performance of the services had become obvious during the League's agitation in January and February 1947 when they took no action against Leaguers who defied the ban on processions and meetings. British officers, uncertain of their future allegedly told Indians who came to them for help to go to their future rulers, the Congress and the League![38] That the police were infected by communalism was illustrated not only by the reluctance of Muslim administrators against Muslim mobs but also by the fact that police weeded out for corruption in Amritsar resigned and joined the Muslim League.[39] A few days before the transfer of power, the situation worsened in Amritsar and Lahore as the Hindu Superintendent of Police in Amritsar disarmed the Muslim Police, and, according to a British report, Sikh and Hindu police declined to protect the Muslims from attacks by their co-religionists.[40] Already by June 1947, Jenkins had concluded:

[36] Governor of Punjab to Viceroy, 8 March 1947, (T 35-G); Jenkins to Wavell, 17 March 1947; Jenkins to Mountbatten, 4 August 1947; R/3/1/89, pp. 56, 131 ff., 221 respectively. See also Note by Jenkins of interview with F.K. Noon, 24 March 1947; and with Liaqat Ali Khan on 26 May 1947, R/3/1/176, pp. 55, 185 respectively; and Liaqat Ali Khan to Mountbatten, 15 April 1947 and Jenkins' note of 16 April 1947, R/3/1/90, pp. 5–10, 12–6 respectively.

[37] Jenkins to Mountbatten, 13 August 1947, L/P&J/5/250, p. 6.

[38] Statement by J.P. Narain, 21 March 1947, HP file no. 33/11/47.

[39] Jenkins to Mountbatten, 25 June 1947, R/3/1/176, p. 212.

[40] Memorandum by Minister of State for Commonwealth Relations, 3 September 1947, to India and Burma Committee, CAB 13/346.

'So far as the services are concerned, we are going through a very difficult period, with some men yearning to leave India, others trying to please new masters, and others again upset and apprehensive. The old administrative machine is rapidly falling to pieces.'[41]

Jenkins probably faced the toughest task that any provincial government had faced until March 1947. In the past communal violence had seldom occurred in two places simultaneously. The administration had been able to concentrate its resources and to come down very heavily on each outbreak as it occurred.

But when outbreaks were widespread, it was impossible to make reinforcements at all points and district officers and military commanders were left to deal with each situation as it occurred. Only five days after the outbreak of rioting in Lahore, the Army Commander told Jenkins that if trouble developed in the rural areas of a large number of districts 'it would be virtually uncontrollable'. The administration had little experience of large-scale disturbances in rural areas with bad communications. Conditions in many of the villages were unknown, since they were approachable only by bridle-path or tracks. The average rural police station had a strength of only a dozen men, to deal with some 100 villages scattered over an area of 100 square miles.[42] About 20,000 troops were used to suppress the violence during March 1947, and on 15 April, Jenkins asked Mountbatten for 60,000 more 'if partition were to be avoided'.[43] A month later, he was informed that no more troops were available for the Punjab, as the British expected disorder in other parts of India following an official announcement in June.[44] Jenkins' reason for not accepting Nehru's suggestion to introduce martial law in the Punjab was revealing: troops were not the answer to 'cloak and dagger' activities; martial law might well fail, and troops would be exposed to the same communal attacks as the police.[45]

The British acknowledged that they did not possess the power to stem the violence; writing retrospectively in September 1948,

[41] Jenkins to Mountbatten, 15 June 1947, L/P&J/5/250, p. 32.

[42] Jenkins to Wavell, 9 March 1947, R/3/1/89, pp. 22, 27–8.

[43] Jenkins to Mountbatten, 15 April 1947, Ibid.

[44] Governor of Punjab to Viceroy, 22 May 1947, and Viceroy to Governor of Punjab, (T 1155-S), 24 May 1947, R/3/1/90, pp. 57, 90.

[45] Jenkins to Mountbatten, 24 June 1947, R/3/1/176, p. 207.

Mountbatten believed that it was 'precisely' in those cases 'where there had been failure to curb movements of violence by sufficiently strong and quick use of armed force, that the massacres had spread'.[46] The communal frenzy was 'without parallel' in any other province in India, and 'nothing which the Governor or his officials had it in their power to do could have altered these fundamentals and removed the sense of insecurity to which they gave rise'.[47] By the beginning of May 1947, Hindus had started retaliatory attacks on Muslims in Eastern Punjab. In the Gurgaon district, six companies of troops were inadequate to deal with a disturbed area of 1000 square miles. Arson ruled the roost in Lahore and Amritsar, and on 27 June, Mountbatten admitted that they would 'soon be burnt to the ground'.[48] The Sikhs, who had faced the brunt of the attack in Rawalpindi, had lost faith in the administration.[49] Those who had suffered could not know what the problems of the administration were. The only fact obvious to them was that the *sarkar* had not been able to defend themselves—in other words, to take the law into their own hands. There were reports of Hindus and Sikhs organizing private armies. The prospects of vengeance being waged on Muslims induced the provincial League to set up a Muslim Central Vigilance Committee in Lahore, with sub-committees all over the province. *Janbazees*—persons ready to sacrifice themselves in their comunity's cause—were being enrolled: they would play the role of storm troopers.[50] By May, the communities had settled down to the 'maximum amount of damage to one another while exposing the minimum expanse of surface to the troops and police'. The police could do little against burning, stabbing and bombing by individuals.[51] Indeed, over a greater part of northern India, in an

[46] Mountbatten's *Secret Report of the Last Viceroyalty, 22 March–15 August 1947* (London, 1948), PREM 8/1002, p. 61.

[47] Memorandum by Minister of State for Commonwealth Relations, 3 September 1947, CAB 134/346.

[48] S.E. Abbott-Abell, 10 June 1947, (T) R/3/1/90, p. 153, and Viceroy's personal report no. 10, 27 June 1947, *TOP*, vol. 11, p. 680.

[49] *Civil and Military Gazette*, 25 March 1947; *Statesman*, 16 March 1947, note by Jenkins on interview with Tara Singh, 19 May 1947, R/3/1/176, p. 168.

[50] FR for Punjab for second half of April 1947, received by Central Intelligence Officer, Lahore, R/3/1/90, pp. 28–9.

[51] Jenkins to Mountbatten, 31 May 1947, L/P&J/5/250, pp. 38ff., Jenkins to Mountbatten, 4 August 1947, R/3/1/89, p. 221.

area bound by Peshawar, Calcutta, Bombay and the Central Provinces, communal clashes were reported daily by the first week of April.[52] Civil war was inevitable. As Jenkins wrote on 4 August 1947: 'Nor can all the King's horses and all the King's men prevent—though they may be able to punish—conflict between communities interlocked in villages over wide areas of country'.[53]

Having experienced the attitude of the League in the Interim Government, the Congress had, by February 1947, despaired of achieving an independent united India. The Congress would not press the British for an immediate announcement on the dismissal of the League from the Interim Government but the issue would have to be faced in the near future. Attlee's statement meant that the Mission Plan would continue to apply only if the League entered the Constituent Assembly. If not, other consequences would follow.[54] Nehru was thinking of the partition of Bengal and the Punjab if the Mission Plan ultimately failed.[55] With the League's intentions made clear in the Punjab after 3 March, the Congress Working Committee passed on 9 March a resolution calling for the partition of the Punjab. It was not easy for the Congress to contemplate such a course but it was preferable to an attempt by either party to impose its will on the other. Large non-Muslim minorities could not be coerced into joining Pakistan any more than Muslims could be made to join the union.[56]

However, the British still hoped that Jinnah would come round. Instructed by Attlee to do his best to secure a united India within the Commonwealth and the imperial defence system,[57] Mountbatten, who, on his own admission, was 'governing by personality',[58] wanted, by April, to announce a quick decision in favour of Pakistan so that it would fail on its merits. The problem would be to reveal the limits of Pakistan so that the League could revert to a unified India with honour. He presented the draft of his "Balkan Plan" to the Governors' Conference on 15 April. This envisaged the trans-

[52] *Times*, 9 April 1947.

[53] Jenkins to Mountbatten, 4 August 1947, R/3/1/89, p. 221.

[54] Nehru to Wavell, 24 February 1947, L/P&J/10/77.

[55] Wavell to Pethick-Lawrence, (T), 22 February 1947, *TOP*, vol. 9, p. 785.

[56] Nehru to Wavell, 9 March 1947, Ibid., p. 898 and enclosure, Ibid., pp. 899–900.

[57] Attlee to Mountbatten, 18 March 1947, L/P&J/10/78, pp. 44ff.

[58] Mountbatten's interview with S. Gopal, 28 May 1970, quoted in Gopal, *Nehru*, vol. 1, p. 342.

fer of power to provinces, or to such confederations of provinces as might decide to group together, before the actual transfer of power.[59]

Jinnah made it clear that he would not reaccept the Mission Plan, —' "You must carry out a surgical operation; cut India and its army firmly in half and give me the half that belongs to the Muslim League" '. Mountbatten felt that a decision on Pakistan would have to be taken within a month. Though he used every argument Jinnah gave in favour of Pakistan against partition, or against dividing Bengal and the Punjab, Mountbatten failed to bring him round. Jinnah's arguments grew increasingly futile and he ended up by saying, ' "If you persist in chasing me with your ruthless logic we shall get nowhere".' Mountbatten concluded that Jinnah was 'a psychopathic case; in fact until I had met him I would not have thought it possible that a man with such a complete lack of administrative knowledge or sense of responsibility could achieve or hold . . . so powerful a position.'[60] Mountbatten warned Jinnah that he would have to choose between the Cabinet Mission Plan which would give him the five provinces of Pakistan with autonomy and a very weak centre and a very moth-eaten Pakistan, the eastern and north-western parts of which would be economically unsound, and which would still depend for its defence on arrangements with India. Jinnah replied, ' "I do not care how little you give me as long as you give it to me completely." ' He would ask for dominion status for Pakistan within the empire.[61]

Jinnah made clear his opposition to any suggestion that a political settlement might be based on the Mission Plan and that the League might enter the Constituent Assembly at every stage of his discussions with Mountbatten.[62] The League's intentions were underlined by the insistence of Jinnah and Liaqat Ali Khan that the British Indian army should be divided. Liaqat expressed the League's opposition to the reorganization of the armed forces on the basis of a united India: the division of India, he told Mountbatten, implied the division of the armed forces to serve Hindustan and Pakistan.[63] Jin-

[59] Governors' Conference, 15 April 1947, L/P&J/10/79, pp. 474, 473.

[60] Viceroy's personal report no. 3, 17 April 1947, L/P&J/10/79, pp. 488–9.

[61] Ibid., p. 490.

[62] Viceroy's personal reports of 9 and 17 April 1947, Ibid, pp. 506 ff. and 486 ff. respectively.

[63] Ibid. and Liaqat Ali Khan to Mountbatten, 7 April 1947, Ibid., pp. 498–9.

nah opposed the move to partition Bengal and the Punjab,[64] as he wanted the full provinces to be included in Pakistan, but Mountbatten believed that he would not seriously contest the need for partition.

Jinnah now pressed the Viceroy to end Governor's rule in the Punjab. He claimed that Mamdot had the support of 93 MLAs and a majority in the provincial legislature. Mountbatten told him that Governor's rule would not be lifted until a decision had been taken by the British government, as the Sikhs were so bitter about atrocities committed by Muslims that they would never accept a one party government by the League. Jinnah then suggestedthat Mamdot should be allowed to see the Viceroy on his own, and he would telephone Mamdot not to see Jenkins again until the Governor had met Mountbatten in Rawalpindi.[65] Jinnah's move, as Jenkins discerned, was intended to increase the importance of the League and to transfer direct control of the Punjab from the Governor to the Viceroy. Jenkins stood his ground. He did not object to a meeting between Mamdot and Mountbatten, but 'there can be no question' of a joint interview between the Viceroy, Mamdot and himself. Mamdot was only a provincial party leader and any procedure adopted for him would have to be available to all party leaders. There was no need to depart from the established constitutional practice in this matter.[66] On 28 April, when Mamdot reiterated his claim to form a ministry, Jenkins told him that he did not think that a communal ministry, whether Muslim or non-Muslim, would have any chance of succeeding in the Punjab.[67] 'The real point is that once any large section of the population declines to recognize a parliamentary majority, a revolutionary situation supervenes and constitutional government in the ordinary sense becomes impossible.' Whether or not this was sufficient on constitutional grounds for refusing to go out of section 93, there was the 'practical point' that it would be 'foolish' to permit the formation of a ministry when an important

[64] Viceroy to Secretary of State (T 21-SC), 8 May 1947, Ibid., pp. 354, 355 Note by Jinnah, received on 17 May 1947, Ibid., pp. 167–8.

[65] Mountbatten's note of interview with Jinnah on 26 April 1947, and Viceroy to Governor of Punjab (T 902-S), 26 April 1947, Ibid., pp. 172, 171 respectively.

[66] Governor of Punjab to Private Secretary to Viceroy (T 84-G), 28 April 1947, Ibid., p. 176.

[67] Governor of Punjab to Private Secretary to Viceroy (T 86-G), 28 April 1947, Ibid., pp. 177–9.

announcement about the future of India was imminent. A section 93 proclamation could be revoked at any time; but it was arguable that the governor was entitled to demand more than 'a mere capacity' to comply with the technical requirements of the Act of 1935.[68] The Unionist coalition forced out by the League had a larger majority than that now claimed by the League.[69] The League continued to be complacent and had made no approach to the Sikhs. Their attitude was that 'Muslims are entitled to rule' the whole of the Punjab and that 'when this is admitted they will be good enough to treat the non-Muslims with generosity'.[70]

With the administrative machine collapsing, with the knowledge that the League would not enter the Constituent Assembly under the Mission Plan, Mountbatten concluded, by the middle of April 1947, that partition was inevitable, and that the Punjab and Bengal would have to be divided. Mountbatten himself did not believe that non-Muslim minorities could be coerced into Pakistan;[71] nor would the Congress have ever agreed to such a proposal. The Congress had suggested the partition of Bengal and the Punjab as early as March 1947, and on 28 April, Rajendra Prasad, president of the Constituent Assembly, reiterated that no constitution would be forced upon any part of India. This would not mean the division of India, 'but a division of some provinces'. For this the Congress would be prepared and a constitution based on such a division might have to be drawn up.[72] In May, non-Muslim MLAs in the Punjab and Bengal legislative assemblies passed resolutions calling for the partition of their provinces.[73] Mountbatten discussed his proposals for the partitioning of Bengal and the Punjab with Patel and Nehru, and on 3 June, when he announced the British government's plan for a transfer of power to Indians, he had already secured the consent of those two leaders to the proposal that MLAs in those provinces would vote to decide whether or not their respective provinces should be partitioned.[74]

[68] Jenkins to Mountbatten, 30 April 1947, Ibid., pp. 182ff.

[69] Draft of letter from Jenkins to Mamdot, 7 May 1947, Ibid., pp. 188ff.

[70] Jenkins to Mountbatten, 30 April 1947, L/P&J/5/250.

[71] Viceroy's personal report no. 3, 17 April 1947, L/P&J/10/79, pp. 486 ff.

[72] V.P. Menon, *The Transfer of Power* (paperback, Madras, 1968) p. 360.

[73] Ibid. and *Statesman*, 7 May 1947.

[74] See, for example, note by Nehru, 16 May 1947; Nehru to Mountbatten 17 and 20 May 1947, L/P&J/10/79.

Patel and Nehru faced criticism in the AICC for committing the Congress to partition without consulting the party. They in turn pointed to the difficulty of consulting the AICC at every stage of the negotiations, and said that their stand flowed out of the resolutions passed by the AICC itself since1942—that no part of India could be coerced into accepting a constitution against its will. Gandhi opposed partition as a moral failure, but said he would not hinder the Congress Working Committee.[75]

The reasons which led the CWC to propose the partition of Bengal and the Punjab in March, and to accept it by June 1947, were summed up by J.B. Kripalani. Their visits to riot-affected areas in Bengal, Bihar and the Punjab 'were a succession of shocks, one greater than the other.' It was not only that the innocent had been massacred; 'our respective religions were degraded'. Each community had vied with the other in the worst orgies of communal violence. The decision to accept partition had been taken out of fear that things might get worse. Gandhi's non-violence had not been able to tackle the problem on a mass scale. Non-violence was not stopping communal riots in the Punjab. 'There are no definite steps, as in non-violent non-cooperation, that lead to the desired goal.'[76] For the Congress then, partition and the communal violence which accompanied it were a sad finale to a movement which had prided itself on secularism and non-violence—a noble way to achieve a noble end.[77] Even as he fasted for peace in June 1947, Gandhi was filled with foreboding that the disillusion was not over, that the killing would go on.

Ever since their release from prison in July 1945, Congress leaders had stressed the necessity to reorganize and revitalize the party organization so that it could channel popular social and political unrest along constructive lines. But the cabinet mission's offer of independence sooner rather than later induced the Congress leadership to concentrate on the negotiations for the transfer of power, since they believed that only an independent government would have the will to tackle the problems facing India. The involvement in the negotiations, coming as it did so soon after the Congress leaders's term in prison after August 1942, took its toll of organizational

[75] AICC meetings on 1 and 2 June 1947, AICC file no. G-30, 1946–1948, pp. 101–2 respectively.

[76] AICC file no. G-47, part 1, 1946–1947, pp. 168–71.

[77] J. Nehru, *Autobiography* (Indian edition, 1962), p. 73.

work, and in August 1946, Nehru reiterated that the Congress had lost its vitality. The links between the central, provincial and local committees must be tightened up; a labour department would have to be set up to study and to suggest solutions for the increasing social unrest; a special department would be established to deal with the work of the Constituent Assembly.

Nehru had hoped that the entry of the Congress into the Interim Government would open the opportunity to carry out Congress programmes and would relegate communal differences to the background by concentrating on economic issues as 'the real issues faced by all communities together'. But the Congress-League division had dominated the Interim Government, it was reflected in the savage communal violence in Noahkhali, Saran and Garmukhteswar; and Congress leaders had more or less despaired of working together with the League in any government. Yet they remained optimistic, and the British announcement of 20 February 1947 was welcomed by them for giving Indians yet another chance to unite and work for independence. At the same time, they knew that the League might never enter the Constitutent Assembly. With the British departure assured by June 1948, and with partition imminent, they insisted that Hindu and Sikh minorities in the Muslim majority provinces must not be submerged into Pakistan, any more than the Muslim minorities wished to be subjected to the all-India majority. The Rawalpindi massacres broke the last straw on the camel's back, and on 7 March 1947, the Congress Working Committee called for the partition of the Punjab and Bengal.

The Congress accepted the partition plan first, because it was based on the premise of a united India. Knowing of Mountbatten's preference for an undivided India, and also because they believed that India would be at a disadvantage if she left the Commonwealth and Pakistan stayed in, they agreed to temporary dominion status and invited him to act as Governor-General of India until June 1948. Partition and an early transfer of power were seen by them as the best check on the growing communal violence. The British seemed unable to end it; and in the NWFP, the Governor actually seemed to be encouraging the League's campaign to overthrow the Congress ministry. Far better that the Raj were wound up: once the new governments took over administrative problems the old bitterness would fade away and unity might still be realized. Kripalani hoped that once Pakistan was established, 'its government would have enough sense of reality not to discredit themselves by unfair treatment of the minorities'. Until now the Muslim League had held that its interest was to create an atmosphere of conflict and strife. Now its interest would 'obviously' be to create order, for any spirit of lawlessness would, sooner or later, be turned against its own minorities. Minorities in Pakistan should therefore not emigrate out of panic. 'They should wait and watch and not lose faith in their own strength, in the potential sanity of the Pakistan Government and in the ultimate unity of India which can never be permanently destroyed'.[78]

With partition almost a *fait accompli* by the end of May, there remained only the need to fix the date for the transfer of power. Mountbatten himself favoured an early transfer: the Congress might then join the Commonwealth; the Indian parties could get acquainted with administrative problems; the communal violence would, hopefully, be checked with a settlement at the centre, and the decline of the administrative machine stemmed.[79] Both Alan Campbell-Johnson and H.V. Hodson have said that the choice of 15 August 1947 as the date of the transfer of power occurred to Mountbatten at his press conference on 4 June 1947.[80] But in a letter to Lord Listowel, who had replaced Pethick-Lawrence as Secretary of State for India in April 1947, on 3 June, Mountbatten clearly stated that he wanted the British to wind up the Raj on 15 August 1947.[81] It is obvious, then, that by 3 June the Viceroy had already thought of 15 August as 'the appointed day'. Two illustrations will show that civil war was foreseen by the British, and that administrative reasons weighed most with Mountbatten in fixing the date. Immediately after the outbreak of rioting in Lahore on 4 March, Jenkins had warned Wavell that until June 1948, order could be maintained in the Punjab whether under a communal ministry or Section

[78] This account has been based on Nehru's note to presidents and secretaries of PCCs, *National Herald*, 1 July 1946; notes for AICC, 6 August 1946, AICC file no. 69 (Part 2), 1946, pp. 1–7 and 67–9. Also see, J.B. Kripalani to A.A. Chowdhury, 13 May 1947, AICC file no. CL-8/1946–1947, pp. 111–17; Kripalani to Lala Duni Chand, 14 May 1947, AICC file CL-9/1946–1947; press statement by Kripalani, 18 June 1947, AICC file G-47 (part 1) 1946–1947, pp. 158–9.

[79] Viceroy to Secretary of State, (T 1284-S), 3 June 1947.

[80] Alan Campbell-Johnson, *Mission with Mountbatten* (London, 1951), p. 109; H.V. Hodson, *The Great Divide* (London, 1969), pp. 319–20.

[81] Viceroy to Secretary of State, (T 1284-S), 3 June 1947, PREM 8/541/part X.

93 'only by use of force'. Under a communal ministry British officers and the Indian army would be used to conquer the Punjab for 'the community in power'; under Section 93 the administration would have 'limited tenure and would hand over to chaos'.[82] A year after the transfer of power, Mountbatten affirmed that

> '. . . the main factor was the period during which it was likely to be possible to keep the existing Interim Government functioning. Indications were daily growing that it was going to be a task of the utmost difficulty to prevent one side or the other resigning if the Government was kept in being for another month or so at the outside. The chaos which would follow such resignations, which were . . . likely to prejudice the successful implementation of the whole plan, was easy to imagine . . . The August transfer of power was inherent in the Partition solution quite apart from any introduction of Dominion Status.'[83]

As partition and the transfer of power had been dictated by political and administrative exigency, 'contrary to expectations', no provision for formal treaties with the new dominions had been made. Any question of making a conditional transfer of power had vanished with the Statement of 20 February 1947, and British officials were uncomfortably aware that if no defence agreement with India eventuated, Commonwealth defence would be in jeopardy.[84] Meanwhile, the Labour government hoped for defence arrangements with at least Pakistan, and conjured up another sort of "divide and rule" tactic. The cabinet rejected a request from Gandhi for a British assurance that they would not have differential agreements with India and Pakistan. Lord Listowel observed that one of the main Congress objections to partition had been its fear that Pakistan would fortify itself with British, American or other outside assistance, and this fear had induced the Congress to accept temporary dominion status. The British would prefer to have similar defence arrangements with both India and Pakistan if the Commonwealth provided the nexus between the two:

[82] Governor of Punjab to Viceroy (T 28-G), 5 March 1947, R/3/1/176, pp. 21–2.

[83] Mountbatten's *Secret Report of the Last Viceroyalty, 22 March–15 August 1947* (London, 1948), pp. 90, 172.

[84] Secretary of State to Viceroy (T), 3 July 1947, L/P&J/10/21, p. 35; Stapleton to Monteath, 13 June 1947, L/P&J/10/21, p. 3; Cabinet Official Committee on Commonwealth Relations, 8 August 1947, CAB 134/117.

'But we feel that we should be very careful not to say that we shall not in any circumstances have closer relations with Pakistan than with India . . . The best hope of getting an effective relationship with the Congress derives from their fear that if they do not play up we shall have differential and better relationships with Pakistan and possibly with non-acceding Indian States. The probability is that this is the strongest bargaining point we have with the Congress . . . We feel that we should be very ill-advised to throw it away.'[85]

Here was the old game in a new setting: by maintaining the differences, the British hoped to bring about cooperation between India and Pakistan under their aegis. Imperialism still assumed that any means would achieve the desired end.

The League alone got what it wanted: a sovereign Pakistan. Jinnah's delight at the statement of 3 June was 'unconcealed'.[86] Before the Congress decision to accept temporary dominion status for India, the League had wanted Mountbatten as Governor-General of Pakistan, but once Jinnah knew that India would join the Commonwealth, he was silent on the subject. On 4 July he told Mountbatten that he wanted to be Governor-General of Pakistan himself, and that his Prime Minister would do what he said. '"In my position it is I who will give the advice and others will act on it."' Mountbatten warned him that the decision might cost him several crores of rupees in assets, but Jinnah remained unmoved. Mountbatten knew that the Congress had agreed to dominion status to facilitate a smooth transfer of power and not to be at a disadvantage if Pakistan joined the Commonwealth; they had also invited him to serve as Governor-General of India until June 1948 because of his own preference for a united India. Mountbatten himself had never wanted to stay with only one side as Governor-General. But he realized that Jinnah had got his way until the very end. 'I fear [wrote Mountbatten] that I have unintentionally led Nehru and all the Congress leaders up the garden path and that they will never forgive me for allowing Jinnah once more to have his own way'.[87] That Jinnah could not be persuaded against taking up the Governor-Generalship

[85] Listowel to Mountbatten, 27 June 1947, L/P&J/10/99, p. 3.

[86] Viceroy to Secretary of State, (T 1277-S), 3 June 1947, PREM 8/541/part X.

[87] Viceroy's personal report no. 11, 11 July 1947, L/P&J/10/81, pp. 51–2. Attlee favoured Mountbatten's accepting the Congress invitation because it was 'a great boost for Britain, and for the Commonwealth . . . If Mountbatten *had* left India, it would have looked like a victory for that twister, Jinnah!' Quoted in Kenneth Harris, *Attlee* (London, 1982), p. 384.

of Pakistan ruled out any hope of eventual unity between the two dominions and signalled that India and Pakistan would be what he had always intended—two sovereign nations, having no links with each other except by treaty.

Conclusions

From the Statement of 3 June 1947 to 15 August 1947, the date chosen by Mountbatten for the British to transfer power to Indians, only a vote of the legislative assemblies of the Muslim majority provinces—and in the NWFP, of a plebiscite—remained to decide whether India would be partitioned. Non-Muslim MLAs in Bengal decided by 58 to 21 votes that the province should be partitioned, and that it should join the existing Constituent Assembly. Muslim MLAs decided by 106 to 35 votes against partitioning the province. Paragraph 6 of the 3 June statement laid down that if a simple majority of either part of the Legislative Assembly decided in favour of partition, the province would be divided. Hence, the vote of the non-Muslim MLAs decided the issue of partition in Bengal. In the Punjab, the vote of non-Muslim MLAs also decided that the province was to be partitioned. The Sind Legislative Assembly decided by 30 votes to 20 to join a new Constituent Assembly. The boycott of the referendum in the NWFP by the provincial Congress contributed to the League winning 50.49 per cent of the votes cast for Pakistan. It had a walkover in the province.

Mountbatten asserted that the British decision to partition was based on the will of the Indian people, as expressed by their representatives in the legislatures of the Muslim majority provinces; but did this expression of the 'will of the people' imply that the communal differences between Hindus and Muslims had made partition inevitable? To establish such inevitability would surely require a remarkably Whig interpretation not only of the partition of India, but of several centuries of India's history. Although a sense of social division in religious terms was pervasive in Indian society, Hindus and Muslims belonging to the same class or locality often had more in common with each other than with their co-religionists in other sections of society. The religious distinctions existed along with, and cut across, tribal, class and caste divisions. The question to be confronted is when and how religious feeling came to be 'politicized' to the point where partition became inevitable.

The answer to this question may be sought not only in the emergence of the Muslim League with its demand for a sovereign Muslim state from March 1940 and its mobilization of Muslim provincial support, but also in British and Congress tactics which contributed to the rise of the League and the solidification of its communal support. And the circumstances of a declining empire may have contributed as much to Muslim political unification as the League's appeals to the nationalism supposedly inherent in Muslim religious communalism.

Historiography offers a variety of suggestions for answering the question, each identifying some element within it. One of these traces back the roots of partition to the Congress refusal to admit League representatives to a share in ministerial power in the UP in 1937. Had they done so, it is argued, the League might not have opted for Pakistan three years later. Admittedly, the failure of the negotiations embittered the provincial Leaguers, but it never turned them into supporters of a sovereign Pakistan. Nor did it drive Jinnah to that extremity as he had opposed the negotiations between the Congress and the UPML throughout. Another suggestion stresses the British contribution made by way of communal representation, provincial responsible government and the extension of franchise to the politicization of communities along religious lines. However, while these institutional innovations promoted political feeling along religious lines, they showed little sign before 1945, of producing widespread Muslim support for the central leadership of the League in the Muslim majority provinces. Moreover, the needs of responsible government often dictated entry into intercommunal alliances, even in Muslim majority provinces. In 1944, in fact, Jinnah's League appeared in danger of political defeat in the Punjab, where it found itself at odds with a major Muslim leader who believed in intercommunal politics. And though Huq in Bengal and Sikander Hyat Khan in the Punjab appeared to adhere nominally to the League in all India matters, Jinnah found them utterly intractable when it came to representing the League's policies at the provincial level.

Of the political unification of Muslims before the war there is little evidence; and the lack of it explains Jinnah's fear that the British would introduce the scheme of federation provided for in the Act of 1935. Given the weakness of the League in the Muslim majority provinces, it would have been left high and dry at the all India level if federation had been implemented.

It was the outbreak of war in September 1939 which 'saved' the League. Even as Linlithgow put federation into cold storage for the duration of the war, Jinnah set out to exploit the British need for the support of the Indian parties for the war effort. At first, he feared that the exigencies of wartime would drive the British into concessions to the Congress, in which the League would be ignored; and he did what he could to prevent such a settlement. The League's resolutions of September and October 1939 declared that India was not a national state; that federation must be jettisoned and the political future negotiated *de novo* with the Muslim 'nation' through its accredited organization the Muslim League. If the League's resolutions of September–October 1939 were calculated to forestall a settlement between Linlithgow and the Congress, they succeeded in their aim. They helped the Viceroy to reject Congress demands for a promise of independence in return for its cooperation with the war effort. The League provided the British with a pretext to tell the Congress that the demand for independence must be weighed against the objections of minorities. But there was more to Jinnah's tactics than diplomacy. On the one hand, Sikander and Huq had come out in support of the war effort; on the other, radicals in the League were urging him to line up in an anti-imperialistic front with the Congress. Jinnah's call for 'Deliverance Day' fell flat in most provinces; and his reliance on the British to allow the League to veto the Congress demand for independence exposed him to the indictment that he was a supporter of imperialism. Unable to suggest any alternative path of constitutional advance to the scheme of federation which he had rejected, Jinnah's stance appeared entirely negative and unconstructive even to Linlithgow. In such circumstances, the demand for Pakistan as a sovereign state served to rebuff the Viceroy's criticism and the charge that in opposing the demand for independence, he was the servant of imperialism. It was not that he was opposed to freedom for Indians, explained Jinnah at Lahore in March 1940, but he must have freedom for Muslims. They would not tolerate domination by the British or by the Congress.

But more than that, the dramatic evocation of a Muslim nation of the future at Lahore might serve to hoist the League out of its political doldrums; for example, in reminding Muslim provincial leaders absorbed in their various provincial interests of the need for unity at the all India level; and that that unity was essential to preserve Muslim interests in the future; or in reminding Muslim voters of grievances, real or imagined, that they might have accumulated against Congress ministries between 1937–9, such as discrimination against Muslims in government service, the imposition of Hindi or the lack of protection for Muslims during communal disturbances. In proclaiming the demand for Pakistan, the League might have expected to reap the political dividends of communal religious sentiment. The slogan of Pakistan tended to identify Congress, in Muslim eyes, with 'Hindustan', and probably contributed to the fact that few Muslims joined the Quit India movement in 1942.

The importance of Jinnah's presidential address at Lahore lay in his assertion that the Indian problem was not an intercommunal but an international one—as between two nations. From that time onwards, Jinnah consistently defined Pakistan in terms of a sovereign state. Evidently, most Muslim politicians did not subscribe to his particular definition at that time or even later. Sir Muhammad Yusuf, for example, who chaired the AIML session in April 1942, saw Pakistan as 'an immeasurable dynamic and potential value for the creation of a united India on the basis of treaties in cooperation with the British government'.[1] Fazlul Huq moved the Pakistan resolution at Lahore, yet soon attacked Jinnah for preaching separatism and was expelled from the League in December 1941. The Unionists paid some lip service to the idea of Pakistan, which they disliked, but Sikander never broke with the League, partly because he seldom seems to have done anything without the permission of the British and was persuaded by Linlithgow in 1940 and 1942 not to come out into open opposition to Jinnah. For the Viceroy was concerned to sustain Sikander for the sake of the Punjab war effort and to sustain Jinnah for the sake of a semblance of Muslim opposition to the Congress at a time when the Congress was engaged in civil disobedience. Linlithgow himself could find, at the beginning of 1942, no genuine enthusiasm for Pakistan among Muslim Leaguers whom he had met, and concluded that they would be content with Pakistan within some sort of a federation. He inferred that whatever the League meant by the term, most Muslims took it as a symbol of a vague resolve against 'Hindu domination', which rarely implied a positive commitment to creating a sovereign state of Pakistan.

In the absence of any conclusive support for Pakistan in the Mus-

[1] Pirzada, *Documents*, p. 379.

lim majority provinces, it is difficult to see how Amery and Linlithgow decided, soon after March 1940, that there could be no return to the Act of 1935 as the basis for a political settlement in the future, because 'Muslims' would never accept it. Reading through their despatches, one finds them critical of Jinnah's inability to define the content of Pakistan. On examining its economic and military implications, they found it impracticable and concluded that an intelligent man like Jinnah could not be serious about it. That they were not willing to take his demand for Pakistan as a sovereign state seriously is shown by the fact that they considered his demand for parity with the Congress in the Executive Council absurdly pretentious. In insisting on parity, Jinnah was claiming equality of political weight with the Congress; for *nations* negotiated as equals. In refusing to concede parity, the British made it clear that they considered the League to be no more than a *political and religious minority*.

By the beginning of 1942, nevertheless, the necessities of the war combined with American anti-imperialist pressure were compelling the British to open the question of constitutional advance which they had intended to shelve during the war. Almost fortuitously, the Cripps plan offered provinces a right to opt out of a future Indian Union before the final transfer of power and to form a separate union if they wished to do so. The British thus opened the way to partition before the transfer of power. They appear to have had no constructive reason for doing so, other than to justify their rejection of Congress demands. But whatever their reasons, they had incidentally encouraged Jinnah's League to anticipate that, when power had to be transferred after the war, Pakistan would be in sight, whereas hitherto its prospect had been visionary. The Cripps offer gave plausibility to the Lahore resolution and strengthened the popular appeal of the League in the Muslim majority provinces; except that at the time, the League had neither the provincial organization, nor, more important, the majorities in the provincial legislatures to take advantage of the Cripps offer.

If, as Cripps promised, Pakistan could come into being simply by a majority vote in the legislatures of the Muslim majority provinces, then the next step for Jinnah was to create a greater following there. But he does not appear to have had much success in his efforts to draw provincial Muslim legislative parties and ministries in those provinces into the League's fold after the Cripps offer than he had

had previously. More than that, there is no strong evidence of the League organizing among the Muslim masses in the rural areas of these provinces until the election campaign of 1945–6. Provincial Leagues resisted his efforts to dictate to them, and the Muslim League's Committee of Action was unpleasantly surprised to find, in June 1944, that in the NWFP, the Muslim League was only a misnomer for party functions and had undertaken no organizational work. It was only in Bengal, where, because of the provincial League's tactic of undermining Huq's support among the poor peasants, that the League's propaganda was carried out in rural areas, while Suhrawardy's radical brand of politics made it popular in urban areas. Within the League, no one challenged Jinnah's stand on all India issues. When they differed with him, for example, in July 1944, over the desirability of a Congress-League settlement, Jinnah's threat to resign as President of the League silenced them. Provincial Leaguers appear to have paid little attention to him in provincial matters, while they gave him a comparatively free hand at the all India level.

Considering the tenuous relationship of the League to various provincial leaders, the variety and ambiguity of their different understandings of, and reactions to, the Lahore resolution, it does not appear that Jinnah's call for a sovereign Pakistan welled up from an emergent Muslim nation from below. The possibility is that the demand was proclaimed from above, and so it held no great significance or effect on the divisions among Muslims politicians in the majority provinces before 1945–6.

If this is so, it is surprising that both the British and the Congress, during the war, should have given Jinnah the position of a contender for the spoils of power at the all India level, regardless of his weakness in the provinces. A strong case can be made for thinking that the British deliberately built up his prestige at the all India level for their war purposes, though at the provincial level they subordinated this objective to the prime necessity of operating the war machine with maximum efficiency. In any event, British officialdom traditionally calculated their 'collaboration equation' in Indian politics in terms of loyal and disloyal elements, of 'Muslim' and 'Hindu'.[2] It suited Linlithgow, as we have seen, to accept Jinnah's claim to speak for all Muslims at the centre from 1939 onwards, to

[2] Anita Singh, 'Nehru and the Communal Problem', pp. 13ff.

justify rejection of the Congress demand for independence. The prestige thus acquired from the British helped make Jinnah's League the only plausible representative of Muslims at the all India level. To an extent British recognition compelled the Congress to recognize Jinnah's claim, though its aim of winning the League into a united anti-imperialist front pointed in the same direction. For instance, Rajagopalachari since 1940 had urged the Congress to accept the idea of Pakistan within a federation with a view to winning Jinnah's cooperation against the British, even though Jinnah was not interested in a settlement with the Congress. After turning a deaf ear to Rajagopalachari's pleas for four years, Gandhi himself entered, in September 1944, into discussions with Jinnah for the same purpose. The talks took place soon after Jinnah's setback in the Punjab at the hands of the Unionists, so they allowed Jinnah to adopt the position of one who spurned what had been offered, and so contributed to his standing and prestige with Muslims. But there was more than a desire for publicity behind Jinnah's talking to the Congress. At a time when the League ministries were battling for survival in other Muslim majority provinces, Jinnah was under considerable pressure from provincial Leagues to talk to Gandhi. Punjab Leaguers wanted him to work out a settlement with the Congress at the centre so that the two parties could then join hands to throw out the Unionist ministry. By entering into negotiations not likely to succeed—for he must have known that Gandhi would never offer him a sovereign Pakistan—Jinnah satisfied his followers that he had done his best to protect Muslim interests and maintained his prestige at the all India level. As it was the first time that the two leaders had met since 1939, Gandhi's apparent acceptance of the principle of Pakistan—that is, of Pakistan within a federation—was taken as a symbolic victory for Jinnah not only by the British and Muslim Leaguers, but also by many Congressmen who were bewildered at Gandhi's stance.

It was however at Simla that the British consolidated Jinnah's monopoly of Muslim representation at the centre in allowing his demand to nominate all Muslims to the Executive Council to break up the conference, instead of going ahead without him. The Congress had agreed to work the proposals. At that time Jinnah was under great pressure from provincial Leagues to join the Executive Council with the Congress, especially as the League considered entry in the Viceroy's Council as the only chance of maintaining themselves in the political limelight. Apparently even at this time Jinnah's demand for a sovereign Pakistan had not turned the balance of power in Muslim provincial politics in its favour. For all these reasons, it seems unlikely that Jinnah would have been able to stand exposure of his obduracy to the world, had the British stood firm. However, he was 'saved' by Whitehall's directive in July 1945 that the world should not come to know that his intransigence had led to the break up of the conference. The League, after all, had been, if not their friend, the enemy of their arch enemy the Congress, and it would not do to put the Congress in a favourable light. The result of Whitehall's decision was that Jinnah, by refusing anything less than parity at Simla, brought the British to a point, by March 1946, where they would offer him the possibility of a sovereign Pakistan if negotiations with the Congress on the basis of a united India were to fail.

But Pakistan was still not inevitable. The elections of 1945–6 provided the League's opponents with an opportunity to defeat it, but they failed to rise to the occasion. In the Punjab, the Unionists relied largely on influence to win mass support. The League, on the other hand, greatly extended its party organization, and organized mass meetings, student volunteers and ulema; it offered Pakistan as the panacea for all Muslim grievances. The League won 76 per cent of the Muslim vote in the elections, which offered the first convincing evidence of its support among Muslims in the majority provinces. The League triumphed by calling on Muslims to unite politically and avert the danger of Hindu domination and win 'Pakistan' in one sense or another. The result of the elections represented a great stride forward in the political unification and solidification of the Muslim community, but the extent of this unification need not be exaggerated into a communal mandate for a sovereign Pakistan. It has been shown that even among League politicians, let alone those who voted for them, 'Pakistan' meant all things to all men. It is not unlikely that the effects of peace, bringing the British departure into close prospect, rallied a majority of the Muslim community to the League. If a British departure was imminent, the competing interests of all Muslim provincial politicians, indeed of the entire Muslim community, could no longer be secured at the provincial level. All now depended on the negotiations proceeding at the centre. It seems probable that the circumstances of peace dictated the swing of Muslim provincial leaders behind the all India League in

1945–6, rather than any positive decision in favour of partition and a sovereign Pakistan.

Though the League's victory in Muslim constituencies in 1945–6 might be recorded as a mandate in some senses, it certainly did not make a sovereign Pakistan inevitable. That depended on how the British would work out the mechanics of the transfer of power in negotiation not only with the League but also with the Congress. The expression of widespread Muslim support for it in the elections did not lessen British opposition to Pakistan, any more than the absence of widespread Muslim support for it before the elections had prevented them from incorporating the principle of partition in the Cripps offer of 1942. Until 1945, the British had worked on the assumption that the empire must survive; and Pakistan had been a useful counterpoise to the Congress demand for independence. But by March 1946, the British announced that the Cabinet Mission would negotiate with Indian parties the basis on which power could be transferred to Indians, and they preferred to transfer power to a united India. No long term British decision to wind up empire by any date existed; there is no evidence to substantiate the Whiggish theory that it was 'always' on the cards, especially after the introduction of provincial self-government in 1919. The constitutional reforms of 1919 and 1935 were aimed at preserving, not terminating empire; the British offer of independence in 1946 was taken in the interests of maintaining the concreteness of their imperial power. This lay at the core of British opposition to Pakistan and their presumption that an agreement between the Indian parties would not for them be a sufficient condition for transferring power—that would depend on whether the agreement catered for their military concerns. This secret but overriding calculation influenced British tactics during the negotiations for the transfer of power in 1946–7 which rules out any labelling of Labour policy as one of an unforced voluntary withdrawal from India.

A complex set of circumstances led to the British announcement of 22 March 1946. One was their realization that their ability to enforce law and order had greatly diminished. The war and the non-cooperation of the Congress and the League had made evident to them the precariousness of their position in India. Despite their breaking the Quit India movement by early 1943, they confessed their inability to deal with large-scale disturbances in future. The loyalty of Indians at all levels of the administration could not be taken for granted. After November 1945, when Indian members of the ICS and armed forces showed sympathy with the rising wave of anti-imperialist sentiment, it was obvious that the civil and military services were not staunch bulwarks of the Raj. The air force and naval mutinies in January and February 1946 respectively confirmed the split in the military base of the empire. Britain's own post-war domestic and international commitments made impossible the trying out of the only alternative method of reviving the administration—the recruitment of more British citizens to the ICS and armed forces—assuming that Whitehall went in for all out repression and that it would have succeeded. So when the Cabinet Mission came to India in March 1946, it worked on the premise that the negotiations must succeed, preferably on the basis of an undivided India.

But a transfer of power to a united India was not an end in itself for the British, as it was for the Congress. The reason why the British were against Pakistan was their desire to keep an undivided, independent India within the imperial security system and to use India's army and economic resources for military purposes. The possibility that the Congress might object to such arrangements had made Wavell envisage, in February 1944, that British military interests must be guaranteed by treaty *before* the transfer of power took place. The way to counteract Congress objections would be to let the threat of Pakistan hang over the heads of Congress so that they would be obliged to give the British the military facilities they wanted.

The British wanted both the Congress and the League to agree to a plan for a transfer of power to a united India. But the opposition they expected from the Congress, not only with regard to their long term aims, but also in respect of the Viceroy's special powers, made them want to keep the League as a counterpoise to the Congress. In other words, the British wanted the two parties to agree on how to make the Mission Plan work in the British interest, and not to agree on how to work against them. One of the conclusions to their attitude that could be taken was of the League working for partition, the Congress against it, the British against it but somehow hoping or thinking that the League's hostility to the Congress would make it more pliable to their intentions—this would mean that the League would work against partition! There is no evidence that the British thought out the logical implications of their tactics. They probably tried to please both parties so that both would enter the Constituent Assembly for an undivided India—where the British would have the last word and get the concessions they wanted—otherwise they would not transfer power.

The Mission Plan of 16 May 1946 provided that Hindu and Muslim majority provinces would form separate groups, and that groups would frame constitutions for their provinces. That this form of grouping could have been avoided in the first instance is suggested by the opinion of, for example, Khizar, that provincial rivalries would militate against the successful working of grouping.[3] The NWFP was in any case a Congress province, and would have preferred a provision for provinces to decide whether they should join a particular group, instead of being pushed into one from the very outset.

Grouping was then a major step on the road to Pakistan. Their obsession with using the League as a counterpoise to the Congress also made the British rule out any alternative which would have given the League less influence in the Interim Government. Azad's suggestion that provinces, not parties, should nominate members to the Interim Government was turned down by the Mission as an example of the diabolical cleverness of the Congress. Under this arrangement, the Congress would have got 8, the League 2 and the Unionists 1, seats in the Interim Government. With provincial tendencies raising their head even in the Muslim majority provinces at that time, it is not inconceivable that Suhrawardy, for example, would not have lined up with Jinnah as a matter of course—Suhrawardy was working with the Bengal Congress for a united Bengal in March 1947.

Perhaps because some provincial Leaguers suggested that Pakistan within a federation would be quite acceptable; perhaps because neither Jinnah nor any other Leaguer could define the content of Pakistan; perhaps because an undivided India favoured the British interest;—for one or more of these reasons the British concluded that Pakistan within a federation would be accepted by the League. But Jinnah had made it very clear to the Mission that he would accept nothing less than a sovereign Pakistan. Even as the negotiations were in progress, he declared before a convention of League legislators in Delhi on 16 April 1946, that the 'idea of a single consti-

[3] *TOP*, vol. 7, p. 148.

tutional body has then no place, and we shall never accept it, for it means our consent to proceed on the basis of a united India, which is impossible . . .'[4] The British ignored, or did not note, the reason behind the League's acceptance of the Mission Plan;[5] and happily concluded that a spirit of compromise had got the better of Jinnah's intransigence.

But there lay a rub. Jinnah and the League accepted the 16 May statement after an assurance given by Pethick-Lawrence and Cripps to members of the Working Committee on 16 May that it was the intention of the Mission that sections would determine the constitutions of their provinces. Sovereignty would not be transferred until the new constitution had been framed. Jinnah's suspicions were therefore roused when the British accepted, a little later, a Congress resolution accepting the 16 May statement with the intention of working *against* grouping in the Constituent Assembly the asserting that no one would dictate to the Assembly what it should nor should not do. Cripps and Pethick-Lawrence stated in Parliament on 17 July that the British aim was *only* to get the parties into the Constituent Assembly. Taken with British ignoring League's demand for parity, and its refusal to form a government without the Congress; these statements put Jinnah up in arms. Accusing the British of bad faith, the League passed, on 29 July, a resolution rescinding its earlier acceptance of the 16 May statement and calling on Muslims to resort to Direct Action—dangerous in its implications because it was never defined.

Could the British have gone ahead with only the Congress in the Interim Government? The alternative was considered by Whitehall, but raised the uncomfortable question whether the British would be prepared to back the Congress in suppressing a possible mass movement organized by the League. Then there was Wavell's attitude. A man who had always disliked and mistrusted the Congress to an extent that he preferred to have no government at all than one which included only the Congress, simply refused to govern without the League. What may have seemed politically logical to the men in Whitehall was, for the man on the spot, psychologically impossible.

Wavell's belief that the League would come into the Constituent Assembly if only the British would clarify their intentions on grouping, was the sort of self-deception that can only be explained

[4] Pirzada, *Documents*, p. 508. [5] *TOP*, vol. 7, pp. 837–8.

by his intense dislike of the Congress. He never upbraided Leaguers for preaching violence even as they sat in his government; he justified and backed up their refusal to work as a team with the Congress. Neither he nor Whitehall ever faced squarely the possibility that Jinnah was intent on a sovereign Pakistan; and their need of the League as a counterpoise to the Congress in the Interim Government made them rule out the possibility of going ahead without it.

The contradiction in British thinking was also evident from the concern of both Wavell and Whitehall that the Viceroy's veto should not be abolished. The veto, they thought, would be needed to protect the services and to prevent the Congress from interfering in the Muslim majority provinces while it sat in the interim government. But if the Viceroy would not have the *power* to do anything against the wishes of the majority of his Executive, preserving the veto served no purpose except to create a barrier between him and the Congress. Of what use would the veto have been if the Congress had resigned from the Interim Government and started mass civil disobedience, which, fearing their inability to control, Wavell suggested that the British withdraw from India by 1 January 1947?

The final question is why mass feeling got out of hand. Communal temperature had remained fairly high, especially in the Punjab, after the Cripps mission. But the Punjab remained free from internecine disturbances during the war. Communal propaganda by the League reached a peak during the elections of 1945–6 and was kept up while the negotiations between the Cabinet Mission and the Indian parties were in progress. There are reports of the League, Akalis and the RSS organizing private armies. There is no mention of provincial action against them, or of the Congress trying to counteract them, so that communal propaganda had a free hand at the time.

Was it the mere prospect of Pakistan or Hindustan which roused mass feeling? It would depend on what they meant. In March 1947, Jenkins believed that the Sikhs could have reached a settlement with the provincial League had it not been for the fact that the latter were taking orders from Jinnah. The League had concentrated on getting Pakistan without ever telling the minorities what their position in it would be. If Pakistan was going to be an Islamic state, as Jinnah himself had suggested on occasion, Hindus and Sikhs would not walk willingly into it. Jinnah's refusal to define the content of Pakistan, and the prospect that he might get it, made the Hindus and

Sikhs quite delirious. Muslims, on the other hand, could not have been greatly enamoured of Hindustan, as stories of 'atrocities' committed on them under Congress rule remained in circulation; and the League carried out its anti-Congress propaganda through the war years, uninterrupted by any party, least of all by the Congress, most of whose leaders were in jail during that time.

Direct Action in Calcutta and Noahkhali, in the organization of which the League ministry connived, provided the spark which lit the fires of civil war. Rape, forced marriages, conversions—the fact that the atrocities had been committed on a fairly large scale before the disturbances could be brought under control—meant that stories and rumours spread like wildfire, arousing the deepest hatred and the fiercest desire for revenge; and stirred Hindus into waging the most bloody and brutal vengeance on Muslims in Bihar and the UP. *This was the breaking point*. A handful of riots in a few cities would not have led to it. But atrocities committed on a mass scale could not be forgotten on either side, and they lent the most sinister definition to Pakistan or Hindustan. As thousands of people lost their lives and as hundreds of refugees fled from their homes, the impression was created in the public mind that the *sarkar* was incapable of doing its job and that it was therefore incumbent on them to be able to defend themselves—in other words, to take the law into their own hands. All these factors came to a head in the Punjab in March 1947, where the outbreak of communal violence simultaneously in several districts meant that the police and the military could only deal with a few areas at a time: there were large areas which were affected by the disturbances but over which no action would be taken. Civil war was on its way.

Would the disturbances have stopped if Jinnah had entered the Constituent Assembly? It is difficult to answer this question. With mass hatred aroused to an extreme, it might not have been possible, given the administrative limitations. The communal disturbances exposed not only the political abyss that separated the Congress from the Muslim League but also the essential weaknesses of Congress strategy. The political division between the Congress and League lay in the latter's wish that any political settlement must be guaranteed by the British, whereas the Congress worked British-sponsored constitutions to free India from imperialist rule. The schism had its roots in the 1920s and 1930s and never changed in its essentials; and it was the reason why Jinnah never accepted the

Congress offer of parity, forwarded by Bhulabhai Desai, in January–February 1945. It was not merely that the League's demand for a sovereign Pakistan was unacceptable to the Congress; but also its desire that it should be awarded by the British and to have post-independence military ties with them. The League's logic was simple. For, if the Congress majority could swallow up the League in a constituent assembly, what except a British guarantee could forestall Congress tactics against Pakistan in the assembly and subsequently protect a sovereign Pakistan from the aggressive designs of a Congress-led India? The League's dependence on the British after 1940 was actuated by its intention first, to achieve a sovereign Pakistan under their aegis, then to enlist their military umbrella for its survival.

Both the British and Congress discerned the meaning behind the League–Congress rift, but each for their own reasons, shied away from its extreme implications, taking refuge in the argument that Pakistan was unviable and that the League could not be serious about it—that it was only a ploy with which to secure a vantage point at the centre. So the British did their best to prevent a Congress–League agreement until 1945—then, assuming that the League, as a political minority, would be ever amenable to their wishes, tried to bring it into a united India while offering it the possibility of achieving the sovereign Pakistan that it demanded. A distinction can be made between their dislike of the Pakistan solution, and the contribution of their tactics to its materialisation: their short-term tactics worked against the achievement of their own long-term aims. The Congress found Jinnah intractable; it conceived the weapon of Muslim mass support against the League in 1937 but never sharpened it, partly because of an idealistic naivete that all Indians would eventually unite against the British, partly because its use of mass sanctions and non-cooperation was more of a temporary tactic in its long-run strategy of compromise-pressure-compromise.[6] In 1940, Nehru observed that Congress ministries had made insufficient progress towards implementing their social and economic programmes,[7] but he did not relate the effects of this inadequacy on a definitive solution to the communal problem. In 1945–7, his

[6] For an elucidation of the compromise-pressure-compromise strategy, see Bipan Chandra, 'The Indian Capitalist Class and Imperialism before 1947', in his *Nationalism and Colonialism in Modern India* (New Delhi, 1979), pp. 144–170.

[7] Nehru, *Autobiography*, pp. 603–4.

view that Pakistan should not succeed because it was the medievalistic, anti-democratic idea of a politically reactionary organization[8] seemed to gloss over the possibility and the fact that such ideas do succeed, often with mass support. Not having fully developed mass organization even for the anti-imperialist struggle, the Congress could not have done it to resolve an issue to which it accorded secondary priority. Jinnah's success in the elections of 1945–6 signified his realization of the necessity of mass backing for a political line; the Congress rout in the Muslim constituencies meant that it could override Pakistan or divide and rule machinations only in negotiations—in which the British acted as arbiters. In March 1946, the Congress coalesced with one of the greatest of loyalists—Khizar Hyat Khan Tiwana and his Unionist party—proving that Pakistan had become one of foremost issues of the day. Criticizing *divide et impera*, the Congress contradictorily joined the British-sponsored Interim Government in September 1946. In 1946, even more than in 1937, the acceptance of office by the Congress was its greatest tactical mistake as it made the party the focus of popular Muslim discontent, even hatred, which eventually burst into civil war.

Yet the fact remains of Jinnah's insistence on a sovereign Pakistan—at the very least, of his lack of interest in a settlement with the Congress unless it was backed up by the British. What agreement was possible with a leader who declared, even as communal massacres spread through the Punjab in March 1947, that the British had 'deliberately fostered' the idea of a united India as 'part of machinations for destruction and bloodshed in the country after their departure'?[9] Between March and May 1947, Jinnah's efforts at the centre to persuade Mountbatten to allow a League ministry in the Punjab symbolized his keenness to obtain the whole province for the League before June 1948. Gandhi alone discerned that Jinnah would not be wooed into a united India, but he had no answer to prevent the realization of a sovereign Pakistan. Jinnah achieved a sovereign Pakistan partly because he knew where he was going, while the 'muddling through' tactics of the British and the Congress were no match for his melange of obduracy, dialectical skill and deliberate, dogged negation of anything less than a sovereign Pakistan.

[8] See, for example, *National Herald*, 8 February, 4 April, 16 July 1946; *Hindustan Times* 30 August 1945.

[9] *The Times*, 28 March 1947.

In any case, given his blend of vanity, ambition, idealism and principle—and all these qualities have been attributed to him, with the emphasis depending on the perceptions of admirers or critics—it is difficult to see how he would have agreed to a united, secular India in which he would have had to play a likely second fiddle to Gandhi and Nehru. In the end, he left the British with the choice of scuttle or allowing the League to capture the NWFP and the Punjab by force—both alternatives reflecting their administrative impotence. Always underestimating the seriousness of the call for a sovereign Pakistan, neither the British nor the Congress formulated a strategy to challenge or to resist it. In August 1947, the Muslim League was the only party to achieve what it wanted. There was no possibility of the British securing any military treaties with India as the price for transferring power, and they faced the prospect of losing their whole eastern empire. Lord Dufferin's warning of 1887 that British attempts to 'divide and rule' would recoil on them rang true in 1947[10]. India paid a heavy price for the achievement of freedom, a consequence of the fact that communal forces were not defeated, nor unity totally achieved.

[10] Dufferin to Cross, 4 January 1887, Cross papers, vol. 22, p. 5.

List of Important Persons

Only the most important positions held by the prominent persons in this book are mentioned below.

ALEXANDER, A. V., First Earl Alexander of Hillsborough, Labour M.P. 1935–50; First Lord of the Admiralty 1940–5 and 1945–6; member of Cabinet Mission to India 1946.

AMERY, Leo, Secretary of State for India 1940–5.

ATTLEE, C. R., First Earl. Opposition leader 1935–40; Lord Privy Seal 1940–2; Deputy Prime Minister 1942–5; Prime Minister 1945–51.

AUCHINLECK, Field Marshal Sir Claude, Commander-in-Chief India 1941 and 1943–7; Commander-in-Chief Middle East 1941–2; Supreme Commander in India and Pakistan 1947.

AZAD, M. A. K., Congress President 1940–6.

BAKSH, Allah, Leader of Sind United Party 1937; Prime Minister of Sind at various times during 1937–42.

BALDEV SINGH, Minister in Punjab 1942–6; member of interim government 1946–7.

BOSE, Sarat Chandra, Leader of Congress Parliamentary Party in Bengal 1937–9; fell out with Congress in 1946 when he formed the Socialist Party.

BOSE, Subhas Chandra, Congress President 1938–9; organized Indian National Army 1942.

BURROWS, Sir Frederick, Governor of Bengal 1946–7.

CAROE, Sir Olaf, Foreign Secretary to Government of India 1939–45; Governor of NWFP 1946–7.

CASEY, Baron R. G., Governor of Bengal 1944–6.

CHHATARI, Nawab Hafiz Ahmad Said Khan, Leader of NAP in UP; Prime Minister of Hyderabad 1941.

COLVILLE, Sir John, Governor of Bombay 1943–7.

CRIPPS, Sir Stafford, Member of war cabinet and deputed by it to India in 1942; Minister of Aircraft Production 1942–5; President of Board of Trade 1945–7; member of cabinet mission to India.

CUNNINGHAM, Sir George, Governor of NWFP 1937–46.

DAULATANA, Mian Mumtaz, Unionist who joined Muslim League in 1943; General Secretary, Punjab Provincial League 1944–7.

DESAI, Bhulabhai, Member of Central Legislative Assembly, one of the authors of Desai-Liaqat Pact of 1945; defended INA men in 1945.

DOW, Sir Hugh, Governor of Sind 1941–6; Governor of Bihar 1946–7.

EMERSON, Sir Herbert, Governor of Punjab 1933–8.

GANDHI, Mahatma, the father of the Indian nation; made personal efforts to promote communal harmony in 1946–7 and only reluctantly accepted partition.

GLANCY, Sir Bertrand, Political Adviser to the Crown Representative 1939–41; Governor of Punjab 1941–6.

HAIG, Sir Harry, Governor of UP 1934–9.

HALLETT, Sir Maurice, Governor of Bihar 1937–9; Governor of UP 1939–45.

HASAN, Syed Wazir, Muslim League President 1936; joined Congress 1937.

HERBERT, Sir John, Governor of Bengal, 1939–43.

HIDAYATULLAH, Sir G. H., Premier of Sind 1937–8, 1942–7.

HUQ, Fazlul, KPP President in 1936; joined Muslim League 1937; Prime Minister of Bengal 1937–43.

HUSAIN, Fazli, Prime Minister of Punjab at the time of his death in 1936; founder of the Unionist Party.

ISPAHANI, M. A. H., prominent Bengal Muslim Leaguer and on its Working Committee 1936–47.

JENKINS, Sir Evan, Private Secretary to Viceroy 1943–5; Governor of Punjab 1946–7.

JINNAH, Muhammad Ali, reorganized Muslim League after 1934, President of League after that date; under his leadership the Muslim League won the independent state of Pakistan in 1947.

KHALIQUZZAMAN, Choudhury, prominent Muslim Leaguer and one of the leading figures in the coalition controversy in UP in 1937; on MLWC 1945–7.

KHAN, Aurangzeb, Prime Minister of NWFP 1943–5.

KHAN, Liaqat Ali, Muslim League General Secretary 1937–47.

KHAN, Muhammad Ismail, with Khaliquzzaman was one of the leading figures in UP coalition controversy in 1937; on MLWC 1945–7.

KHAN, Raja Ghazanfar Ali, member Punjab Legislative Assembly 1937–45; member Interim Government 1946–7.

KHAN SAHIB, Prime Minister of NWFP 1937–9 and 1945–7.

KHAN, Sikander Hyat, Unionist Party leader after 1936, Prime Minister of Punjab 1937–42.

KHUHRO, M. A., MLWC member 1942; Minister Public Works Department in Sind 1946–7.

KRIPALANI, J. B., General Secretary of Congress 1934–46 and President in 1946.

LINLITHGOW, Second Marquis of, Viceroy and Governor-General of India, 1936–43.

LISTOWEL, 5th Earl of, Secretary of State for India April–August 1947.

LUMLEY, Sir Roger, Governor of Bombay 1937–43.

MAMDOT, Nawab of, President, Punjab Provincial League 1942–7.

MIEVILLE, Sir Eric, Assistant Private Secretary to King George VI 1937–45; member of Lord Mountbatten's staff in India 1947.

MONTEATH, Sir David, Permanent Under Secretary of State for India and Burma from 1942.

MOUNTBATTEN of Burma, First Earl, Chief of Combined Operations 1942–3; Supreme Allied Commander South East Asia 1943–6; Viceroy of India March–August 1947.

MUDIE, Sir Francis, Chief Secretary to UP government 1939–44; member Viceroy's Executive Council 1944–5; Governor of Sind 1946–7.

NAZIMUDDIN, Khwaja, Prime Minister of Bengal 1942–5.

NEHRU, Jawaharlal, Congress President 1936–7; member CWC 1936–47; played leading role in negotiations for transfer of power in 1946–7.

NISHTAR, Abdur Rab, Minister of Finance in NWFP 1943–5; on MLWC 1945–6; member of Interim Government 1946–7.

NOON, Firoz Khan, in Viceroy's Executive Council 1941–5, leading Punjab Muslim Leaguer.

PANT, G. B., Congress Prime Minister of UP 1937–9.

PATEL, Sardar Vallabhai, leading Congressman and member of Interim Government 1946–7.

PETHICK-LAWRENCE, First Baron, Secretary of State for India 1945–7; member of Cabinet Mission to India 1946.

PRASAD, Rajendra, Congress President 1939 and 1947; President of Constitutent Assembly 1946–50.

RAJAGOPALACHARI, C., Congress Prime Minister of Madras 1937–9.

SAADULLAH, Muhammad, Chief Minister of Assam 1937–8, 1939–41 and 1942–6.

SYED, G. M., President Sind Muslim League 1938; nominated to MLWC 1941; expelled from League 1946.

SUHRAWARDY, H. S., Muslim League minister in Bengal 1937–45 and Chief Minister 1946–7.

TARA SINGH, prominent Akali leader for four decades; led movement for Azad Punjab in the forties.

TIWANA, Malik Khizar Hyat Khan, Prime Minister of the Punjab 1943–7; expelled from League in 1944, formed coalition with Congress and Akalis 1946–7; resigned after British government's announcement of 20 February 1947.

TWYNAM, Sir Henry, Governor of CP and Berar 1940–6.

WAVELL, Sir Archibald, later First Earl, Commander-in-Chief Middle East 1939–41; Commander-in-Chief India 1941–3; Viceroy of India 1943–7.

WYLIE, Sir Francis, Political Adviser to Crown Representative 1940–1 and 1943–5; Governor of UP 1945–7.

ZETLAND, Second Marquis of, Secretary of State for India 1935–40.

Bibliography

On a subject on which the reading list is seemingly endless, I have included in this bibliography only those sources which I found especially useful or stimulating.

UNPUBLISHED SOURCES

Private Papers

Bodleian Library, Oxford
Attlee papers

India Office Library and Records, London

Allan Arthur	Mss. Eur. D.943
Viscount Cross	Mss. Eur. E.243
Sir George Cunningham	Mss. Eur. D.670
Sir John Erksine	Mss. Eur. D.596
Sir Harry Haig	Mss. Eur. F.115
Sir Maurice Hallett	Mss. Eur. E.251
Lord Linlithgow	Mss. Eur. F.125
Sir Robert Reid	Mss. Eur. E.278
Lord Zetland	Mss. Eur. D.609

Centre of South Asian Studies, Cambridge
J.M.G. Bell
E.C. Benthall
M.O. Carter
H.J. Frampton
O.M. Martin
I.M. Stephens
S.G. Taylor

Churchill College, Cambridge
A.V. Alexander

Gandhi Smarak Sangrahalaya, New Delhi
Mahatma Gandhi

National Archives of India, New Delhi
M.R. Jayakar
Rajendra Prasad

Nehru Memorial Museum and Library, New Delhi
Bhulabhai Desai
Syed Mahmud
Jawaharlal Nehru
T.B. Sapru (Microfilm)
B. Shiva Rao
Purshottamadas Thakurdas

Government Records
India Office Library and Records, London
L/E
L/I
L/P & J/5
L/P & J/10
L/WS/1
R/3/1
R/3/2

National Archives of India
Home Establishments Department
Home Police Department
Home Political (Internal) Department
Reforms Office

Public Records Office, London
CAB 127
CAB 134
PREM 1/216/1937
PREM 1/414/1939
PREM 4/47/1
PREM 8

Party Papers
Nehru Memorial Museum and Library, New Delhi
All-India Congress Committee
Hindu Mahasabha

PUBLISHED SOURCES

Cmd. 3568 (1930) *Report of Indian Statutory Commission*, Vol. 1.
Report of Indian Statutory Commission, Vols. IV-XIV (HMSO, 1930).
Cmd. 3778 (1932) *Proceedings of Indian Round Table Conference, Second Session*, 7 September 1931–1 December 1931.
Cmd. 4086 (1932) *Report of the Indian Franchise Committee.*
Cmd. 4147 (1931–2) *Communal Decision*
Government of India Act, 1935 (Delhi, 1936).
Census of India 1941 (Delhi, 1942).
Constitutional Relations between Britain and India: The Transfer of Power

1942–7, Vols. I–IX. Editor-in-Chief, N. Mansergh (HMSO, 1970–80).
Bengal Legislative Assembly Debates 1937–46.
Central Assembly Debates 1944.
NWFP Legislative Assembly Debates 1937–46.
Punjab Legislative Assembly Debates 1937–46.
Sind Legislative Assembly Debates 1937–46.
Ahmad, Jamiluddin, *Speeches and Writings of Mr. Jinnah*, Vol. 1, 6th edn. (Lahore, 1960).
Collected Works of Mahatma Gandhi (75 vols. 1958–79).
Durga Das (ed.) *Sardar Patel Correspondence 1945–50* (10 vols., Ahmedabad, 1971–74).
S. Gopal (ed.) *Selected Works of Jawaharalal Nehru* (12 vols., New Delhi, 1972–79).
Gwyer, M. and Appadorai, A. (eds.) *Speeches and Documents on the Indian Constitution 1921–47* (2 vols., Oxford, 1957).
Indian Annual Register
Jafri, S.S. (ed.) *Qaid-e-Azam Jinnah's Correspondence with Punjab Muslim Leaders* (Lahore, 1977).
Pirzada, S.S., *Foundations of Pakistan: All-India Muslim League Documents: 1906–1947*, vols. I (1906–23) and II (1924–47), (Karachi, 1970).
Moon, P. (ed.) *Wavell: The Viceroy's Journal* (Oxford, 1973).
Report of the Inquiry Committee Appointed by the All-India Muslim League to inquire into Muslim Grievances in Congress Provinces (November, 1938).
Zaidi, Z.H. (ed.) *M.A. Jinnah-Ispahani Correspondence 1936–1948* (Karachi, 1976).

Newspapers

Amrita Bazaar Patrika
The Bombay Chronicle
Civil and Military Gazette
Dawn
The Eastern Times
Harijan
The Hindu
Hindustan Standard
The Hindustan Times
The Leader
Morning News
National Herald
Searchlight
Star of India
The Statesman
The Times of India
The Tribune

Secondary Sources

Ahmad, Aziz, *Studies in Islamic Culture in the Indian Environment* (Oxford, 1964).
———, *Islamic Modernism in India and Pakistan 1857–1864* (Oxford, 1967).
Ali, C.M., *The Emergence of Pakistan* (New York, 1967).
Ambedkar, B.R., *Pakistan or Partition of India* (Bombay, 1946).
Amery, L., *My Political Life* (4 vols., London 1953–5).
Ashraf, K.M., *Life and Conditions of the People of Hindustan* (2nd edition, New Delhi, 1970).
Attlee, C.R., *As It Happened* (London, 1954).
Azad, M.A.K., *Indian Wins Freedom* (New York, 1960).
Aziz, K.K., *The Making of Pakistan: A Study in Nationalism* (London, 1967).
Birla, G.D., *In the Shadow of the Mahatma* (Bombay, 1953).
Bolitho, Hector, *Jinnah: Creator of Pakistan* (London, 1954).
Brass, Paul R., *Language, Religion and Politics in North India* (Cambridge, 1974).
Brittain, V., *Pethick-Lawrence* (London, 1963)
Broomfield, J.H., *Elite Conflict in a Plural Society* (University of California, 1968).
Campbell-Johnson, Alan, *Mission with Mountbatten* (London, 1951).
Chopra, P.N. (ed.) *Quit India Movement: British Secret Report* (New Delhi, 1976).
Collins, L., Lapierre, D., *Mountbatten and the Partition of India*, vol. 1 (New Delhi, 1982).
Connell, John, *Auchinleck* (London, 1959).
Connell, John, *Wavell: Supreme Commander* (London, 1969).
Coupland, R., *The Cripps Mission* (Oxford 1942).
Coupland, Reginald, *The Indian Problem* (Oxford, 1944).
Dalton, Hugh, *High Tide and After* (London, 1962).
Das, Durga, *India from Curzon to Nehru and After* (London, 1969).
Das, M.N., *Indian Under Morley and Minto* (London, 1964).
Das, M.N., *Partition and Independence of India* (New Delhi, 1982).
Dixit, P., *Communalism: A Struggle for Power* (New Delhi, 1974).
Durrani, F.H. Khan, *The Meaning of Pakistan* (Lahore, 1944).
El Hamza, *Pakistan: A Nation* (Lahore, 1942).
Faruqi, Zia-ul-Hasan, *The Deoband School and the Demand for Pakistan* (Bombay, 1963).
Ghosh, S., *Gandhi's Emissary* (London, 1967).
Glendevon, Lord, *The Viceroy at Bay* (London, 1971).
Gopal, Madan, *Sir Chhotu Ram: A Political Biography* (Delhi, 1977).
Gopal, Ram, *Indian Muslims—A Political History (1858–1947)* (Bombay, 1959).
Gopal, S., *Jawaharalal Nehru: A Biography*, vol. I: 1889–1947 (Indian Edition, Oxford University Press, 1976).

Grewal, J.S., *Muslim Rule in India: The Assessments of British Historians* (Oxford, 1970).
Griffin, Lepel, *Chiefs and Families of Note in the Punjab*, 2 vols. (Lahore, 1940).
Gupta, A.K., *North-West Frontier Province and the Freedom Struggle 1932–47* (New Delhi, 1979).
Gupta, P.S., *Imperialism and the British Labour Movement 1914–1964* (London, 1975).
Hardy, P., *The Muslims of British India* (Cambridge, 1972).
Hasan, M., *Nationalism and Communalism in Indian Politics* (New Delhi, 1979).
Hodson, H.V., *The Great Divide* (London, 1969).
Husain, Azim, *Fazli Husain* (Bombay, 1946).
Hutchins, F.G., *Spontaneous Revolution* (Delhi, 1971).
Ismay, Lord, *Memoirs* (London, 1960).
Ispahani, M.A.H., *Qaid-e-Azam Jinnah As I Knew Him* (Karachi, 1966).
Jones, K.W., *Arya Dharm* (Berkeley, 1976).
Kaura, Uma, *Muslims and Indian Nationalism: The Emergence of the Demand for India's Partition 1928–40* (New Delhi, 1977).
Khaliquzzaman, C., *Pathway to Pakistan* (Lahore, 1961).
Khosla, G.D., *Stern Reckoning* (New Delhi, 1949).
Krishna, K.B., *The Problem of Minorities* (London, 1939).
Low, D.A. (ed.) *Soundings in Modern South Asia History* (London, 1968).
Low, D.A., (ed.) *Congress and the Raj* (London, 1977).
Lumby, E.W.R., *The Transfer of Power in India 1945–47* (London, 1954).
Madan, T.N. (ed.) *Muslim Communities of South Asia* (New Delhi, 1976).
Malik, Hafeez, *Moslem Nationalism in India and Pakistan* (Washington, 1963).
Mansergh, P.N.S., *The Commonwealth Experience* (London, 1969).
Mansergh, P.N.S., *Prelude to Partition: Concepts and Aims in Ireland and India* (Cambridge, 1978).
Mehta, A. and Patwardhan, A., *The Communal Triangle in India* (Allahabad, 1942).
Menon, V.P., *The Transfer of Power in India* (Paperback, Madras, 1968).
Minault, G., *The Khilafat Movement* (Delhi, 1982).
Molesworth, G.N., *Curfew on Olympus* (London, 1965).
Moon, Penderel, *Divide and Quit* (London, 1961).
Moore, R.J., *The Crisis of Indian Unity 1971–1940* (Oxford, 1974).
———, *Churchill, Cripps, and India 1939–1945* (Oxford, 1979).
———, *Escape from Empire* (Oxford, 1983).
Mountbatten, Lord, *Reflections on the Transfer of Power and Jawaharlal Nehru* (Cambridge, 1968).
Mujeeb, M., *The Indian Muslims* (London, 1967).
Nanda, B.R., *Mahatma Gandhi* (London, 1958).
Nehru, J., *Eighteen Months in India* (Allahabad, 1938).
———, *An Autobiography* (New Delhi, 1962).
———, *The Discovery of India* (Bombay, 1969).

Noman, M., *Muslim India: The Rise and Growth of the All-Indian Moslem League* (Allahabad, 1942).
Noon, Firoz Khan, *From Memory* (Lahore, 1966).
Page, David, *Prelude to Partition* (Oxford 1982).
Philips, C.H. and Wainwright, M.D., (ed.) *The Partition of India* (London, 1970).
Prasad, Rajendra, *India Divided* (Bombay, 1946).
Pyarelal, *Mahatma Gandhi: The Last Phase, vols. 1 and 2* (Ahmedabad, 1956–8).
Rothwell, V., *Britain and the Cold War 1941–1947* (London, 1982).
Saiyid, M.H., *Mohammad Ali Jinnah: A Political Study* (reprint of 2nd edition, Lahore, 1962).
Sayeed, K.B., *Pakistan: The Formative Phase 1857–1948* (2nd edition, London, 1968).
Sen, Shila, *Muslim Politics in Bengal 1937–1947* (New Delhi, 1976).
Sitaramayya, P., *History of the Indian National Congress, Vols. 1 and 2* (Bombay, 1947).
Smith, W.C., *The Muslim League 1942–45* (Lahore, 1945).
———, *Modern Islam in India* (Lahore, 1946).
Taylor, D. and Yapp, M. (eds.) *Political Identity in South Asia* (London, 1979).
Thapar, R. (ed.) *Communalism and the Writing of Indian History* (New Delhi, 1969).
———, *The Past and Prejudice* (New Delhi, 1975).
Thorne, C., *Allies of a Kind* (London, 1978).
Tomlinson, B.R., *The Indian National Congress and the Raj 1929–1942* (London, 1976).
———, *The Political Economy of the Raj 1914–1947* (London, 1979).
Thursby, G.R., *Hindu-Muslim Relations in British India: A Study of Controversy, Conflict, and Communal Movements in Northern India 1923–1928* (Leiden, 1975).
Tinker, H., *Experiment with Freedom* (Oxford, 1967).
Tuker, F., *While Memory Serves* (London, 1950).
Venkataramani M.S., and Shrivastava, B.K., *Quit India: The American Response to the 1942 Struggle* (New Delhi, 1979).
Wingate, R., *Lord Ismay* (London, 1970).
Zetland, Lord, *Essayez* (London, 1956).

Articles

Baxter, C., 'Union or Partition: Some Aspects of Politics in Punjab 1936–45', in L.Ziring el al., *Pakistan: The Long View* (Duke Univestity, 1977), pp. 40–69.
Brass, Paul R., 'Muslim Separatism in the United Provinces: Social Context and Political Strategy before Partition', *Economic and Political Weekly*, Annual Number, January 1970, pp. 167–86.
Chandra, Bipan, 'Secularism: Retrospect and Prospect', *Secular Democracy*, February 1973.
Chandra, Satish, 'Jizyah and the State in India During the 17th Century',

Journal of the Economic and Political and Social History of the Orient, Vol. 12, 1969, pp. 322–40.

Chatterjee, P., 'Bengal Politics and the Muslim Masses, 1920–1947', *Journal of Commonwealth and Comparative politics*, 1982, pp. 25–41.

Freitag, Sandra B., ' "Natural Leaders", Adminstrators and Social Control: Communal Riots in the United Provinces 1870–1925', *South Asia* (September, 1978), vol. 1, No. 2, pp. 27–41.

Gallagher, J., 'The Congress in Bengal: The Period of Decline 1930–39', *Modern Asian Studies*, 7, 7, 1973.

Gupta, P.S., 'The British Raj and the Communal Question Sept. 1939–Jan. 1940', *Indian History Congress Proceedings 1973*, vol. II, pp. 56–9.

Inder Singh, A., 'Imperial Defence and the Transfer of Power in India, 1946–1947', *International History Review*, November 1982, pp. 568–88.

Inder Singh, A., 'Decolonization in India: The Statement of 20 February 1947', *International History Review*, May 1984.

Listowel, Lord, 'The Whitehall Dimension and the Transfer of Power', *Indo-British Review*, vol. 7, nos. 3 and 4, pp. 22–31.

Low, D.A., 'The Indian Schism', *Journal of Commonwealth Political Studies*, vol. IX, No. 2 July 1971, pp. 158–67.

McPherson, Kenneth, 'The Muslims of Madras and Calcutta: Agitational Politics in the Early 1920s', *South Asia*, December 1975, pp. 32–47.

Moon, P., 'May God Be With You Always', *The Round Table*, July 1971.

Moore, R.J., 'The Mystery of the Cripps Mission', *Journal of Commonwealth Political Studies*, vol. XI, No. 3, November 1973, pp. 195–213.

Moore, R.J., 'Mountbatten, India, and the Commonwealth', *Journal of Commonwealth and Comparative Politics*, 1981, pp. 5–43

Moore, R.J., 'Jinnah and the Pakistan Demand', *Modern Asian Studies*, 17, 4, 1983, pp. 529–61.

Morris-Jones, W.H., 'The Transfer of Power, 1947: A View from the Sideline', *Modern Asian Studies*, 16, 1, 1982, pp. 1–32.

Oren, Stephen, 'The Sikhs, Congress, and the Unionists in British Punjab', *Modern Asian Studies*, 8, 3, 1974, pp. 397–418.

Potter, David, 'Manpower Shortage and the End of Colonialism', *Modern Asian Studies*, 7, 1, 1973, pp. 47–73.

Talbot, I.A., 'The 1946 Punjab Elections', *Modern Asian Studies*, 14, 1, 1980, pp. 56–91.

Tinker, H., 'Jawaharlal Nehru at Simla May 1947', *Modern Asian Studies*, October, 1970.

Tomlinson, B.R., 'Indian and the British Empire, 1935–1947', *Indian Economic and Social History Review*, vol. XIII, No. 3., pp. 323–351.

Oral Evidence

Interviews with:

W.H. Saumarez-Smith
Arthur Williams
Henry Taylor
S.E. Abbott

Unpublished theses

Lambert, Richard, 'Hindu-Muslim Riots', Unpublished Sociology Dissertation submitted to University of Pennsylvania for Ph.D. degree, Philadelphia, 1951.

Singh, Anita I., 'Nehru and the Communal Problem 1936–1939', Unpublished M.Phil dissertation submitted to Jawaharlal Nehru University, New Delhi, 1976.

Index